Transitional Economies

Euro-Asian Studies

General Editor: **Christoph Bluth**, Visiting Professor, Centre for Euro-Asian Studies, University of Reading, and Professor in International Studies, University of Leeds

The transition of the countries in Euro-Asia is one of the most important developments affecting the international system since the end of the Cold War. The development of market economies after decades of central planning, the formation of new states and national identities, the creation of new, democratic institutions of state and the reintegration into the world economy pose enormous challenges. Whilst some countries have progressed relatively well and are in the process of joining the European Union, others have experienced several economic and social dislocations, to the point of political disintegration and armed conflicts. The Centre for Euro-Asian Studies at the University of Reading is dedicated to the academic study of the political, economic, social and cultural aspects of this process. This series presents the most recent contributions from leading academics in the field. With an interdisciplinary focus, it seeks to provide a substantial, original and ongoing contribution to our understanding of the region which is of vital importance for academics and of high policy relevance for governments and businesses.

Titles include:

Yelena Kalyuzhnova and Dov Lynch (*editors*)
THE EURO-ASIAN WORLD
A Period of Transition

Yelena Kalyuzhnova and Michael Taylor (*editors*)
TRANSITIONAL ECONOMIES
Banking, Finance, Institutions

Euro-Asian Studies
Series Standing Order ISBN 0–333–80114–8
(*outside North America only*)

You can receive future titles in this series as they are published by placing a standing order. Please contact your bookseller or, in case of difficulty, write to us at the address below with your name and address, the title of the series and the ISBN quoted above.

Customer Services Department, Macmillan Distribution Ltd, Houndmills, Basingstoke, Hampshire RG21 6XS, England

Transitional Economies

Banking, Finance, Institutions

Edited by

Yelena Kalyuzhnova
Director
The Centre for Euro-Asian Studies
The University of Reading
UK

and

Michael Taylor
Senior Economist
International Monetary Fund
Washington
USA

in association with
The Centre for
Euro-Asian Studies

First published 2001 by
PALGRAVE
Houndmills, Basingstoke, Hampshire RG21 6XS and
175 Fifth Avenue, New York, N. Y. 10010
Companies and representatives throughout the world

PALGRAVE is the new global academic imprint of
St. Martin's Press LLC Scholarly and Reference Division and
Palgrave Publishers Ltd (formerly Macmillan Press Ltd).

ISBN 0–333–80144–X

This book is printed on paper suitable for recycling and
made from fully managed and sustained forest sources.

A catalogue record for this book is available
from the British Library.

Library of Congress Cataloging-in-Publication Data
Transitional economies : banking, finance, institutions / edited by
Yelena Kalyuzhnova, Michael Taylor.
     p. cm.
   Includes bibliographical references and index.
   ISBN 0–333–80144–X
   1. Banks and banking—Europe, Eastern. 2. Banks and banking–
   –Europe, Central. 3. Financial institutions—Europe, Eastern.
   4. Financial institutions—Europe, Central. 5. Europe, Eastern–
   –Economic policy—1989– 6. Europe, Central—Economic policy.
   I. Kalyuzhnova, Yelena. II. Taylor, Michael (Michael W.), 1962–
   HG2980.7.A6 T733 2001
   332.1'0947—dc21
                                                    2001021200
10   9   8   7   6   5   4   3   2   1
10   09   08   07   06   05   04   03   02   01

Printed in Great Britain by Antony Rowe Ltd, Chippenham, Wiltshire

For Andrei and Lee

Contents

List of Boxes and Tables

Boxes

Tables

Foreword

This edited collection addresses the financial and banking issues in transitional economies. In particular, the book is focused on three major themes: the development of the banking sector; non-banking financial reforms and institutions; and regulatory and supervision problems. This book claims to be among the first of those devoted to the development of the financial sector in transition. The idea to write such a book came to us after hosting an international conference at the University of Reading (UK): 'Entering the World Financial Market: East and Central Europe and the CIS Countries' (25 September 1998). By that time we realized that in order to understand the difficulties and challenges of transitional finance we needed to carry out a brainstorm with the academics, bankers and specialists working in this area. Through this we recognized our very strong advantage. We have tried to make this book coherent and transparent. The volume represents the output of members of the Centre for Euro-Asian Studies at the University of Reading (UK) with the collaboration of friends of the Centre. Some of these chapters were presented at the conference. Others are the result of the recent research and experience of the contributors.

The whole book has been written in a spirit of collaboration and we are sincerely grateful to all contributors. We especially thank Douglas Arner for his support in the most crucial period of writing this book. Our sincere gratitude goes to Paul Mosley, Christopher Nobes and Pietro Vagliasindi for their helpful comments and encouragement. Thanks are also extended to Togzhan Kassenova, Altay Kenzhebayer and Natasha Shevchik for helping to shape the electronic version of this book and to Sylvia Smelt, Administrator at the Centre, for all the help and care given during the whole project. The team of contributors express their sincere gratitude to Linda Auld for the meticulous and excellent job of proof-reading this volume. Without her contribution this book would not have been possible. Finally, we are extremely grateful for the loving support and inspiration which we constantly had from Andrei and Lee, to whom we dedicate this volume.

Yelena Kalyuzhnova
Reading, UK

Michael Taylor
Washington DC, USA

List of Abbreviations

APEC	Asia-Pacific Econonomic Co-operation
BGZ	Bank Gospodarki Zyznosciowej
BIS	Bank for International Settlements
BOE	Bank of Estonia
BOLAT	Bank of Latvia
BOLIT	Bank of Lithuania
BPH	Bank Przemyslowo-Handlowy
BSD	Banking Supervision Department
CEEC	Central and East European countries
CIS	Commonwealth of Independent States
CPSS	Committee on Payment and Settlement Systems
EAs	European Agreements
EBRD	European Bank for Reconstruction and Development
EC	European Community
ECMH	Efficient capital markets hypothesis
EEC	European Economic Community
EEIG	European Economic Interest Grouping
EU	European Union
FATF	Financial Action Task Force
FDI	Foreign direct investment
FF system	Fully funded pillar
FSU	Former Soviet Union
GATS	General Agreement on Trade in Services
GATT	General Agreement on Tariffs and Trade
GDP	Gross domestic product
GKO	Russian Treasury Bills
G-7	Group of Seven Industrialized Countries
IAS	International Accounting Standards
IASC	International Accounting Standards Committee
ICAS	Institute of Chartered Accountants of Scotland
IFC	International Financial Corporation
IFIs	International Financial Institutions
IMF	International Monetary Fund
IOSCO	International Organization of Securities Commissions
IPO	Initial Public Offering
ISA	International standards of audit

ISD	Investment Service Directive
LLR	Lender of last resort
NAFTA	North American Free Trade Agreement
NATO	North Atlantic Treaty Organization
NBFIs	Non-bank Financial Institutions
NEB	North Estonian Bank
NESB	North Estonian Share Bank
NBP	National Bank of Poland
OECD	Organization for Economic Cooperation and Development
OTC	Over-the-counter
PAYG	Pay-as-you-go
PBK	Powszechny Bank Kredytowy
PBR	Polish Bank of Development
PCA	Partnership and Cooperation Agreement
PCG	Planul Contabil General
PKO	Polska Kasa Oszczednosci
RKB	Riga Kommercbank
SCE	Système Comptable d'Enterprise
SEB	Skandinaviska Enskilda Banken
SOEs	State-owned enterprises
SOF	Substance over form
SPOZ	Special convertible bonds
SROs	Self-regulatory organizations
TCB	Tartu Commercial Bank
TFV	True and fair view
UBB	The Union Baltic Bank
UCITIS	Undertakings for Collective Investment in Transferable Securities
UNDP	United Nations Development Programme
VEB-fund	Vnesheconombank-fund
WTO	World Trade Organization

Contributors

Douglas W. Arner is Sir John Lubbock Support Fund Fellow at the Centre for Commercial Law Studies at Queen Mary & Westfield College, London. He is also an honorary lecturer at the Faculty of Law of the University of Hong Kong and a consultant with the Office of the General Council of the European Bank for Reconstruction and Development in London.

Alex Fleming is Lead Financial Economist in the World Bank's Europe and Central Asian Regional Office, where he is working on financial sector issues in the transition economies of East and Central Europe. Before this he worked on the Latin American economies for the Bank. He was formerly an economist at the Bank of England and a lecturer at the University of St Andrews.

Yelena Kalyuzhnova is the Director of the Centre for Euro-Asian Studies and a lecturer in the Economics Department at the University of Reading. Her research interests include the planning process and industrial policy in the transitional economies, and macroeconomic issues in transition. She is the author of the first major study of the Kazakhstani economy (1998) as well as an editor of *The Euro-Asian World. A Period of Transition* (2000).

Joseph J. Norton is Sir John Lubbock Professor of Banking Law, Centre for Commercial Law Studies, Queen Mary & Westfield College, University of London; Director of the London Institute of International Finance, Banking and Development Law; James L. Walsh Distinguished Faculty Fellow in Financial Institutions Law and Professor of Law, SMU School of Law, Dallas, Texas; and currently Vice-Chancellor's Distinguished Visiting Professor of Law, the University of Hong Kong.

Alan Roberts is a lecturer in international accounting at the University of Reading. He is also a member of the Centre for Euro-Asian Studies. For the year 1999–2000 he was Visiting Professor at the University of Toulouse 1, France.

Animesh Shrivastava is the Deputy Director of the Centre for Euro-Asian Studies and a lecturer at the Department of Economics, Reading University. He holds a Ph.D. from Oxford University where he previously taught.

Krystyna Szymkiewicz is a researcher at the CNRS (Centre National de la Recherche Scientifique) and Deputy Director of ROSES, the Research Centre on Transition Economics, located in Paris, at the University Paris I–Sorbonne. She graduated from the Main School of Planning and Statistics in Warsaw. She took her Ph.D. at the University Paris I. She has published widely on subjects related to Polish international economics and banking sector.

Michael Taylor is a senior economist in the Monetary and Exchange Affairs Department of the International Monetary Fund. He has written extensively on financial regulation as both a journalist and an academic and previously taught at several British universities. He is Visiting Professorial Fellow at the Centre for Commercial Law Studies at the University of London, Visiting Professor at London Guildhall University and Visiting Fellow of the Centre for Euro-Asian Studies.

George Tridimas is a reader at the School of Public Policy, Economics and Law, The University of Ulster, UK and a member of the Centre for Euro-Asian Studies. His research interests include public economics and economics of transition and combine theory, policy and applied econometrics. He has published widely in various leading academic journals.

Introduction

Yelena Kalyuzhnova and Michael Taylor

The process of building a market-based financial system in the countries of the Former Soviet Union (FSU) and other transition economies has been doubly complex. In the first place the transition countries have needed to contend with the problems faced in the 1990s by all developing economies that opened themselves up to the world's financial markets. Access to the international capital markets can bring important benefits, especially financing for much-needed infrastructural and capital projects, given the pressing need for many transition economies to upgrade and replace the capital stock they inherited from the centrally planned system. However, it also can carry significant risks. The potential for such capital flows to induce serious disruptions in the process of development has been widely documented and analysed, and was graphically illustrated by the worldwide financial crisis that began with the Asian currency crises in 1997 and was compounded by the Russian Treasury Bills (GKO) default in 1998. Unless domestic financial systems are especially robust, they will be unable properly to intermediate the flows of international capital, and their failure to do so may result in serious banking or currency crises.

The problem of a weak domestic financial sector intermediating international capital flows is common to both the transition and developing economies. But while institutional development has been an issue for other developing economies as well, in the transition economies this problem has assumed qualitatively different dimensions. They have needed to build a market-based financial system from a starting-point in which financial institutions had played little more than a passive record-keeping role, and in which market prices and property rights were almost completely absent under the socialist system. This book is concerned with the process of building viable, market-based financial institutions in the transition economies, and with the problems and issues that have arisen during the past decade in which they have attempted to enter the world financial market.

In a market-based economy the financial system performs two vital functions. It both allocates resources over time, and provides a mechanism for coordinating economic activity. The coordinating function has both a regulatory and an enabling aspect. A properly functioning financial system regulates real economic activity since the cost of finance and its availability for a particular use is fundamental in determining which productive investments are undertaken. Financial discipline – the condition that debts incurred must finally be repaid – is essential in ensuring that investments undertaken are socially efficient. At the same time the regulatory role of the financial system is combined with an enabling one. Provided that some entrepreneur or investor is prepared to assume the risks of undertaking a project with borrowed funds and that some lender believes that the loan will be repaid, the project can go ahead. Thus a competitive financial system is also central to the decentralized decision-making that is a hallmark of the market economy.

In contrast, allocative decisions under the socialist system were made according to the central plan, with the financial system performing little more than a book-keeping role. Indeed, the socialist system has been described as being monetarized more in appearance than in reality, and one leading analyst has described it as a 'semimonetarised' system (Kornai, 1992). The subordinate role played by the banking and financial systems in these countries prior to transition grew out of a clear ideological imperative. At a theoretical level, Marxist theory had anticipated the gradual elimination of money circulation and its replacement by the 'natural exchange' of products under socialism. Although this did not actually happen, another strand of Marxist theory stressed the centrality of the banking system to the capitalist economy (Hilferding, 1903/ 1981). Lenin, impressed by Hilferding's analysis and the powerful political and economic influence of the European banks during the eighteenth and nineteenth centuries, nationalised all Russian banks immediately after the 1917 revolution as the fastest and most effective way of ending capitalism and assuming control over the entire Russian economy. The banking system thus became part of the bureaucratic apparatus of the state, charged with the allocation of resources according to the dictates of central planning.

The state-owned banking system under socialism usually comprised several organizations: the central bank and various specialized banks including an agricultural bank, a foreign trade bank and a savings bank for household deposits. The specialized banks, although nominally independent, were in fact run simply as branches of the central bank. Thus the banking system formed a single, centralized hierarchical operation, with the result that it is frequently described as a 'monobank' (Kornai, 1992; Gros and Steinherr, 1995). In contrast to the market economies, the central bank of a socialist country did more than merely issue money. Through its control over the rest of the monobank system it handled the entire credit supply of both the state and state-owned firms. Each state-owned firm kept an account at the central bank, which thus had an unparalleled picture of firms' monetary transactions. The essence of the system was that credit was allocated according to the requirements of the plan, through direct bureaucratic control and the monitoring of inventories by the central bank, rather than market signals. Although the banking system paid interest on deposits and charged interest on loans, all interest rates were centrally administered and there was no differentiation for risk. Moreover, interest rates under the socialist system were frequently negative once hidden rather than official inflation rates were taken into account.

A further feature of this system was that money had ceased to be the textbook 'universal medium of exchange'. Precise rules governed the amount of cash each firm could keep and what it could be used for. The firm was required to keep an account at the central bank, and this was in turn divided into sub-accounts between which there was no fungibility. Thus funds intended to pay for materials and other semi-finished products could not be used to pay wages; money for wages could not be used for materials and so on. In consequence the national currency was not convertible within the country, since 'materials money' could not be converted into 'wages money' or 'investment money'. Moreover, all financial relations with the outside world were strictly centralised in the central bank or its foreign trade arm. Money was thus not convertible but was governed by detailed rules and case-by-case adjudication.

A final feature of the socialist financial system was that the only financial assets were bank deposits. For households and individuals, the only savings instrument, apart from hoarding cash, was to place it on deposit with the savings bank. Firms also, through their accounts with the central bank, held their financial assets in the form of bank deposits. By definition there are no private ownership rights under socialism, and hence no market for equities, and there were virtually no negotiable debt instruments such as bonds. Firms and the government obtained virtually all their financing needs from the banking system, with the exception of the comparatively small amount of financing that was raised on international financial markets.

Most studies of the development of financial systems in the transition economies begin from the starting-point of monetary reform. In order that market prices can properly perform their signalling function it is clearly essential that money should be able to operate as a universal medium of exchange and as a store of value. Hence much of the existing literature on the sequencing of reform policies and the efforts to construct a modern financial sector have emphasized the importance of ensuring the convertibility and stability of the currency at least domestically, with a view to subsequent capital account liberalization. What has received less attention has been the process of financial institution-building itself. Monetary reform is undoubtedly the central pillar of the transition effort and no viable market-based financial system can exist without it. However, the institutional infrastructure provided by the financial system – what may be described as the 'plumbing' of the market economy – is also of immense importance. Without sound plumbing, the benefits of monetary reform will almost literally leak away. Accordingly, the focus of this volume is on the process of institution-building as it concerns the development of financial systems in transition. Its chapters are each concerned, in their different ways, with the process by which the transition countries have moved from a monobank system, with its centrally administered allocation of credit, to a market-based system in which market signals are employed to calculate a trade-off between risk and return that governs the allocation of credit.

Because the process of building institutional structures lends itself to analysis from more than one theoretical or academic perspective, the contributors have been deliberately chosen for their broad range of expertise. Thus as well as academics working in the economics of transition, we have also incorporated chapters by lawyers and an accountant, and in a number of cases our contributors have the benefit of first-hand experience, gained as advisers and consultants, in building institutional capacity in the transition economies. Because our aim is to try to provide a blend of theory and practice, the choice of topics is deliberately eclectic. No one volume can do justice to the wide range of issues raised by the process of financial sector reform, and hence in a number of instances our contributors have focused on case studies based on their experience of specific countries in transition. From these case studies we none the less hope that the reader will be able to draw some more general conclusions about the problems and issues that arise for the transition economies in entering the world financial market.

Reform, institutional design and complementarities

Although analysis of institutional capacity-building in the transition economies cannot be confined to economics, it would be none the less misguided to argue that economic analysis has nothing to offer by way of an understanding of the change process. The apparent failure of a number of early attempts at reform, in which reformers were accused of adopting strategies that grew out of economic textbooks rather than the actual conditions in the late-period socialist systems, may have contributed to this perception. It was widely alleged that the failure of the reformers' early efforts demonstrated how far economic theory had become divorced from institutional reality; indeed, it was the neglect of institutional reality and other initial conditions of reform that was often seen as the root cause of the failure of a number of early reform efforts, especially in Russia. However, as Animesh Shrivastava discusses in his contribution, there is no necessary connection between the failure of the reformers' textbook models and the alleged redundancy of economic analysis in understanding the transition process. Recent developments in economic theory, especially transaction costs economics and the new institutional economics, have provided ways in which traditional economic models – constructed on the assumption of maximizing behaviour by individuals – can provide a way of better understanding the relationship between institutions and the reform process. Shrivastava's chapter stresses the importance of identifying complementarities in the reform process and each of the subsequent chapters can be seen as illustrations of the difficulty of identifying these, and of the problems that occur when one set of institutional changes fails to take into account the incentives created by another set.

Banking sector reform

Banking sector reform is at the core of the process of institution-building with which this volume is concerned. As discussed earlier, in the transition economies only the banking sector performed any form of financial intermediation function. The only financial assets were bank deposits, and the only financial institutions the various arms of the monobank system. Turning the monobank system into a decentralized, market-based system in which credit is allocated according to price rather than bureaucratic decree has been a major undertaking in institution-building that is still far from complete.

Under the central planning system the solvency of firms was irrelevant to the bank's lending decision. The criterion according to which funds were allocated was that the activity for which the funds were needed must be stipulated by the plan. Hence the budget constraint confronting borrowers from the monobank system was 'soft' to the extent that new credit would be forthcoming for any enterprise that continued to operate in accordance with the requirements of the plan. The fact that the firm was making losses was irrelevant to the credit-rationing decision; losses in one state enterprise would be made good by surpluses generated elsewhere in the system, the distribution between surplus and loss taking place across the balance sheet of the monobank system. However, once the banking system moves from credit-allocation decisions that were based on the dictates of the plan to one in which credit is rationed by price, the solvency of the borrower and its repayment capacity does become of fundamental importance. Under a market-based system the losses in one state enterprise can no longer be made good from the surpluses of another. The firm faces a hardening of its budget constraint. In this environment, credit extended by the state banking system to loss-making state enterprises is unlikely to be repaid; the banking system faces a loss of both principal and interest on the substantial amount of credit it had granted to loss-making state enterprises under the socialist system. This is the problem referred to as the overhang of bad loans.

In a market-based system, with a well-functioning set of prudential regulations, a bank would be required to allocate capital against its 'bad' (non-performing) loans; that is, in accountancy terms it would be required to make provisions that have the effect of writing down their book value by the amount of anticipated losses. However, the size of the bad debts under the transitional banking systems means that a realistic level of provisioning will result in the insolvency of most state-owned banks. They would then need to be recapitalized, at substantial cost to the central government's budget. Moreover, if the state-owned banks were prevented from extending credit to loss-making state enterprises, many of the latter would be forced into bankruptcy. Hence the state-owned banks often face powerful political pressures to continue to extend credit to enterprises which may be a major source of employment.

Permitting state-owned banks in transition to continue to extend credit to loss-making enterprises is widely regarded as creating serious inefficiencies in the process of financial intermediation. However, this traditional view is challenged by George Tridimas in his chapter (Chapter 1). Tridimas's results are interesting and challenging to the current policy consensus in favour of removing bad loans from the banking sector's balance sheet as soon as possible.

A very different approach to the issue of transforming a monobank into a competitive, market-based banking system is found in Krystyna Szymkiewicz's review of the process of bank restructuring in Poland (Chapter 2). She looks at the origins of the current system and presents the results of bank restructuring since 1989. A particular problem has been the lack of credit assessment skills and a commercial approach on the part of bank management.

Poland's transformation of its banking sector is neatly paralleled by the chapter on banking-sector crises in the three Baltic republics, Estonia, Latvia and Lithuania. In Chapter 3, Alex Fleming argues that although each country took a different approach to the reconstruction of its monobank system, there were also a number of similarities in other aspects of their policies towards developing a competitive banking sector. Echoing Szymkiewicz, he stresses the problems that resulted from a lack of human capital in the early phases of transition, especially the lack of proper credit and management skills. In the Baltic republics, which were fortunate in that their banking crises were relatively quick to die down, the crises may also have been a salutory experience, as they have resulted in a stronger banking system and stronger banking supervision than before.

The development of a non-bank financial sector

As the European Bank for Reconstruction and Development *Transition Report* (EBRD, 1998) notes, banks have tended to play an even bigger and wider role in financing economic activities in transition economies than in developing countries. This is probably inevitable given the legacy of the monobank system which, as we have seen, meant that the financial sector of the centrally planned economies consisted entirely of the *de facto* branches of a monopolistic state bank. Reducing the role of banks in the transition economies thus requires a fundamental reorientation in their financial systems. In addition, unlike the construction of a competitive banking sector, it goes beyond the restructuring of the previous state banking system and instead requires the construction of an entirely new set of institutions. Even in those countries which had enjoyed flourishing stock markets and other nonbank financial sectors before the imposition of a centrally planned economic system, the socialist system involved the abolition (rather than merely the nationalization) of these institutions.

Given the very substantial task of constructing a nonbank financial sector, it is worth raising the issue of why it matters. In particular, since Gerschenkron's (1962) classic study emphasised the role of the banking systems in the economic development of Germany, France and Italy in the nineteenth century, it may appear that the need for a nonbank financial sector is largely redundant in the specific circumstances of the transition economies. However, there are two main reasons why the existence of nonbank financial institutions (NBFIs) matters: one concerns economic development and the other relates to financial stability.

In the first place, banks offer assets (deposits) that claim to be capital certain. If this promise is to be honoured, then there must be limits to the range and nature of assets that a bank can reasonably take on to its balance sheet. Notwithstanding the existence of universal banking in many parts of the world (that is, banks also engaging in securities market activities), this consideration implies that bank-based financial systems will tend to have a smaller range of equity-type assets than those with a more broadly based structure including a wide range of NBFIs. More generally, NBFIs play a range of roles that are not suitable for banks, and through their provision of liquidity, divisibility, informational efficiencies and risk-pooling services they broaden the spectrum of risks available to investors. In this way they encourage and improve the efficiency of investment and savings; and through the provision of a broader range of financial assets that, unlike deposits, are not capital certain, they also foster a risk management culture by encouraging those who are least able to bear risk to sell risks to those better able to manage them. Thus NBFIs complement banks by providing services that are not well suited to banks and fill the gaps in financial services that otherwise occur in bank-based financial systems.

Secondly, from the point of view of financial stability, in financial sectors in which NBFIs are comparatively undeveloped banks will inevitably be required to assume risks that otherwise might be borne by the stock market, collective investment schemes, or insurance companies. However, as already noted, there is a basic incompatibility between the kinds of financial contract banks offer and their performance of these other financial functions. Banks may thus become more likely to fail as a result. One way of minimizing financial fragility in the transition economies may be to encourage a diversity of financial markets and institutions, where investors are able to assume (and hedge) a variety of risks outside the banking system itself. Without this diversity, there is a tendency for all risks to be bundled within the balance sheet of the banking system, which arguably makes a severe financial crisis more likely. This point was widely noted by policy-makers in their analysis of the lessons of the Asian currency crisis: as Greenspan (1999) pointed out, the impact of the currency crisis in Thailand might have been significantly less if some of the risks borne by the Thai banks had instead been borne by the capital markets.

Thus there are several good reasons for seeking to develop capital markets and a nonbank financial sector in parallel with the banking system, but, to quote Greenspan, this alternative is possible

> only if scarce real resources are devoted to building a financial infra-structure – a laborious process whose payoff is often experienced only decades later. The process is difficult to initiate, especially in emerging economies that are struggling to edge above the poverty level, because of the perceived need to concentrate on high short-term rates of return to capital rather than to accept more moderate returns stretched over a longer horizon.
>
> (Greenspan, 1999)

Given the high costs involved, the attempts by many of the transition economies to construct capital market institutions have not so far generated significant returns.

Some of the issues (especially the European Union system of securities regulation which could be used as a potential model for transitional economies) involved in the construction of a capital market in transition are considered in the chapter by Joseph Norton and Douglas Arner (Chapter 4).

There is also a close linkage between the development of a nonbank financial sector and the shift towards fully funded as opposed to pay-as-you-go (PAYG) pension systems. In theory, the shift towards fully funded schemes should increase the savings rate and encourage the development of capital markets and NBFIs that invest with the time horizon needed to match future pension liabilities. It should also help reduce government fiscal burdens, especially the large contingent liabilities that exist in the form of governments' commitment to pay pensions to future generations of pensioners under PAYG systems. However, the extent to which fully funded pension provision is feasible given the relatively low state of development of the financial sectors of many transition economies is an issue that has not been fully analysed. In Chapter 6, Yelena Kalyuzhnova uses the example of Kazakhstan to consider this issue.

Building a sound financial system infrastructure

The institutions of a sound financial system, whether exclusively bank-based or involving capital markets as well, in turn depend on the existence of a sound infrastructure, especially that provided by accounting standards and legal and regulatory norms. Accounting standards are intended to provide assurance of the reliability of the basic raw material of a financial system – information. Neither bankers nor investors in a competitive market economy will willingly provide credit without being able to perform an analysis of the repayment capacity of a potential borrower or potential profitability of the project in which they are invited to invest. In contrast to the informational monopoly enjoyed by the monobank, with its control over all cash flows between state-owned enterprises, bankers and investors in a competitive environment must instead rely primarily on publicly disclosed information (although in this respect banks do enjoy an advantage in that they often have access to the firm's internal management information), and the efficiency of the financial system will depend to a large degree on the quality and availability of information. This means ensuring that firms are audited according to a set of reliable and consistent accounting principles.

The question for many transition economies, which under the socialist system had lacked this aspect of the financial infrastructure along with many others, was what set of accounting standards they should adopt. Drawing on the experience of Romanian accounting reform, Alan Roberts (Chapter 5) considers the factors that weighed in the decision of the Romanian authorities to adopt a set of accounting principles based on Anglo-Saxon practice. However, Roberts expresses some doubts, which arose during the implementation of the reform, about the appropriateness of following such principles.

Another aspect of the infrastructure of finance is the need for sound legal and regulatory frameworks. Since the Asian crisis the impetus towards developing international codes and standards of regulation has gained an unstoppable momentum. Effective prudential regulation and supervision of financial markets and institutions are now recognized as essential to the financial stability and efficient functioning of any economy. The effectiveness of prudential regulation can now be assessed against a number of international standards: the Basel Committee's Core Principles for Effective Banking Supervision, the International Organization of Securities Commission's Objectives and Principles, and the similar document promulgated by the International

Association of Insurance Supervisors. Doug Arner's chapter (Chapter 7) considers the relevance of these standards documents to the transition economies, and he stresses that they should best be seen as an overlay to a set of prior requirements, such as an independent judiciary, functioning legal process, and bankruptcy procedures.

In Chapter 8, Michael Taylor takes up the theme of developing a sound regulatory infrastructure. As Taylor remarks, one of the most difficult aspects of developing regulatory systems in the transition economies is that the purposes of regulation are often poorly understood by politicians, the public and even by the regulators themselves.

References

EBRD, *Financial Sector in Transition (Transition Report)* (1998).

A. Gerschenkron, *Economic backwardness in historical perspective, a book of essays* (Cambridge, MA: Harvard University Press, 1962).

A. Greenspan, 'Lessons from the Global Crises', speech delivered on 27 September 1999, available at the Federal Reserve Board website: http://www.federalreserve.gov/boarddocs/speeches/1999/199909272.htm

D. Gros and A. Steinherr, *Winds of Change: Economic Transition in Central and Eastern Europe* (Harlow: Longman Group, 1995).

R. Hilferding, *Finance capital: a study of the latest phase of capitalist development*, edited with an introduction by Tom Bottomore; from translations by Morris Watnick and Sam Gordon (London; Boston: Routledge & Kegan Paul, 1981 [1903]).

J. Kornai, *The Socialist System* (Oxford University Press, 1992).

Overview: Developing Market Institutions in Transitional Economies

Animesh Shrivastava

Writing in 1991, Robert Solow cautioned: 'There is not some glorious theoretical synthesis of capitalism that you can write down in a book and follow. You have to grope your way'.[1] Indeed, attempts to develop a market economy in the transitional countries represent experimentation on a gigantic scale. There are several reasons for this. First, the market economy is a *system* comprising a set of supporting institutions, ranging from economic to legal, political, social and beyond. This means that the set of potential 'components' of a market economy is quite large and diverse. Further, observationally, there are marked differences between the institutions of the leading market economies. Hence the desiderata for transformation to a market economy are by no means either unique or uncontroversial. Second, the *raison d'être* of institutions is to modify the behaviour of economic agents: unless institutions do so they fail in their purpose. However, mere existence or formal adoption of institutions does not necessarily change economic behaviour. An institution's rules and arrangements have to be credible to induce that. But credibility is a complex and somewhat amorphous attribute, having roots in enforcement mechanisms, expected durability of institutional change, commitment to complementary policy changes and so on. Moreover, institutional credibility can be acquired and enhanced in a number of different ways. Thus, even if the 'targets' for requisite institutional change are uniquely identifiable, the 'instruments' for bringing them about will not necessarily be so. Third, the problem of unclear guiding principles has been compounded by insufficient practical experience. The scale and scope of the attempted transformation to a market economy in the transitional economies is without parallel.

Reforms in China have provided only limited insights since they have occurred in a markedly different economic and political setting. And reform in Latin American economies was concerned more with macro-economic stabilization than large-scale systemic change.

Like all experiments, the development of market institutions in transitional economies has been a two-way process. Existing conventional wisdom about reforms shaped initial approaches; and subsequent experience has challenged working assumptions and theories, forcing a re-thinking of the overall reform framework in many cases. In particular, the reform experience has produced a number of 'puzzles' and interesting patterns. First, the extent and severity of the economic downturn that followed reforms were not anticipated, at least publicly, by the early reformers. Second, countries that adopted a rapid programme of reform ('shock therapy') as opposed to a gradualist one appear to have experienced less severe economic decline and faster subsequent growth (World Bank, 1996; Aslund et al. 1996). Third, even among rapid reformers there have been important differences. For instance, despite following the shock therapy, the Russian economy has not experienced the rate of output growth and strong emergence of the private sector seen in Poland. Finally, and most piquantly, despite explicit moves towards a market economy through privatization and de-statization, the transition economies have not shown the growth rates that China has managed without any significant privatization or relinquishing of state control (McMillan and Naughton, 1992; Bolton, 1995).

This Chapter surveys issues in the development of market institutions and reviews the experience of the transition economies in this regard. The experience of transition so far is utilized to build a framework for understanding the issues and problems in the development of market institutions. The first section emphasizes the fact that introduction of a market economy differs from other policy-induced changes in that it involves large-scale interconnected changes. As such, the 'mechanics' of such a transformation differs significantly from that of other policy changes. The second section argues that the main role of markets as economic institutions is to provide appropriate incentives and to coordinate agents' actions. However, to do this efficiently the market mechanism requires the support of a number of complementary institutions which help address the problems of information, quality, contract formation and contract enforcement that lie at the heart of any impersonal, arm's-length transaction. In particular, the character of the legal system has an important influence on the development of market-based mechanisms.

The third section discusses issues in the design of a reform package. It stresses the notion that reforms are essentially incentive devices and, as such, can complement or substitute each other. More importantly, elements of an optimum reform package can be obtained by taking into account the incentive features of different reforms and the context within which they will be implemented. This framework is used to address the issue of optimal speed of reform or, alternatively, of 'big bang' versus 'gradualism'. The fourth section deals with political aspects of market reform. It focuses in particular on the issue of maintaining political support for reform programme in the interim phase, when costs of disruption to the old system are realized but the benefits from establishment of the new system have yet to be obtained. In this context, the strategic use of a 'window of opportunity' is discussed. The fifth section concludes.

Modelling institutional change

The move to a market economy does not merely represent an economic change (like 'liberalizing' the exchange rate or the interest rate) but a deeper transformation of the social framework. While market-oriented reforms were motivated by a number of goals in practice (ideological, political, social, maximization of government revenue, and so on), the economic case for market economy is based on allocative efficiency. The task of an economic system is to provide incentives to agents within the economy and to coordinate their actions. The case for a market mechanism rests on the claim that as an economic institution for incentive provision and coordination, it is the best in the sense that it leads to the most efficient allocation of resources.

Standard microeconomic analysis, which helps in understanding and critiquing this claim, focuses on price determination and on incentive and efficiency aspects of the price system. Such a focus on the price system can convey the impression that market reforms are synonymous with (in particular, limited to) price liberalization: institutional context does not matter. This view is of course erroneous. As discussed in the next section, the price system is highly institution-intensive, and probably more so than other forms of economic coordination (such as a command economy).

Accepting that markets are economic *institutions* has a number of implications for the design of economic reforms. To begin with, institutions are, as North (1990, p. 3) puts it, 'humanly devised constraints that shape human interaction'. Voluntary behaviour can be shaped or modified only to the extent that there are carrots and sticks of personal gains and losses respectively. In other words, all institutions need to generate incentives and have some kind of enforcement mechanism which makes them credible. In practice, credibility of institutions rests on a complex set of formal rules, informal sanctions and behavioural norms. This embeddedness of institutions in informal rules and behavioural norms means that quick, policy-induced changes are not feasible. While the formal characteristics of a system may be changed overnight through political or judicial processes, the informal rules, traditions and behavioural norms may be impervious to deliberate policy. This is of course a major lesson learnt from the transitional experience. While ambitious privatization and liberalization programmes were adopted, behaviour of individual managers, workers, banks and so on did not change since many of the supporting legal, contractual and transactional structures which would make the changes credible were not in place.

A related problem is that the outcome of a policy-induced institutional change is not entirely predictable. Experience of both developed and transitional economies shows that institutions grow through a dialectical process: individuals respond to 'opportunities' (positive and negative) created by a set of formal rules; and rules adapt either to enlarge or foreclose some of these 'opportunities'. Moreover, the path and pattern of development are determined to a considerable extent by the local conditions (that is presence or absence of the right set of supporting institutions). Thus privatization and market reform were presumably aimed at facilitating anonymous, arm's-length transactions which form the basis of competitive markets in advanced market economies. However, lack of supporting institutions means that they have in many cases strengthened relationship-based transactions. For instance, privatized banks in Ukraine had to operate without any systematic set of laws on collateral, debt recovery and bankruptcy (Jimenez, 1997). As a result, their lending activities, instead of being market-based (that is, determined by risk–return characteristics of loans) became largely network-based. Banks would lend mainly to customers with whom they had a personal relationship. Thus liberalization in banking, instead of creating an economy-wide credit market, actually fragmented it along network-based lines.

The third problem in effecting institutional change relates to the self-enforcing characteristic of most institutions. Arthur (1988, p. 10) has pointed out that there are four sources of self-enforcing mechanisms: (a) large set-up or fixed costs, which serve to bring down operating cost as more people use a system; (b) learning effects, which lower transaction costs of operating the system as it gets used more intensively; (c) coordination effects, which raise the payoffs for all agents by better coordination over a larger set of actions; and (d) adaptive expectations, where greater adoption or use of a system leads to enhanced expectations about its durability and credibility. It is clear that institutions possess all the four self-enforcing properties. This can explain why old systems and institutions in transitional economies have proved so difficult to dislodge, despite obvious evidence of their inefficiency. More importantly, though, it suggests that small-scale attempts to introduce a market economy will not work. Given the reinforcing character of existing systems and forces, piecemeal reforms would typically be either reversed or perverted. As some of the transitional experience suggests, reform has to be strategically organized on a broad front if it is to succeed.

Finally, there is the paradoxical problem of state power with respect to market-oriented reforms. As noted in the next section, successful development of market institutions requires change on large number of economic, legal, political and social fronts. This raises an interesting political-economy question: is the state powerful enough to introduce all these changes? If not, then what is the case for attempting wholesale transformation of the economic system? If it is, then what is the guarantee that the state will not become acquisitive and use its power to promote its own interests and a structure of the economy that suits it best? Shleifer and Vishny (1998) have argued that one of the major lessons of transition is that political transformation (in the sense of responsible exercise of state power) is an important concomitant of economic transformation. They contend that the difference between the post 'shock therapy' performance of Russia and Poland can be explained to a large extent by the nature of their respective governments.

Developing market institutions

The goal of transition to a market economy is not achieved simply by establishing markets where commodities can be bought or sold. Market outcomes in many cases, such as monopolies or oligopolies, can be worse than outcomes achieved under non-market systems. To achieve allocative efficiency, which is the goal of economic transformation, markets need the support of a whole host of complementary institutions and practices.

Mechanisms for enterprise efficiency

To begin with, the benefits of price competition can be realized on the production side only if the supplying firms attempt to maximize profits. Otherwise, establishment of even a competitive market for firms' outputs can worsen things. Privatizing state-owned enterprises, for instance, is not likely to enhance productive efficiency unless accompanied by extensive restructuring which makes cost-effective, profit-maximizing behaviour possible. Such a restructuring has several elements: change of management skills and personnel, provision of appropriate incentives (both short-term and long-term), reform of corporate governance and imposition of hard budget constraints. The cross-section of experience in transitional economies shows the importance of these factors. In Russia privatization took place without any significant attempt to replace existing management and infuse new skills. Earle et al. (1995) found the following pattern of ownership in privatized enterprises: in 55 per cent of the enterprises the insiders (managers or workers) predominated; in 34 per cent it was the state; and in the remaining 11 per cent it was the outside owners. One consequence of this strong insider bias was that the performance of the privatized companies did not appear to be significantly different from that of state-owned enterprises. A similar situation prevailed in many of the other East European countries. Exceptions to this trend, which highlighted the importance of internal restructuring, were the Czech Republic, Hungary and East Germany. In these cases significant management changes can be associated with the involvement of foreign firms with domestic enterprises (Carlin et al., 1995). This effect was particularly strong in East Germany, where many of the enterprises were purchased by West German firms and where management restructuring was seen as an important part of the privatization process (Schott and Reilly, 1994).

Similarly, the allocative efficiency of the market mechanism can be enhanced by imposing financial discipline upon firms through capital markets and banks. However, this requires development of complementary institutions. Privatization, for instance, does not necessarily resolve the problem of the 'soft' budget constraint and the pervasive losses that engenders. In Poland, for example, Calvo and Coricelli (1992) found that enterprises had a complex web of inter-enterprise credit as a legacy of central planning. In 1990 the volume of inter-enterprise credit was more than twice the volume of bank credit for working capital. However, in the planning era, information about the 'quality' of these loans, the implied risk exposure of the relevant enterprises, creditworthiness of

the counterparties and so on was not available. As a result, even privatized firms had interconnected balance sheets which made it difficult to
distinguish viable from non-viable firms. Hence, before external financial discipline can be responsibly imposed, appropriate information,
accounting and evaluation systems need to be in place to disentangle
and assess the economic characteristics of each enterprise.

Institutions for supporting exchange

One of the main advantages of the market mechanism is its low operating or transaction cost. In an efficient market any (anonymous) trader
can turn up and either buy or sell as he wishes. The ease of this must be
contrasted with alternative, non-market arrangements where time and
resources have to be expended in locating counterparties and agreeing
terms of trade. However, the paradox of anonymous exchange, which
epitomizes the advantages of the seemingly institution-free market
mechanism, is that it is probably more institution-intensive that any
other form of exchange.

Buyers and sellers typically have a number of concerns about any
trade, the main ones being the quality of the goods being bought and
the price being paid. If the transaction involves passage of time
(between, say, agreement of contract and its execution or between
delivery of goods and payment), then additional concerns arise, such
as: (a) creditworthiness of the counterparty; (b) reliability of the counterparty (to honour the contract rather than renege); (c) external enfor-
ceability of the contract; and (d) remedies for contractual breach. For
transactions to be successful, whether in the market or non-market
mode, these issues must be addressed. When trades occur in unorgan-
ized settings, these issues are typically tackled by the buyers and sellers
themselves through a variety of methods such as information-gathering,
monitoring, private enforcement of contractual agreements and use of
reputational mechanisms in repeated trade settings. While feasible, such
a mode of transaction clearly involves high transaction costs which
eventually get factored into the price of the commodity being traded.
Consequently trade volumes, and eventually level of economic activity
in such high-cost trading environments, are reduced.

Progress towards low-cost, anonymous trading can be made by developing institutions for dealing with each of these various dimensions of
the trading problem. Once this is done, any buyer or seller can operate
on any market without incurring large transaction costs. Development
of such supportive institutions for organizing trade brings considerable
advantages. First, there are likely to be high 'set-up' costs for an

individual trader who wishes to perform these functions himself. Since these costs are repeated over traders, organizing them through a common source can significantly lower the cost per unit trade. This brings down the overall cost of trades and therefore expands the volume of economic activity. Second, organizing these activities commonly brings scope for specialization and hence further increase in the efficiency of transactions.

The market ideal of anonymous trade therefore relies on a number of complementary institutions to sort out the various problems and concerns relating to any trade or exchange. Hence introducing a market economy involves not just price liberalization (that is determination of price by market forces rather than government fiat) but also the development of the various institutions that support market exchange. The experience of transitional economies suggests just how important these measures are.

Consider the problem of information. Successful markets require several kinds of information and hence information-processing institutions. First, information needs to be collated about potential demands and supplies. This is what contributes to 'thickness' of markets and to the discovery of competitive prices (that is, prices which ensure that goods come from lowest-cost producer and go to the highest-value consumer). In many transitional economies where coordination of demand and supply was previously done through plans, there were no natural mechanisms (for example business associations, business directories and so on) to facilitate search that produces information about potential trading partners. In Romania, introduction of markets initially worsened the situation. There was considerable local variation in prices and, with the partial abandonment of the planning framework, the coordination of inputs and outputs became more difficult (Ben-Ner and Montias, 1991). Similarly, Carlin et al. (1995) report that enterprise managers in Poland, the Czech Republic and Slovakia, Hungary and Russia cited collapse of wholesale distribution networks as an important constraint in their attempts to restructure operations in response to market forces. Such problems can have two effects. First, trading activity of firms is restricted to information available from their personal networks. Thus each firm operates in a narrower market with fewer economic prospects than need be the case. Second, the informational barriers which segment a potentially large (national) market into local, network-based ones also create, in effect, a multitude of monopolies which would again have the effect of lowering the quantities traded. In transitional economies, few information-processing institutions were created around the time of market reform. However, the need for information in order to have successful market organization has brought about several responses. Trade associations, brokerage houses, wholesale traders and so on have emerged to intermediate between buyers and sellers, to reduce search costs and to gather as well as spread information. In Russia, for instance, markets for wholesale farm produce and for commodities such as aluminium and oil have evolved (McMillan, 1997).

The second informational problem is one of quality. If trade is to occur freely outside the personal network of firms, then doubts about quality need to be resolved. If the trade concerned is a 'spot market' trade, where delivery of commodity and payment occur simultaneously, the main problem is one of adverse selection. However, in the case of trades in which time elapses between the first steps and the final completion (say between delivery and payment or contract agreement and execution), the adverse selection problem is compounded by a moral hazard problem as well.

The adverse selection problem affects the ability of the market mechanism to match up feasible trades (that is, trades which both buyer and seller would be willing to undertake if doubts about quality were cleared up) and in some cases, as the literature shows,[2] can prevent the emergence of the market altogether. In well-functioning market economies, a number of mechanisms exist to address the adverse selection concerns regarding quality. For instance, firms attempt to signal quality by offering a variety of warranties on product (for example money-back guarantees or no-quibble replacement) or price (for example lowest price guarantee or promise to match the lowest offer). Screening mechanisms of various kinds grow up (for example government-backed certification bodies or self-regulation of quality by producers' associations). Again, in transitional economies these quality issues were not systematically addressed as part of the market reform programme. However, as expected, a number of solutions have appeared over time. For instance, in Russia the government introduced a law on quality and on a national certification body (Goldberg, 1992). Russian commodity exchanges attempted to resolve informational problems about quality through various routes: trade was focused on branded commodities; an extensive system of certification regarding nature, quantity and quality of goods on offer was used; and compensation guarantees were offered to buyers against broker malfeasance (Davis, 1998).

The moral hazard problem of ensuring agreed-upon contractual performance has to be addressed through a different set of institutions.

Fundamentally, there are two ways of dealing with moral hazard problems: monitoring and incentive alignment. Monitoring can be done through a number of institutions such as consumer associations, watchdog bodies, public regulators and so on. Incentive alignment can, in principle, be done by drawing up a 'complete' contract covering all contingencies. Completeness of contract refers to the provision that the contract specifies what is to be done by each party in each possible contingency. However, such complete contracting is infeasible for a number of reasons. First, it may not be possible to anticipate all contingencies. Second, it may not be possible to agree the terms of transaction for each contingency. Third, it may not be possible credibly to enforce all the terms of a contract. Hence economic contracts are inevitably incomplete in the sense that they do not cover many of the contingencies. Incentive alignment, in this case, requires appropriate *ex post* distribution of bargaining power (Grossman and Hart, 1986). This is effected, to a large extent, by the legal system.

The role of the legal system

Transactions in a market-based economy can be broadly divided into two types: (a) arm's-length trades that do not involve the buyer and seller in any interrelated activity; and (b) other transactions in which there is some degree of joint 'production' or interaction between the trading parties. Examples of the first type range from the simplest purchases of goods in ordinary ('spot') markets to agreements to buy or deliver at future dates (as in future deliveries of grain, oil, imported inputs, or futures contracts of a financial nature). Examples of the second type are employment relationships, relationships between various producers using a common resource, or relationships between governments and private businesses. The legal system performs an important facilitating role for both these types of exchanges, which considerably lowers their transactions costs.

For 'arm's-length' transactions the legal system supplies standardized contract 'shells' (regarding, for example, the implications of the various terms of offer or guarantee) and a judicial-cum-penal system for interpreting and enforcing contractual obligations. This requires a framework of rules (regarding freedom to contract and exchange, protection of consumers, other consumer rights, suppliers' obligations, quality, health and safety, and so on) and a network of institutions for enforcing them. Such laws and institutions were not adequately developed in command economies, where most of the goods and resources were moved by fiat and in which the state (or a state-owned enterprise) was typically one of the parties involved in economic transactions.[3]

Transactions involving joint production or, more generally, coordination between the various parties typically involve interactions over time. As mentioned above, drawing up complete contracts for these dynamic transactions can be difficult, especially if the transactions involve inputs and outputs that are difficult to measure (for example effort and its marginal product or externalities relating to a trader's activity). Hence such transactions are organized under 'incomplete' contracts which cover only the more important or standardized contingencies. This leaves open the issue of what happens in other possible contingencies. But, as Grossman and Hart (1986) and Hart and Moore (1990) point out, the way these gaps in the contract are filled crucially affects initial (relation-specific) investments and overall economic efficiency.

The legal system turns out to have a crucial role in filling these contractual gaps and thus encouraging long-term transactions. First, a routine function of the legal system is to solve disputes which, reinterpreted, means adjudicating on the gaps in the actual contract between the disputing parties. Second, the legal system empowers other institutions of social ordering such as corporations, industry associations, arbitration bodies and so on which play a vital role in filling contractual gaps. The legal system does this by legitimizing the institutions' procedures and decisions.[4] The most important contribution of the legal system is perhaps an indirect one. In any social system the overwhelming majority of dispute settlement takes place in the 'shadow of the law' in the sense that disputes are privately resolved largely on basis of disputants' expectations of the nature, uncertainty and cost of securing a formal settlement through courts (Galanter, 1981). Therefore the nature of the legal system – its extensiveness and reach, the predictability of its decisions, and the delay, cost and complexity of seeking legal redress – significantly affects long-term economic relationships and overall efficiency.

In transitional economies there were no significant institutions for supporting private contractual exchange. This was especially so with respect to institutions for either 'completing' incomplete contracts or providing low-cost dispute settlement and contract enforcement. The main source of authoritative precepts was the state. But given the 'grabbing-hand' nature of many states (Shleifer and Vishny, 1998) and the lack of effective institutions to curb the state's power to renegotiate, this did not provide a congenial legal environment for market-based activity.

As McMillan (1997, p. 226) notes, 'The existing legal system suited central planning, not a market economy.'

Legal sanctions are not the only means to uphold contractual behaviour. The literature on repeated non-cooperative games suggests that there are various circumstances and mechanisms under which self-interested players would adhere to an agreed outcome (Fudenberg, 1992). In other words, business relations can develop ahead of developments in formal law. This has been the case in transitional economies. Banks have lent money, business deals have been struck and exchanges have been organized in the absence of a secure contracting environment. While encouraging in itself, the way in which these trades have been done suggest the inherent limitations of such spontaneous developments. Thus banks have had to rely on personal contacts and extensive screening; and lending has been short-term to reduce risk exposure. Businesses have had to screen potential partners and cultivate long-term relationships. In the absence of efficient and reliable judicial systems, contracts have had to be enforced through illegal or criminal means (Grief and Kandel, 1995). It is clear that the 'transactions technology' underlying these exchanges is highly inefficient. Trade relations are limited to an (arbitrary) network of personal contacts; costs are high and can be physically and socially disruptive. This is in sharp contrast to the low-cost, economy-wide trade that the transactions technology of a market-based system permits.

The final part of the legal transformation required for a market economy is the development of countervailing institutions to rein in state power and make it more accountable. Historically, the state in transitional economies has enjoyed supreme economic, political and legal powers and unchallenged discretion in its use. But, as noted above (Grossman and Hart, 1986), such power to renegotiate contracts discourages, in effect, long-term relationships and dissuades economic partners from investing in specific assets. This effect is quite general and holds beyond transitional economies. For instance, Borner et al. (1995, p. 36) find that in 'discretionary' states, in which power is not exercised in a 'credible' manner 'the private sector reacts by keeping its resources liquid and retreating into informal relationships'. Consequently, savings, investment, technological growth and, eventually, per capita income growth are lower. Borner et al. find empirical support for this proposition in a study of 28 developing countries where political credibility provides a potentially very important explanation of the differences in economic growth. In the context of transition economies, Shleifer and Vishny (1998) put forward a similar hypothesis to explain the relatively poor growth experience of Russia in comparison with Poland. They argue that despite similar economic reforms (including the common 'shock-therapy' approach) the state in Russia has retained more substantial control over economic life and acts, in general, in a more acquisitive manner. Consequently, they argue that a central part of market reforms must be the 'transition of the government from a Communist police state to an institution supporting a market economy' (p. 230).

Application: the development of equity markets in transitional economies

The development of capital markets is important for all transitional economies. Capital markets are crucial for raising equity capital as well as for efficient risk-bearing and risk-shifting that is made possible by forward trades and trades in derivative instruments. Despite the predominance of bank-based debt finance in transitional countries there is evidence that (external) equity capital is an important source of finance in these economies (Singh, 1994). Indeed, debt and equity finance appear to be complements rather than substitutes (La Porta et al., 1997).

The task of establishing fully functional, efficient equity markets illustrates well the complex set of institutional, legal and governance-related changes required. To begin with, note that the setting up of a trading floor (or electronic trading system) in which securities of a few firms are infrequently traded does not have much economic significance. For stock markets to play their full economic role, they must be liquid and assist in 'price discovery' and the allocation of resources (see Allen, 1993). Each of these characteristics requires a particular legal-institutional underpinning. Liquidity or 'immediacy' is the ability to trade instantly without a significant impact upon price. Markets possess this characteristic only if there is a significant number of traders (speculators/market-makers) willing to spread the risk of any 'shock' felt by some of the investors. The scope for provision of such liquidity depends upon various aspects of the market structure (Grossman and Miller, 1988). If transaction and operating costs are high, if trading rules prevent flexible trade practices and restrict the ability of market-makers to bear risk, if credit facilities available to them are inadequate and rigid, then the liquidity of the market as a whole suffers. This affects the efficiency of the markets since illiquid equity markets are essentially ineffective markets.

Price discovery is perhaps the most important function of financial markets. In stylized analyses, 'price discovery' (realization by the markets of a price best approximating the security's net present value) occurs through the efforts of private investors. Investors gather price-sensitive information to profit from it; and the pattern of their trades 'conveys' the information to the market (Glosten and Milgrom, 1985). But for this mechanism to work, investors must be willing to trade on the market or, alternatively, have 'confidence' in the marketplace. Confidence depends upon a number of things. First, there should be as little market manipulation or insider trading as possible. Insider trading acts like a tax on other investors (Copeland and Galai, 1983); extensive insider trading can restrict participation by ordinary investors and lead to a market collapse. Protection against insider trading requires a set of inter-related legal, institutional and policy measures. For instance, at the legal level, laws prohibiting insider trading must be enacted. At the institutional level, some formal body such as the stock exchange needs to take responsibility for monitoring trades to detect 'unusual patterns'. At the governance level, there should be some authority (either a regulator or a special court) for pursuing suspected cases of insider trading and imposing credible penalties. Second, investors should have reliable information about the operating details and cost and revenue profiles of the firms they invest in. Therefore stock market operations must be backed by extensive information disclosure regimes as well as standardized accounting and auditing systems to ensure consistency and accuracy of information. Third, investors need to be reassured about receiving their returns at the end of the investment period. Several risk are involved here: performance (or default) risk relating to the investment being financed, counterparty risk, settlement risk and so on. Again, in order to develop trading activity, mechanisms and institutions must be devised to deal with these problems.

For example, in futures trades which require delivery of some underlying 'commodity' at a specified future time, counterparty and settlement risk are key risks since non-delivery negates the entire purpose of undertaking the futures transaction. For private investors wishing to undertake futures trades, it is extremely expensive to check details of potential counterparties, especially regarding their ability to deliver in the future. A key institutional innovation which has historically helped in the development of futures markets was to make the futures exchange itself the counterparty to each transaction. For individual traders, this helped lower the risk of counterparty and settlement default. As for the exchanges, their ability to monitor all trades centrally and their ability to diversify risk by acting as counterparty to all trades means that they can provide insurance against the risk at a much lower cost.

Design of the reform package

It is clear from the discussion above that development of a market system requires institutional and policy changes across a very wide front. As Lipton and Sachs (1990) have argued, the required reforms are interlinked in a 'seamless web'; hence the reform process must be comprehensive. While the seemingly all-encompassing nature of the required change is easy to understand, the case for comprehensive reform does not necessarily follow from that for several reasons. First, any reform process entails adjustment costs which are frequently 'convex' in the sense that they rise proportionately faster as the pace of reform increases. These costs may include costs of unemployment generated and the destruction of firm-or sector-specific assets and institutions in the process of structural change. Second, complementarities between reforms may only imply 'connectedness' of reforms over time (within the context of an overall reform package) but not necessarily simultaneity in their implementation. Third, some reform measures may be substitutes and hence need not occur together as a package. Fourth, lack of adequate information about the reform process and outcomes may mean that some experimentation through a limited reform programme may be desirable before attempting full-scale change. Finally, the political or administrative capacity for introducing and managing change as well as the economy's capacity for absorbing it may be more much limited than envisaged by a reform programme. Bold but unrealistic reform programmes (like the 500–Day Plan for the Soviet Union) were common at the beginning of the transition experience and have been tried in other contexts too. For example, commenting on a 'tough' stabilization and structural adjustment plan – which, note, still did not attempt an overhaul of the economic system – introduced in Bolivia in 1985, Williamson (1990, p. 5) noted: 'In short, Paz's advisers planned the equivalent of about five GATT rounds, six Gramm-Rudmans, and more deregulation than had been accomplished by the Carter and Reagan administration together, all overnight.'

In designing an optimum reform package, it is worth noting that development of a market system requires two kinds of reforms: (a) those that align agents' incentives with efficient economic outcomes; and (b) those that reduce transaction costs. As a first approximation, it is reasonable to assume that agents maximize their self-interest (however perceived) in any circumstance. The problem with malfunctioning economic systems is that this could mean that agents maximize leisure or personal gain at social cost (for example through work disruption or through 'diversion' of firms' resources). The allocative merit of a market economy, enunciated first by Adam Smith, was that personal gain was pursued in a manner that promoted social wealth. Development of the market system in transitional economies requires similar incentive restructuring in the production sector. That is why the issue of enterprise reform is central to the proper development of markets.

The alignment of a manager's incentives to socially efficient outcomes contains several elements. First, the manager's compensation must to be tied to profit maximization. Hence changes in corporate governance and compensation arrangements that produce this will be required. Second, for the computed profit to reflect true (social) profit, the inputs and outputs must be traded at their correct (shadow) prices. This requires liberalization of these markets (so that prices can find their shadow value) as well as their 'regulation' to ensure that they operate in a competitive environment. It should be noted here that not only does alignment of managerial incentives require a number of things to be done (that is, induce profit-maximizing behaviour and set correct prices); each of these things can in principle be done through a number of different reform measures. For instance, privatization, regulatory oversight, finance market discipline, threat of takeovers, compensation through stock options and so on can all serve to induce profit-maximizing behaviour. The question, implicitly posed at the start of this section, becomes clearer: which of these seemingly 'seamless webs' of reforms should be chosen and how?

The key insight for analysing this issue is that, as incentive devices, reforms can function as complements or substitutes. A pair of reforms can be defined as complements if the incremental effect on incentives from implementing one is greater if the other is already in place (Milgrom and Roberts, 1990). For example, input price liberalization and capital market discipline are complements. A pair of reforms are substitutes if the effect of both of them together is not greater than the sum of the effects of each reform in isolation. Thus privatization and changes in management compensation schemes can be substitutes in enterprise restructuring. This is shown clearly by the experience of China, which has managed pervasive restructuring and consequent growth without ownership change.

A major element of policy design, therefore, is to concentrate on complementary rather than substitute policies. Even so, the set of complementary reforms can be quite large, raising the issue again of whether a 'big-bang' approach is necessarily implied. Some progress can be made in this direction by employing additional considerations beyond that of complementarity between reform instruments. The first concerns expectations about behaviour over time. If a reform which is expected to be implemented tomorrow (such as introduction of competition) produces offsetting behaviour today (such as erection of costly industry defences), then it may be better to bring forward the implementation of tomorrow's plan. The second consideration is uncertainty regarding the costs and benefits of reform, and hence the need both for experimentation as well as keeping open the option of reform reversal. Dewatripont and Roland (1997) generate several interesting insights in this regard. They show that in a situation where there is uncertainty about outcomes, where reversal of reforms is costly and where reforms are complementary, gradualism or partial reform is costly. However, gradualism does provide the benefit of an option for early reversal (if reform outcomes are not as desired). Hence, if learning (about reform outcomes) is fast enough compared to the potential costs of partial reform, then gradualism is to be preferred; otherwise, big bang is optimal. More generally, they argue that complementarity of reforms implies connectedness but not necessarily simultaneity: complementarity, it turns out, is also a necessary condition for gradualism to be optimal.

Over and above the reversal costs are the adjustment costs, discussed at the beginning of this section. How do these costs affect the debate about optimal pace and sequencing of market-oriented reforms? Friedman and Johnson (1996) have obtained some interesting results in this regard. First, they argue that the worse the initial condition of an economy, the more ambitious and the faster the reform programme should be. The intuition is that in critical situations a package of radical reforms may not appear too costly and the benefits of rapid change may be easier to sell. Thus it is argued that the depth of the Polish crisis in 1989 made it a more natural candidate for shock therapy than the gradually reforming Hungary. Second, Friedman and Johnson argue that if the economic characteristics are more congenial to a market economy, then a faster-paced reform is more desirable. Finally, the less credibility a government has, the more intense or far-reaching its reforms need to be. The idea is that reforms succeed only to the extent that they influence behaviour of economic agents. A halting reform process from a seemingly insecure government would not induce rational agents to change their behaviour and expectations. However, a more radical package may cross a 'threshold' such that agents are also induced to make appropriate changes. In this context It is notable that in China even small policy changes produced significant results, perhaps because of their perceived stability.

Overall, a large number of factors impinge upon the choice of a policy package, so that designing it may be more akin to art rather than science, requiring astute judgements based on context-specific factors. However, ideas regarding complementarity between reform instruments, time complementarity, the trade-off between inefficiency of partial reform and the option to exit with low costs if reforms do not work, the depth of economic crisis and the reform credentials of the state can be used to help identify a core package of reforms and a time sequence for its implementation.

Political economy

Reforms do not occur in a political vacuum or as trial runs in an experimental setting. Benefits and costs are necessarily distributed unevenly as the structure of the economy is altered and resources are shifted from some sectors into others. Since these reforms cannot be Pareto improving, policy-makers typically back them on the basis that they increase aggregate wealth. However, this approach has a number of pitfalls. Since (full) compensation of losers by winners is not typically part of a reform programme, the argument about increase in aggregate wealth is not sufficient to secure general consensus for reform. The consensus becomes more difficult to maintain if even the goal of increase in aggregate wealth becomes difficult to reach.

In nearly all transitional economies, post-reform output fell sharply as economies slid backwards. 'After five years of transition economics', Amsden et al. (1998, p. vii) note, '[t]he popular mood is one of anger over rising unemployment, inflation, deteriorating living standards, the collapse of social services, and soaring crime'. Assuming that both market-oriented reform and its continuation are desirable, the challenging issue is how to create and sustain consensus for reform, especially in light of the adverse effects it has generated. Both economic analysis and experience of transitional economies help to show the problems and prospects in this regard.

To begin with, the size and sequencing of the reform plan depends crucially upon initial conditions and the nature of the political process. Dewatripont and Roland (1997) have argued that if a gradualist approach to reform is preferred, then it is advisable to start with the implementation of highest-payoff reforms and reforms which benefit the median voter in order to maintain support for the reform. More generally, support for reform from key constituencies may have to be bought by relevant transfers. The experience regarding the nature and type of reform in transitional economies can be read as evidence of the significance of this factor. For instance, the Russian privatization programme has generally been criticized for favouring existing management and other stakeholders. However, Boycko et al. (1993) have argued that that was the only politically feasible method of privatization. In Poland, the mass voucher privatization programme was blocked for more than three years by insiders who did not want the benefits to accrue to the public at large (Roland, 1994).

If a gradual path of reform may be difficult to sustain over time (since costs of disruption arise before the benefits of restructuring), then the idea of a 'window of opportunity' to introduce a programme of radical reform becomes appealing. A window of opportunity should be understood as any set of circumstances in which the proposed reform plan is *ex ante* acceptable to the population. *Ex ante* acceptability may arise either because the current economic situation is critical ('no way but forward' argument) or there are sizeable benefits to acceptance (such as conditional loans from international organizations and banks) or the costs of reform are not well known or widely understood. The scale of reforms a government may attempt to squeeze through any window of opportunity would depend upon several factors. If there is a threshold level beyond which reforms are too costly to reverse, then a 'big bang' that takes the reform programme beyond that threshold will be adopted. If there is a pair of reforms *A* and *B* such that *B* becomes much more desirable or acceptable once *A* is in place, then the initial programme may include only reform *A*. In this way a government can build up future momentum for change. Similarly, governments may include reforms in the initial programme which constrain successor governments to change. Hence discretionary elements (like reducing subsidies or cutting expenditures) may be tackled in the initial reform programme since successive governments cannot be constrained to specific policies in those spheres.

Conclusion

This chapter has selectively surveyed the literature on the development of market institutions and the experience of transitional economies in this regard. The central theme that emerges is that impersonal, competitive exchange, which the market system ideally produces, is perhaps more institution-intensive than any other arrangement for organizing exchange. Typically, each supporting institution serves to enhance transactional or operational efficiency (by reducing costs and aligning

incentives) so that it is economically desirable on its own. More importantly, however, these institutions are also complementary in the sense
that the efficiency of each is enhanced by the presence of others. Consequently, development of market institutions involves a whole set of
interrelated institutional changes. The experience of transitional economies has shown not only how complex the transformation process is,
but also how context-and culture-specific some of the supporting institutions can be. Still, the reform process in the transitional economies
has in general proved robust and forward-moving. Significant reversals
have not been experienced and, perhaps because of their complementary character, initial reforms have been followed by more market-
oriented ones. There has also been a significant growth in quasi-legal
and social institutions supportive of market reform. In due time this
should lead to the realization by each country of its own specific 'brand'
of the market economy.

Notes

1   *The New York Times*, 29 September 1991, p. E1.
2   See Salanie (1997) for a recent review.
3   This means that there was little room for development of (independent)
    institutions for monitoring and supporting exchange transactions. For
    instance, in the event of poor quality, delay in delivery or other types of
    non-performance of contracts by state enterprises there was little scope for,
    or point in, appealing to the state itself. Consequently, there was a general
    absence of third-party monitoring, evaluation and enforcement institutions
    on which much market-based exchange relies. In a similar vein, Rapaczynski
    (1996) has argued that a state that exercises most of its policy through prop-
    erty rights (and the discretion that goes with it) tends to rely less on regulatory
    and quasi-judicial processes (which involve transparency and, hence, proce-
    dural restrictions on the arbitrary exercise of authority).
4   It can do so, for example, through explicit rulings about the authority of
    arbitrators in labour disputes (Getman, 1979) or commercial disputes (Gold-
    berg, 1976), or through immunity in the form of non-admittance of cases
    involving certain kinds of regulatory activity.

References

F. Allen, 'Stock Markets and Resource Allocation' in C Mayer and X Vives (eds),
  Capital Markets and Financial Intermediation (Cambridge: CUP, 1993).
A. Amsden, J. Kochanowicz and L. Taylor, *The Market Meets its Match* (Cambridge,
  MA.: Harvard University Press, 1998).

W. B. Arthur, 'Self-Enforcing Mechanisms in Economics', in P. W. Anderson, K. J. Arrow and D. Pines (eds), *The Economy as a Complex Evolving System* (Reading, MA: Addison-Wesley, 1988).

A. Aslund, P. Boone and S. Johnson, 'How to Stabilize: Lessons from Post Communist Countries', *Brookings Papers on Economic Activity*, 1 (1996), 217–314.

A. Ben-Ner and J. M. Montias, 'The Introduction of Markets in a Hypercentralized Economy: the Case of Romania', *Journal of Economic Perspectives*, 5 (1991), 163–70.

P. Bolton, 'Privatisation and the Separation of Ownership and Control: lessons from Chinese enterprise reform', *Economics of Transition*, 3 (1995), 1–12.

S. Borner, A. Brunetti and B. Weder, *Political Credibility and Economic Development* (Basingstoke: Macmillan – now Palgrave, 1995).

M. Boycko, A. Shleifer and R. Vishny, 'Privatizing Russia', *Brookings Papers on Economic Activity*, 2 (1993), 139–92.

G. A. Calvo and F. Coricelli, 'Stagflationary Effects of Stabilization Programs in Reforming Socialist Countries: enterprise-side vs household-side factors', *The World Bank Economic Review*, 6 (1992).

W. Carlin, J. van Reenan and T. Wolfe, 'Enterprise Restructuring in the Transition: the case study evidence from central and eastern Europe', *Economics of Transition*, 3 (1995), 427–58.

T. Copeland and D. Galai, 'Information Effects and the Bid–Ask Spread', *Journal of Finance*, 38 (1983), 1457–69.

J. D. Davis, 'Russian Commodity Exchanges: a case study of organized markets in the transition process, 1990–96', *Economics of Transition*, 6 (1998), 183–96.

M. Dewatripont and G. Roland, 'Transition as a Process of Large Scale Institutional Change' in D. M. Kreps and K. E. Wallis (eds), *Advances in Economics and Econometrics: theory and applications*, Volume II (Cambridge: CUP, 1997).

J. Earle, S. Estrin and L. Leschenko, 'The Effect of Ownership on Behaviour: Is privatization working in Russia?' CEPR Discussion Paper (LSE: London, 1995).

E. J. Friedman and S. Johnson, 'Complementarities in Economic Reform', *Economics of Transition*, 4 (1996), 319–29.

D. Fudenberg, 'Explaining Cooperation and Commitment in Repeated Games', in J.-J. Laffont (ed.), *Advances in Economic Theory* (Cambridge: CUP, 1992).

M. Galanter, 'Justice in Many Rooms: Courts, Private Ordering, and Indigenous Law', *Journal of Legal Pluralism*, 19 (1981), 1–47.

J. Getman, 'Labor Arbitration and Dispute Resolution', *Yale Law Journal*, 88 (1979), 916–49.

L. Glosten and P. Milgrom, 'Bid, Ask, and Transaction Prices in a Specialist Market with Heterogenously Informed Traders', *Journal of Financial Economics*, 13 (1985), 71–100.

P. Goldberg, 'Economic Reform and Product Quality Improvement Efforts in the Soviet Union', *Soviet Studies*, 44 (1992), 113–22.

V. Goldberg, 'Regulation and Administered Contracts', *Bell Journal of Economics*, 7 (1976), 426–48.

A. Grief and E. Kandel, 'Contract Enforcement Institutions: historical perspectives and current status in Russia', in E. Lazear (ed.), *Economic Transition in Eastern Europe and Russia: Realities of Reform* (Stanford: Hoover Institution Press, 1995).

S. Grossman and O. Hart, 'The Costs and Benefits of Ownership: a theory of vertical and lateral integration', *Journal of Political Economy*, 94 (1986), 691–719.

S. Grossman and M. Miller, 'Liquidity and Market Structure', *Journal of Finance*, 43 (1988), 617–33.

O. Hart and J. Moore, 'Property Rights and the Nature of the Firm', *Journal of Political Economy*, 98 (1990), 1119–58.

J. Jimenez, 'Issues for Banking Reform in Ukraine', in P. K. Cornelius and P. Lenain (eds), *Ukraine: Accelerating the Transition to Market* (Washington, DC: IMF, 1997).

R. La Porta, F. Lopez-de-Silanes, A. Shleifer and R. Vishny, 'Legal Determinants of External Finance', *Journal of Finance*, 54 (1997), 471–517.

D. Lipton and J. Sachs, 'Creating a Market Economy in Eastern Europe: the case of Poland', *Brookings Papers on Economic Activity*, 1 (1990).

J. McMillan, 'Markets in Transition', in D. M. Kreps and K. E. Wallis (eds), *Advances in Economics and Econometrics: theory and applications*, Volume II (Cambridge: CUP, 1997).

J. McMillan and B. Naughton, 'How to Reform a Planned Economy', *Oxford Review of Economic Policy*, 8 (1992), 103–43.

P. Milgrom and J. Roberts, 'Rationalizability, Learning, and Equilibrium in Games with Strategic Complements', *Econometrica*, 58 (1990), 1255–77

D. C. North, *Institutions, Institutional Change and Economic Performance* (Cambridge: CUP, 1990).

A. Rapaczynski, 'The Role of the State and the Market in Establishing Property Rights', *Journal of Economic Perspectives*, 10 (1996), 87–103.

G. Roland, 'The Role of Political Constraints in Transition Strategies', *Economics of Transition*, 2 (1994), 27–41.

B. Salanie, *The Economics of Contracts* (Cambridge, MA: MIT Press, 1997).

V. Schott and B. Reilly, 'Privatization in Germany – 1993', in A. Bohm and M. Simoneti (eds), *Privatization in Central & Eastern Europe 1993* (Ljubljana: CEPN, 1994).

A. Shleifer and R. Vishny, *The Grabbing Hand* (Cambridge, MA: Harvard University Press, 1998).

J. Williamson, 'The Progress of Policy Reform in Latin America' (Institute for International Economics), 28 (1990).

A. Singh, 'How do Large Corporations in Developing Countries Finance their Growth?', in R. O'Brien (ed.), *Finance and the International Economy* (New York: OUP, 1994).

World Bank, *World Development Report: From Plan to Market* (Washington, DC: World Bank, 1996).

Part I

The Development of the Banking Sector

1
Bad Loans as Alternatives to Fiscal Transfers in Transition Economies

George Tridimas

The failure of state-owned-enterprises (SOEs) in post-socialist economies to repay their debts to the banking sector, the so-called 'bad loans problem', is considered as one of the most important impediments to successful economic transition. Accumulation of bad loans, the argument runs, distorts the allocation of scarce capital and delays the restructuring of enterprises, restricts lending to the public sector, jeopardizes the health of the balance sheet of banks and imperils the privatization process of firms and banks alike. The quantitative significance of the problem is recorded in Table 1.1, which presents the profile of the ratio of bad loans to total loans for the transition economies during the period 1994–98. From an (unweighted) average of almost a quarter of the total stock of loans, the share has decreased over time, but still claims 14 per cent of the total. Although the precise size of bad loans and its pattern of change varies from country to country, no transition economy has been spared its far-reaching consequences. Partly as a result of deliberate policy action and partly as a result of unpredicted economic shocks, in some countries, such as Albania, Azerbaijan, Romania, the Czech and the Slovak Republics, the ratio has remained stubbornly high (and often increasing), while in other countries significant progress has been made towards decreasing it, for example in Hungary, Poland, Latvia, Lithuania, Kyrgyzstan and Armenia, although in the latter countries the move has not necessarily signalled the establishment of hard budget constraints on enterprises. It is also clear that the problem of bad loans is an endemic one that afflicts vulnerable countries irrespective of the stage of transition, level of economic development and progress towards liberalization.

Non-performing bank loans to state-owned-enterprises in transition economies have long been recognized as a covert method of

Table 1.1   Bad loans (in percent of total loans, end of period)

	1994	1995	1996	1997	1998
Albania	–	35	40	91	–
Armenia	34	36	23	8	–
Azerbaijan	16	22	20	20	20
Belarus	8	12	14	13	17
Bosnia and Herzegovina	–	–	–	–	–
Bulgaria	7	13	15	13	–
Croatia	12	13	11	10	15
Czech Republic	36	33	28	27	27
Estonia	4	3	2	2	4
FYR Macedonia	–	–	42	36	33
Georgia	24	41	7	7	7
Hungary	18	10	7	4	6
Kazakhstan	–	15	20	8	7
Kyrgyzstan	92	72	26	8	2
Latvia	10	19	20	10	6
Lithuania	27	17	32	28	13
Moldova	16	9	17	10	5
Poland	36	35	24	15	12
Romania	19	38	48	57	34
Russian Federation	–	6	5	4	5
Slovak Republic	30	41	32	33	44
Slovenia	22	13	14	12	11
Tajikistan	–	–	3	3	3
Turkmenistan	–	11	11	14	2
Ukraine	5	13	12	11	–
Uzbekistan	–	8	2	4	–
Mean (unweighted)	23.1	22.4	19.0	17.9	14.0

– not available
Source: EBRD (1998 and 1999).

government assistance to loss-making enterprises. That is, rather than using explicit fiscal taxes-cum-transfers paid directly through the budget, the government subsidizes the SOEs indirectly by forgoing payment of interest on their debt, which amounts to levying implicit taxes on financial intermediaries and their customers and transferring the proceeds to the recipient SOEs.[1] However, although the distortionary effects of the bad loans for the incentives of both lenders and borrowers, and the consequent misallocation of resources, have been discussed at length in the literature,[2] no formal account of the redistributive tax-cum-transfer effects from bank depositors and 'good' borrowers to

SOEs has been offered.[3] The aim of this chapter is to address this issue.

Specifically, the present study examines systematically the equivalence between bad loans to SOEs and fiscal transfers. For this purpose it treats bad loans to SOEs as a policy instrument whose size is decided by the government.[4] Using a standard firm-theoretic model of bank behaviour, bad loans to SOEs are modelled to (a) reduce the size of bank portfolio that can be used to grant loans to good borrowers and (b) affect negatively bank profitability by reducing the expected net return on loans and by increasing the expected cost of servicing deposits. The first section traces the effects of bad loans on the total volume of deposits channelled through the official banking sector and bank credit granted to the profitable private sector. However, the model focuses on the equilibrium of the banking sector and the aggregate levels of deposits and loans and does not raise issues relating to the distribution of bad loans across different banks, nor the possibility that some banks burdened with large sums of bad loans may fail. Recognizing that a possible settlement of the bad loan issue would be for the government to pay the interest due, the second section compares the effects of bad loans with the effects of government borrowing, when the government borrows at the market interest rate an amount equal to the size of the bad loans.

Bank behaviour in the presence of bad loans

The model used in the present chapter is an extension of the standard Monti–Klein model of monopoly bank behaviour. The assumption of a monopoly banking system is adopted since, at best, bank competition in the transition economies has been rather limited. The break-up of the monobank that characterized central planning has hardly led to a competitive banking structure. On the contrary, with few exceptions only, it was followed by high concentration in deposit and loan markets (with the saving banks being the dominant institutions in the former and the specialized sector-specific banks in the latter), continued state ownership of banks and restricted foreign bank entry. More specifically, in 1997 the shares of the five largest banks in total bank assets in the countries of Central and East Europe and the countries of the Commonwealth of Independent States were 68 per cent and 66 per cent respectively (down from 69 per cent and 79 per cent respectively), while the equivalent figure for the countries of the OECD and the EU were 52 per cent and 49 per cent (EBRD, 1998).[5]

Formally, a single-period decision-making horizon is assumed and, focusing on the portfolio transformation function of financial intermediaries, the banking sector is modelled to purchase deposit-inputs and produce loan-outputs acting as interest-rate setter in both the deposit and loan market. However, unlike the standard Monti–Klein framework, and similar, to the models of Courakis (1984 and 1987), which studied the effects of bank portfolio constraints on the size of financial intermediation in less developed countries, banking in the transition economies is characterized by the absence of a large securities market, where the banking sector always deals as rate-taker. The absence of the latter implies that the opportunity cost of funds at which the banking sector can acquire or dispose of extra funds is no longer constant and exogenously given, but is variable and endogenously determined by the demand and supply of loans and deposits, and consequently, bank decisions about deposits cannot be separated from bank decisions about lending.[6]

Let the volumes of bank deposits, 'good' or serviced loans to the private sector and bad or non-performing loans to state-owned enterprises be denoted by D, L and N respectively. Abstracting for simplicity, but without loss of generality, from other items of the portfolio the balance sheet of the banking sector at the beginning of the period is then written as

$$D = L + N \tag{1.1}$$

Of the above variables only deposits and serviced loans are endogenously determined, while the size of bad loans to SOEs is exogenously decided by the government, which is the ultimate recipient of such funds. The latter treatment is in the spirit of the practice by which for reasons of political expediency, the state forces banks to finance loss-making enterprises, which they do by means of rolling over the outstanding debts, capitalizing interest arrears and providing new credit. As in standard practice, the demand for bank loans by the private sector is assumed to be decreasing in the loan interest rate (r_L), while the supply of deposits by savers is increasing in the deposit interest rate (r_D). Formally, we may then write

$$L = a - br_L, \text{ with } a \text{ and } b > 0 \tag{1.2}$$

$$D = c + hr_D, \text{ with } c \text{ and } h > 0 \tag{1.3}$$

By definition, the bad loans of the SOEs are not serviced;[7] interest is earned only on bank loans to the private sector, while interest services have to be paid on all deposits held by the banking sector. Abstracting from resource costs (since they are not essential to the present analysis) and denoting the expected return and cost per loan granted and deposit accepted by $E(r_L)$ respectively $E(r_D)$, the expected bank profit at the end of the period is expressed as

$$E\left(\prod\right) = E(r_L)L - E(r_D)D \tag{1.4}$$

It is further posited that the expected return per unit of bank loan, $E(r_L)$, is lower than the interest rate charged on bank borrowers r_L. Two reasons account for this difference. First, the distortions and inefficiencies that bad loans generate for the decision-making process of the banking sector and the indebted firms, as well as the heightened probability that good borrowers may also default (when they are exposed to failed enterprises), imply that for the banking sector the expected return per unit of bank loan, $E(r_L)$, is lower than it would have been in the absence of bad loans, r_L. More specifically, it is assumed that the larger the sum of bad loans, the larger the reduction in the expected rate of return. In addition, incomplete information regarding the quality of good private sector borrowers and their ability to repay their bank debts implies that some borrowers will default, which again reduces the expected rate of return below r_L. In the latter vein, following Stiglitz and Weiss (1981), it is recognized that because of incentive effects in the form of adverse selection and moral hazard the probability of loan default may depend positively on the size of the interest rate charged,[8] which further implies that beyond a certain value, say, R, as r_L rises $E(r_L)$ falls.[9] Formally, these notions suggest that we may express the expected bank return on loans as

$$E(r_L) = \beta r_L - \gamma N^2 - \delta N \quad \text{for } r_L < R \quad \text{with } 0 < \beta \leq 1, \gamma \text{ and } \delta > 0 \text{ and}$$
$$E(r_L) = \beta R - \gamma N^2 - \delta N \quad \text{for } r_L \geq R \tag{1.5}$$

which obviously depends negatively on N for all $N \geq 0$. Equation (1.5) implies that the banking sector will not charge borrowers an interest rate higher than that which maximizes $E(r_L)$, that is, R. Since the empirical relevance of the assumed relationship that a higher interest rate may lower the expected return on the bank is not indisputable, an alternative interpretation of R is also sought. Specifically, R may be considered as a measure to pursue credit policy objectives of the kind that have not been uncommon in financially repressed economies.

Similarly, recognizing that bad loans cause depositors to worry about the financial health of banks and the safety of their deposits, implies that the expected cost per unit of bank deposit, $E(r_D)$, is greater than the interest rate banks pay on deposits, r_D, so that we may write

$$E(r_D) = \varepsilon r_D + \theta N^2 + \lambda N \quad \text{with } \varepsilon \geq 1, \text{and } \lambda > 0 \tag{1.6}$$

which is obviously increasing in N for all $N \geq 0$. However, granted the various explicit or implicit state guarantees on the banking sector (that is, 'too big to fail' or 'too political to fail'), adverse selection and moral hazard effects on the side of depositor behaviour are assumed away.

Upon using the balance sheet (1.1), substituting from (1.2) and (1.3) into (1.5) and (1.6) and then the resulting expression into (1.4) the profit equation can be stated as

$$
\begin{aligned}
E\left(\textstyle\prod\right) &= \{\beta[(a + N - D)/b] - \gamma N^2 - \delta N\}(D - N) - \\
&\quad \{\varepsilon[(D - c)/h] + \theta N^2 + \lambda N\}D \quad \text{when } r_L < R \\
E\left(\textstyle\prod\right) &= \{\beta R - \gamma N^2 - \delta N\}(D - N) - \\
&\quad \{\varepsilon[D - c]/h] + \theta N^2 + \lambda N\}D \quad \text{when } r_L = R
\end{aligned}
\tag{1.7}
$$

In effect, bad loans are modelled to have the following negative consequences. The first is an implicit portfolio tax on the activity of the banking sector from forcing banks to hold non- interest-bearing credits, which causes the cost of funds per unit of deposit to differ from the cost of funds per unit of private loans, since only part of the deposits is now invested in profitable private loans. Such changes cause the bank to adjust its deposit liabilities and profitable assets in comparison with the case where there are no portfolio restrictions. As the ultimate owner of the SOEs, the state is obviously the beneficiary of the implicit tax and reaps a tax revenue equal to the amount of the corresponding interest charges. The second negative consequence of bad loans is the adverse impact on the expected net return from banking activity (where the latter can be thought of as measuring the benefit that the economy derives from the operation of the banking sector), which reduces the revenue and increases the cost per unit of banking business.

In a monopolistic setting banks maximize profits by setting the interest rates on loans and deposits.[10] Assuming that the banking sector is risk-neutral, the equilibrium volumes of deposits and loans and corresponding interest rates are found upon maximizing the profit function (1.7) with respect to D. In general, there are two solutions to this problem, namely, (a) when the optimum loan rate is below its maximum limit, $r_L < R$, and (b) when the interest rate is equal to its maximum limit, $r_L = R$.

(a) When $r_L < R$:

Focusing first on the former case (a), we obtain the following equilibrium solutions:

$$D^* = \{-bh(\gamma + \theta)N^2 + h[2\beta - b(\delta + \lambda)]$$
$$N + ah\beta + bc\varepsilon\}/2b(b\varepsilon + h\beta)$$
$$r_D^* = \{-bh(\gamma + \theta)N^2 + h[2\beta - b(\delta + \lambda)]$$
$$N + h\beta(a - c) - c(b\varepsilon + h\beta)\}/2h(b\varepsilon + h\beta) \tag{1.8}$$

$$L^* = \{-bh(\gamma + \theta)N^2 - b[2\varepsilon + h(\delta + \lambda)]$$
$$N + ah\beta + bc\varepsilon\}/2(b\varepsilon + h\beta)$$
$$r_L^* = \{bh(\gamma + \theta)N^2 + 2b[\varepsilon + h(\delta + \lambda)]$$
$$N + b\varepsilon(a - c) + a(b\varepsilon - h\beta)\}/2(b\varepsilon + h\beta) \tag{1.9}$$

The resulting equilibrium expressions are quadratic, and therefore non-monotonic functions of the size of bad loans, which implies a rather complicated pattern of responses of bank credit and deposits to the bad loans.

Probing further into Equations (1.8) and (1.9) and differentiating the equilibrium expressions for loans and deposits we obtain

$$dD^*/dN = h\{-2b(\gamma + \theta)N + 2\beta - b(\delta + \lambda)\}/2(b\varepsilon + h\beta) \geq 0$$
$$\text{for } N \leq [2\beta - b(\delta + \lambda)]/2b(\gamma + \theta)$$
$$(dr_D^*/dN = \{-2b(\gamma + \theta)N + 2\beta - b(\delta + \lambda)\}/2(b\varepsilon + h\beta) \geq 0$$
$$\text{for } N \leq [2\beta - b(\delta + \lambda)]/2b(\gamma + \theta) \tag{1.10}$$

$$dL^*/dN = -b\{2h(\gamma + \theta)N + 2\varepsilon + h(\delta + \lambda)\}/2(b\varepsilon + h\beta) < 0$$
$$\text{for all (positive values) of } N$$
$$dr_L^*/dN = \{h(\gamma + \theta)N + \varepsilon + h(\delta + \lambda)\}/(b\varepsilon + h\beta) > 0$$
$$\text{for all (positive values) of } N \tag{1.11}$$

Equation (1.11) reveals that the equilibrium volume of private loans is decreasing in the size of bad loans, since for all positive values of N the L^* function is declining. This result formalizes the intuition that bad loans to SOEs crowd out bank credit to the private sector.

On the contrary, Equation (1.10) reveals that the overall effect of bad loans on deposits depends on the size of bad loans, the interest elasticities of the loan demand and deposit supply functions, as well as the characteristics of the expected return and cost functions per unit of banking activity. More specifically, the adverse effect of bad loans on the net return on banking activity (captured by the γ, θ, δ and λ parameters) causes an unambiguous reduction in bank deposits, while the implicit portfolio tax effect of bad loans (captured by the product of the h and β parameters) increases bank deposits. Such findings further imply that there is a range of parameter values where a positive relationship between deposits and bad loans may exist, and, consequently, under bad loans the equilibrium volume of deposits may be larger than in their absence. Indeed, from Equation (1.10) we obtain that the volume of bank deposits is maximized when the size of bad loans is set at $N_D^* = [2\beta - b(\delta + \lambda)]/2bh(\gamma + \theta)$, which is positive for parameter values such as $\beta > b(\delta + \lambda)/2$, and negative otherwise.[11] Since in practice mobilization of domestic savings and channelling them through the official banking sector is widely acknowledged to be the key to an efficient payments system and an increase in the availability of investment funds,[12] this result is of considerable importance and relevance for designing and assessing policy. Intuitively, since bad loans reduce the size of the bank portfolio that can be invested profitably, the banking sector seeking to maintain its profits responds by increasing the deposit and loan interest rates, which, in turn, increases the volume of deposits and reduces the volume of loans; this effect, however, is counteracted by the direct reduction of the expected net return brought about by the bad loans.[13]

The combination of the expansionary effect on bank deposits and the contractionary effect on private loans noted above implies that the increase in the size of financial intermediation, following the increase in bad loan holdings, occurs at the expense of the private enterprise sector. This result can be seen from two different and conflicting perspectives. On the one side, if private investment is more productive than public investment, and therefore more conducive to growth, it is the cause of a harmful (financial) crowding-out effect. On the other side, the increase in the volume of available funds allows the government to finance a larger sum of expenditures than it would have been able to otherwise. If such extra funds serve only to transfer economic rents, they are indeed unproductive, and may generate an additional direct crowding-out effect (which reinforces the previously noted financial crowding out). But if, on the contrary, the government uses them to finance projects that generate positive externalities that the private sector fails to deliver (including, conceivably, social stability), 'bad loans' lead to a crowding-in effect and can make a positive contribution to social welfare.

(b) When $r_L = R$:

Turning to the latter case (b), we obtain after the relevant manipulations

$$D^* = \{h\beta R + c\varepsilon - h[\gamma + \theta)N + \delta + \lambda]N\}/2\varepsilon \quad \text{and}$$
$$r_D^* = (h\beta R - c\varepsilon - h[(\gamma + \theta)N + \delta + \lambda]N\}/2h\varepsilon \tag{1.12}$$

$$L^* = \{h\beta R + c\varepsilon - [h(\gamma + \theta)N + \delta + \lambda + 2\varepsilon]N\}/2\varepsilon \quad \text{and}$$
$$r_L^* = R \tag{1.13}$$

That is, when the banking sector is constrained to charge the maximum loan interest rate R, Equations (1.12) and (1.13) reveal that both loans and deposits depend negatively on the size of bad loans. Notice also that in this circumstance, where the optimum volume of loans $(D - N)$ is determined by the availability of deposits, since the loan interest rate is not freely adjustable, the loan market may be characterized by credit rationing.

The above results are in sharp contrast to those obtained in the standard Monti–Klein setting, where the banking sector has access to a large open market for securities, denoted by B, and which offer a given rate of return rB. In the latter case, the balance sheet of the banking sector and the profit function are written as $L + B + N = D$ and $\prod = E(r_L)L + r_B B - E(r_D)D$. Upon substituting from Equations (1.2) and $(1.3)^{14}$ and maximizing profits with respect to L and D, we obtain the equilibrium volumes of deposits and loans.

(a) When $r_L < R$

$$D^* = \{c\varepsilon + h[r_B - (\theta N + \lambda N]\}/2\varepsilon$$
$$r_D^* = \{-c\varepsilon + h[r_B - (\theta N + \lambda)N]\}/2h\varepsilon \tag{1.14}$$

$$L^* = \{a\beta - b[r_B + (\gamma N + \delta)]N\}/2\beta$$
$$r_L^* = \{a\beta + b[r_B + (\gamma N + \delta)]N\}/2b\beta \tag{1.15}$$

That is, bad loans will have unambiguously negative effects on the equilibrium values of all stock variables. Moreover, it is worth noting that the negative influences operate entirely through the impact of bad loans on the expected return and costs of loans and deposits (the parameters γ, δ, θ and λ) rather than through the portfolio tax impact of bad loans. The reason for this is that in the present setting, the optimal volume of deposit is decided with reference to the exogenously given return on funds which is represented by r_B, and, similarly, the optimal volume of loans is decided with reference to the exogenously given opportunity cost of funds which is also represented by r_B, which makes the deposit and loan decisions of the bank separable.

(b) When $r_L = R$:

In this circumstance bank profits become $\prod = (\beta R - \gamma N^2 - \delta N - r_B)L - (E(r_D) - r_B)D - r_B N$, which yields $D^* = \{c\varepsilon + h[r_B - (\theta N + \lambda)N]\}/2\varepsilon r_D^* = \{-c\varepsilon + h[r_B - (\theta N + \lambda)N]\}/2h\varepsilon$; that is, as in (1.14), while loans to the private sector will be granted only for parameter values such as $R \geq [(\gamma N + \delta)N + r_B]/\beta$, and may also imply some credit rationing. If the reverse inequality holds, the entire portfolio will be invested in bonds and no loans to the private sector will be provided at the R interest rate.

Bad loans and government borrowing

Drawing on the equivalence of bad loans to an implicit form of tax on depositors cum a transfer to the recipient borrowers, this section turns to a formal comparison of bad loans with the case where the government decides to fulfil the obligations of the SOEs and pays the market interest rate on the outstanding balance of the bad debts. This latter is equivalent to a situation where the government borrows from the banking sector the same amount N at the market interest rate r_L, while it also increases the transparency of government policy by making explicit the sum of the subsidy paid to the SOEs. In such a setting two different modes of financing the interest expenditure can be distinguished: (i) from tax revenues raised outside the banking system; and (ii) from taxes that are levied on banking activities. We examine the two in turn. In the first instance it is assumed that the interest expenses $r_L N$ are financed from general tax revenue, which is in effect equivalent to the circumstance where the non-banking part of the economy finances the government debt. The banking sector balance sheet now becomes

$$L = D \tag{1.1'}$$

while in the absence of bad loans the demand for loans, expected loan return and expected deposit cost functions respectively take the forms

$$L = a + N - br_L \tag{1.2'}$$

$$E(r_L) = \beta r_L \quad \text{for } r_L < R \quad \text{with } 0 < \beta \leq 1 \quad \text{and}$$
$$E(r_L) = \beta R \quad \text{for } r_L = R \tag{1.5'}$$

$$E(r_D) = \varepsilon r_D \quad \text{with } \varepsilon \geq 1 \tag{1.6'}$$

That is, the demand for interest-yielding bank loans increases by an amount equal to the size of bad loans and simultaneously the negative effects of bad loans on the expected return and cost of banking activity disappear. Substituting from $(1.1')(1.5')$ and $(1.6')$ into the profit function we obtain

$$E\left(\prod\right) = \beta[(a + N - D)/b]D - \varepsilon[(D - c)/h]D \quad \text{when } r_L < R$$
$$E\left(\prod\right) = \beta RD - \varepsilon[(D - c)/h]D \quad \text{when } r_L = R \tag{1.16}$$

Maximizing the latter with respect to D, after the relevant manipulations, we derive the equilibrium volumes of deposits as

(a) When $r_L < R$:

$$D^G = [h\beta(a + N) + bc\varepsilon]/2(b\varepsilon + h\beta) = L^G$$
$$r_D^G = \{h\beta(a + N - 2c) - bc\varepsilon\}/2h(b\varepsilon + h\beta) \quad \text{and}$$
$$r_L^G = \{(2b\varepsilon + h\beta)(a + N) - bc\varepsilon\}/2b(b\varepsilon + h\beta) \tag{1.17}$$

(b) When $r_L = R$:

$$D^G = [h\beta R + c\varepsilon]/2\varepsilon = L^G \quad \text{and}$$
$$r_D^G = [h\beta R - c\varepsilon]/2\varepsilon \quad \text{and} \quad r_L^G = R \tag{1.18}$$

Comparing the equilibrium under bad loans and under government borrowing when $r_L < R$ we obtain for the volume of loans to the private sector

$$L^* - L^G = -N\{bh(\gamma + \theta)N + b$$
$$[2\varepsilon + h(\delta + \lambda)] + h\beta\}/2(b\varepsilon + h\beta) < 0 \quad \text{for all } N > 0 \tag{1.19}$$

which shows that the alternative of government borrowing at market terms secures a higher volume of equilibrium credit to the private sector. For the volume of deposits, comparison of (1.17) with (1.11) renders

$$D^* - D^G = hN\{\beta - b[(\gamma + \theta)N + \delta + \lambda]\}/2(b\varepsilon + h\beta)$$
$$> 0 \quad \text{for } N < [\beta - b(\delta + \lambda]/b(\gamma + \theta) \tag{1.20}$$

Obviously, the latter is positive for parameter values such that $\beta > b(\delta + \lambda)$. That is, contrary to what a priori arguments against support for the SOEs through the banking system might have led us to believe, the replacement of the implicit portfolio tax-cum-subsidy implied by the bad loans with government borrowing at market rates may well yield a lower total of deposits, thus diminishing social welfare.

On the other hand, when the loan rate is set at its maximum level R the equilibrium of the banking sector is independent of the size of government borrowing, so that, as comparison of equations (1.12) and (1.18) makes clear, replacement of bad loans by serviceable government debt will increase the equilibrium volumes of both deposits and loans.

We now turn to the second method of financing government borrowing, that is the case where, rather than using tax proceeds earned outside the financial sector, the interest payments on government borrowing are financed by levying a tax on bank activities. Assuming that the tax takes the form of an *ad valorem* tax t on bank deposits (or equivalently, an *ad valorem* tax u on bank loans), total cost in terms of deposits is written as

$$E(r_D) = \varepsilon(1 + t)r_D \quad \text{with } \varepsilon \geq 1 \quad \text{and } tr_D D = r_L N \tag{1.6''}$$

Substituting from (1.1′) (1.5′) and (1.6′) into the expected profit function we find

$$E(\textstyle\prod) = [(a + N - D)/b(\beta D - \varepsilon N) - \varepsilon[(D - c)/h]D \quad \text{when } r_L < R$$
$$E(\textstyle\prod) = (\beta D - \varepsilon N)R - \varepsilon[(D - c)/h]D \quad \text{when } r_L = R \tag{1.21}$$

which upon maximization with respect to D yields

(a) When $r_L < R$:

$$D^t = [ah\beta + bc\varepsilon + h(\beta + \varepsilon)N]/2(b\varepsilon + h\beta) = L^t$$
$$r_D^t = [h\beta(a - c) - bc\varepsilon + h(\beta + \varepsilon)N]/2h(b\varepsilon + h\beta) \quad \text{and} \qquad (1.22)$$
$$r_L^t = [(2b\varepsilon + h\beta)(a + N) - \varepsilon(bc + hN]/2b(b\varepsilon + h\beta)$$

(b) When $r_L = R$:

$$D^G = [h\beta R - c\varepsilon]/2\varepsilon = L^G, \text{ that is, as in Equation (1.18).}$$

Comparison of (1.22) with (1.8) gives that when $r_L < R$

$$D^* - D^t = hN\{\beta - \varepsilon - b[(\gamma + \theta)N + \delta + \lambda]\}/2(b\varepsilon + h\beta)$$
$$< 0 \quad \text{for all } N, \text{since } \beta < 1 < \varepsilon \qquad (1.23)$$

which shows that when the interest cost of government borrowing is financed by an explicit tax on bank deposits, government borrowing results in a larger volume of deposits (and loans) than an equal sum of bad loans – implicit tax.

Conclusions and policy implications

With regard to the costs of bad loans to SOEs in transition economies, it is common to subscribe to the notion that such costs include 'either an increase in total bank lending or the alteration of the composition of a given quantity of lending, an increase in the spread between loan and deposit interest rates ... [which] drives a huge wedge between the incentive to save and the cost of investment ... [and] crowding out of lending to the private sector through an inadequate quantity of credit and unduly expensive credit' (Begg and Portes, 1993, p. 237). Such claims were put under scrutiny by the present study using an extension of the Monti–Klein model of bank behaviour.

The analysis was based on the following premises. The banking sector lacks access to a large open securities market where it always deals as a rate-taker, while the government is assumed exogenously to set the size of the bad loans in order to assist ailing state-owned Enterprises. By reducing the size of bank portfolio that can be profitably invested, bad loans impose a lump-sum tax on the banking sector. Furthermore, recognizing the damage that bad loans may do to the ability of the banking sector to intermediate funds between savers and investors and allocate credit efficiently to the most profitable uses, bad loans are modelled to directly reduce the net return per unit of banking activity. The latter influence is unlike other taxes on financial intermediation and obviously stacks the deck against the use of bad loans as a policy instrument. Assuming that the banking sector sets the interest rate on both the deposit and loan markets to maximize profits, the chapter explored the effects of bad loans on the equilibrium volumes of deposits and loans and the corresponding interest rates when (i) there are no constraints on the highest level of the loan interest rate, and (ii) a binding upper limit on the loan interest rate prevails.

The chapter showed that irrespective of whether there are restrictions on the lending policy of the banking sector, the volume of loans to the private sector decreases as a result of bad loans, as has been suggested in the literature. However, with respect to bank deposits, only in the case of a binding loan-interest ceiling will bad loans unambiguously reduce the volume and interest on deposits, and possibly lead to credit rationing. On the other hand, when no such binding constraint exists, there are two forces in operation; first, the portfolio tax effect of the bad loans, which induces banks to increase deposit-taking; and second, the net return reduction from bad loans, which tends to reduce deposit-taking. The analysis then showed that, contrary to the presumptions of the literature (epitomized by the previous quotation), there exist values for the size of bad loans which imply that in equilibrium the banking sector will hold a larger volume of deposits, but provide a lower volume of loans to private borrowers, offering a higher interest on deposits and charging a higher interest on loans than it would in the absence of bad loans to SOEs. This result is entirely driven by the portfolio tax effect of bad loans.

The main policy implication from this analysis relates to the latter effect. That is, to the extent that the government is interested in increasing the volume of funds intermediated through the official banking sector and keeping afloat some SOEs in order to ease the social tension of the transition, constraints on the portfolio of banks, which eliminate the negative effects of bad loans on bank returns, but retain the expansionary effects on deposits, have a useful role to play. An example of such a policy instrument would be a policy of zero- interest reserve requirements on bank deposits that the government may decide to vary at its own discretion.

Therefore, if it is so desired, policies which are designed and implemented to resolve the problem of bad loans can be complemented with a policy which will require banks to place a sum of their deposits equal to the size of bad loans to SOEs in non-interest-yielding reserves. The elimination of bad loans would then clean bank balance sheets, restoring the efficiency of the banking sector in the process of financial intermediation, but the government would also be able to maintain a source of implicit revenue through a portfolio tax on banks. At a minimum, such a tax would secure the same level of deposits as government borrowing at a market rate financed from an explicit-fiscal tax on financial intermediation, while if the interest payments are financed from a tax revenue raised outside the banking system, the reserve requirement results in a larger volume of deposits than in its absence.

Notes

1 For example, the essence of the issue is succinctly summarized by the following two (independent) quotations: 'In most Reforming Economies, the state transferred the burden of ailing state-owned enterprises from the Treasury to the banking system. Banks had little choice: they rolled over non-performing loans, accumulated interest arrears, and extended new credits to otherwise bankrupt clients. Good borrowers paid for these subsidies in the form of high borrowing rates. What had been a transparent fiscal support for ailing borrowers turned into an opaque support intermediated by banks' (Steinherr, 1997, p. 118). And, 'In leaving commercial banks burdened with bad (inherited) loans, the state substituted its earlier transparent support of ailing companies through direct fiscal subsidies with non transparent financial redistribution...The healthy segment of the commercial sector supported ailing companies by paying high fees for financial services and high rates for loans.' (Abel and Bonin, 1998, p. 8). Obviously, by obscuring the state of public finances and concealing the true cost of financial restructuring and bank recapitalization accumulation of bad loans may have certain political advantages, which in turn may have contributed to the delay of necessary reforms and painful adjustment.
2 See for example, Begg and Portes (1993), Mitchell (1993), Steinherr (1997), Abel et al. (1998).
3 See Repullo (1993) and Tridimas (1998) for exceptions to this.
4 In such a setting, queries regarding the incentives of bank managers to report truthfully the true worth of bank loans and the implications of the latter for the appropriate bank recapitalization policy are not of direct relevance.
5 Discussions of the competitive structure of the financial sector in transition economies and their implications for the profitability of financial institutions, economic efficiency and financial stability can be found in, among other publications the *Forum Report* of Anderson et al. (1996) and the study by Anderson and Kegels (1998).

6 See Freixas and Rochet (1997) for a detailed discussion of this point and various extensions of the standard Monti–Klein bank behaviour model.

7 Although excluded from this section, bank loans to the government sector on which the government pays the market interest rate are included in the next section.

8 That is, a rise in the loan interest rate is likely to deter low-risk borrowers and attract higher-risk loan applicants (adverse selection) and a higher loan interest rate is likely to encourage borrowers to pursue projects characterized by higher risk and higher return when successful (moral hazard), so that as the loan interest rate rises, the probability of default rises too.

9 Making R endogenous, that is, dependent on L, as in Courakis (1987) complicates the algebra, but does not alter the thrust of the results.

10 More specifically, we assume a setting where the banking sector is monopoly supplier of loans to the private sector and monopsony buyer of deposits.

11 It is easily checked that the second-order condition for a maximum is satisfied; that is, $d^2D^*/dN^2 = -h(\gamma + \theta)/(b\varepsilon + h\beta)$.

12 For example, the EBRD has put it as 'increasing the depth and breadth of banking activity is of vital importance to transition' (EBRD, *Transition Report, 1998*, p. 117).

13 These results trace the aggregate size of bank loans and deposits upon assuming that the banking sector as a whole is solvent; they do not preclude the possibility that some banks may be insolvent and need to be recapitalized.

14 For simplicity the possibility of substitutability relationships between deposits and other securities and complementarity relationships between loans and other securities is ignored.

References

I. Abel and J. P. Bonin, 'State desertion and credit market failure in the transition', in Abel Istvan, Pierre Siklos and Istvan Szekely (eds), *Money and Finance in the Transition to a Market Economy* (Cheltenham: Edward Elgar, 1998), pp. 1–15.

I. Abel, P. Siklos and I. Szekely, 'The gradual approach to banking reform and the anatomy of the bad loans problem', in Abel Istvan, Pierre Siklos and Istvan Szekely (eds), *Money and Finance in the Transition to a Market Economy*, (Cheltenham: Edward Elgar, 1998), pp. 115–24.

R. W. Anderson and C. Kegels 'Transition Banking'. *Financial Development of Central and Eastern Europe*', (Oxford: Clarendon Press, 1998).

R. W. Anderson, E. Berglof and K. Miszei, *Forum Report of the Economic Policy Initiative, No. 1: Banking sector development in Central and Eastern Europe* (Centre for Economic Policy Research and Institute for East West Studies, 1996).

D. Begg and R. Portes, 'Enterprise debt and economic transformation: financial restructuring in Central and Eastern Europe', in Colin Mayer and Xavier Vives (eds), *Capital Markets and Financial Intermediation* (Cambridge: CUP, 1993), pp. 230–55.

A. S. Courakis, 'Constraints on bank choices and financial repression in Less Developed Countries', *Oxford Bulletin of Economics and Statistics*, 46 (1984), 341–70.

A. S. Courakis, 'In what sense do compulsory ratios reduce the volume of deposits?', in C. Goodhart, D. Currie and D. Llewellyn (eds), *The Operation and Regulation of Financial Markets* (Macmillan – now Palgrave, 1987), pp. 150–86.

European Bank for Reconstruction and Development, *Transition Report, 1998* (EBRD, 1998).

European Bank for Reconstruction and Development, *Transition Report, 1999* (EBRD, 1999).

X. Freixas and J.-C. Rochet, *Microeconomics of Banking* (Cambridge, MA: MIT Press, 1997).

Michael Klein, 'A theory of a banking firm', *Journal of Money, Credit and Banking* (1971), 3: 205–18.

J. Mitchell, 'Creditor passivity and bankruptcy: implications for economic reform', in C. Mayer and X. Vives (eds), *Capital Markets and Financial Intermediation* (Cambridge: CUP, 1993), pp. 197–224.

M. Monti 'Deposit, credit and interest rate policies under alternative bank objective functions', in G. Szego and K. Shell (eds), *Mathematical Models in Investment and Finance* (Amsterdam: North Holland 1972). 431–54.

R. Repullo, 'Discussion of Enterprise debt and economic transformation: financial restructuring in Central and Eastern Europe', in C. Mayer and X. Vives (eds), *Capital Markets and Financial Intermediation* (Cambridge: CUP, 1993), pp. 255–9.

A. Steinherr, 'Banking reform in Eastern European countries', *Oxford Review of Economic Policy*, 13 (1997), 106–25.

J. Stiglitz and A. Weiss, 'Credit rationing in markets with imperfect information', *American Economic Review*, 71 (1981), 393–410.

G. Tridimas, 'Bad loans and the scale of financial intermediation in transition economies', in E. Miklaszewska (ed.), *Global Tendencies in East European Banking*, (Krakow: Jagiellonian University Press, 1998), pp. 260–9.

2
The Second Stage of Banking Transformation in Poland

Krystyna Szymkiewicz

In 1989, new banking legislation opened the way to the establishment of a banking system adapted to the market economy. Ten years later, the vast majority of Polish banks are organized and function along the same lines as Western European banks. After having undergone systemic transformation in record time, the young Polish banking sector is now confronted with the problems arising from the liberalization of the financial markets. By becoming a member of the OECD in November 1996 and beginning negotiations with a view to joining the European Union, Poland has taken it upon itself to open its financial markets to the free movement of capital. This is a true challenge facing both the economy and the financial system in general, as well as the banking sector in particular. The latter, which remains the key feature of the Polish financial system, has thus been forced to accelerate its consolidation through bank privatization as well as mergers aimed at concentrating capital and thereby reinforcing the competitive position of merged banks.

According to Hanna Gronkiewicz-Waltz, governor of the central bank of Poland, 'over the previous years, the Polish banking sector has quite naturally moved from quantitative development to qualitative development' (Gronkiewicz-Waltz, 1998). The analysis of this new phase in the evolution of Polish banking constitutes the main objective of the present study.

The first section of the chapter offers an overview of bank restructuring in Poland. Following a brief look at the origins of the current system, we present the results of bank restructuring achieved since 1989. In the following section, we indicate the progress made in elaborating a legal framework corresponding to European norms. Next, we provide data that shed light on the principal characteristics of the Polish banking sector.

In the second (and main) section of the chapter, we analyse changes in the capital structure of the Polish banking system: foreign banks' increasing presence, the progress of privatization and the advancement of consolidation of the banking sector. The last section indicates the financial situation of the banking system in 1998–99, with a few forecasts as to its future.

A general overview of the evolution of the Polish banking system

A radical reform of the Polish banking system began in January 1989 with the promulgation by the Polish parliament of two important laws: the Banking Act and Act on the Narodowy Bank Polski, NBP (National Bank of Poland).[1] These laws made it possible to set up a two-tier system, composed of the central bank and the universal commercial banks.

Until then, the organization of the banking sector had followed the Soviet model for over 40 years. A powerful state bank, the NBP behaving both as a central bank and a commercial bank, had branch offices spread across the country. A handful of specialized banks carried out specific services. For instance, Bank Handlowy SA was in charge of operations linked with foreign trade. Bank Polska Kasa Opieki SA managed the population's foreign currency accounts, fed, in large part, by transfers carried out by the large Polish diaspora. Polska Kasa Oszczednosci (PKO), the national savings bank, drained private savings and financed certain small individual projects. Finally, Bank Gospodarki Zywnosciowej (BGZ), a large bank covering the food industry, financed the agricultural sector. These banks were officially independent but, in reality, the NBP and the Ministry of Finance strictly controlled their activity. In fact, they were nothing more than one of the links in the monobank system. Before 1989, the banking system underwent a few partial reforms that, however, failed to bring about radical change. In this system, the banks' role consisted of distributing centrally planned funds. There was, therefore, room for neither autonomous credit policy nor for competition between the various banks.

Before the Second World War, the Polish banking sector had been relatively well developed. In 1938, Poland was endowed with a modern central bank, 3 large state banks, 27 private banks in the form of joint stock companies, 19 building societies, 353 savings banks, 975 local savings bank branches and 5597 cooperative banks (credit cooperatives). After the war, toeing the line of the new ideology, all these establishments were nationalized (Bury et al., 1999). Since 1989, Poland has been trying to erase this 40 year 'parenthesis' in its history, by once again privatizing the sector and helping it adapt to the market economy.

The effects of bank liberalization in 1989

In accordance with the new legislation, in February 1989, nine regional agencies of the NBP were transformed into independent and universal public commercial banks (see. Table 2.A1 in the Appendix). Freed from its commercial activities, the NBP should have played the role of a classical central bank, carrying out its functions of issuing, setting up and controlling monetary policy and supervising the activity of commercial banks. In reality, it was not until 1994 that the NBP put an end to its commercial activities once and for all, by transferring investment financing to the Polish bank of investment, created on 2 November 1994.

The Banking Act of 1989 equally opened the way to creating new banks which would help to diversify the banking network and encourage competition between the banks. From 1989 onwards, a group of state enterprises created the Bank Inicjatyw Gospodarczych, BIG SA.

Between 1990 and 1991, following the introduction of a very liberal policy concerning the creation of banks, there was a multiplication of the number of banks and a diversification of the banking system (during this period, 62 new banks began functioning). Later, due to a tightening of the conditions imposed on new owners, the number of new banks considerably decreased. From 1992 to 1996, a mere 20 new licences were granted, mainly to foreign banks (Baka, 1997).

The introduction of prudential requirements has not, however, gone ahead at the same rate as the multiplication of banks and the liberalization of banking. Consequently, during the first years of transition, bad loans appeared within the new banks, which, from lack of experience, took risks by granting credits with insufficient collateral.

Quite rapidly, the problem of bad loans has become a threat to the stability of the young banking sector. This problem is not due solely to the inexperience of new banks, but also to the fact that the nine big banks born of the NBP have inherited portfolios of bad loans corresponding to the credits directed at companies during the socialist era. At the beginning of transition, these companies were confronted with difficulties stemming from price liberalization, the suppression of subsidies, the break-up of the Comecon and the collapse of the internal market, and have since not been able to pay off their debts. Furthermore, in order to continue functioning, these same companies requested new credits that, in most cases, were granted by the banks.

At the beginning of transition, the unreformed state banks continued financing state companies, without bearing in mind their financial situation. As J. Winiecki remarks, for several decades 'Nobody's Banks' handed out loans to 'Nobody's Industrial Firms' (Winiecki, 1993) and it took a few years to end these old habits.

In 1991, bad debts represented 16.5 per cent of total credits granted by Polish banks as a whole, while in 1993, the figure reached 31 per cent (Fink et al., 1999). By the end of 1993, the banking sector's situation was very worrying: a few dozen cooperative and commercial banks went bankrupt and people were afraid of a possible systemic crisis. This was only just avoided thanks to salvage measures set up by the central bank and the Ministry of Finance that made it possible to save several banks.

It is worth underlining the merits of the restructuring programme for bad loans that was applied as early as 1994. By combining the restructuring of bad loans with the recapitalization of several banks, this programme greatly contributed to the recovery of the banking sector (Szymkiewicz and Moisseron, 1994). The recapitalization of several banks and, just as importantly, the introduction of tighter prudential regulations made it possible to considerably improve the health of the banking sector.

The creation of a legal framework

On 1 January 1998 two important legislative acts which were to regulate the functioning of the Polish banking sector came into effect. They were the Banking Act and the Act on the National Bank of Poland that replaced the 1989 legislation.[2] The content of these two laws comes very close to European standards (rules and regulations), and they should make the banking sector more solid and help Polish banks to function in an environment which is increasingly competitive. In particular, the new laws delimit the banks' sphere of activity and modify and reinforce the system of bank supervision.

The Act on the National Bank of Poland confirms the independence of the central bank and its capacities as far as monetary policy is concerned. The creation of the Monetary Policy Council, as stipulated in the Act, constitutes the main novelty. Other than the governor of the NBP, who is, at the same time, the President of the Council, there are nine members named in equal proportions by the Diet (the Polish parliament), the Senate and the President of the Republic of Poland. Every year, the Council sets the objectives of its monetary policy and informs the Diet of these aims as the Budget is being presented by the government of the day. (Previously, monetary policy objectives had to be ratified by the Diet whereas nowadays it need only be informed of these choices.) During the five months following the winding up of the year's Budget, the Council must present the Diet with a review of the success in reaching its monetary goals. In accordance with article 12, the Council fixes the central bank's interest rates as well as the level of its mandatory capital provisions, it approves the NBP's financial plans and its annual reports. The Council's mandate is of the same duration as that of the governor of the NBP, that is six years.

The task of overseeing the stability of the banking system (the watchdog role) has been entrusted to the Banking Supervision Commission, which, unlike the previous body, is independent of the central bank. Its chairman is the governor of the central bank, and the office comprises representatives from the Ministry of Finance, the Office of the Head of State, the Securities Exchange Commission and the Banking Guarantee Fund. The Commission's decisions are carried out and coordinated by a special structure created within the NBP under the name of the 'General Inspectorate of Banking Supervision'.

The Commission is endowed with considerable powers (some of which previously fell under the control of the governor of the NBP), listed in detail in the Banking Act. They concern licensing policy, the regulation of the banking sector and the supervision of the banks. Among other things, the Commission:

- provides the licences necessary to engage in any banking activity (unlike under previous legislation, at present, two licences are necessary: one to create a bank and the other to begin activity, after having fulfilled the requirements);
- agrees to the nomination of the president and vice-president of the bank's council (the names of other members are also transmitted to the Commission, as well as any changes in the council's make-up);
- initiates liquidation and bankruptcy procedures,
- defines liquidity levels and other prudential standards.

Among the most important dispositions defined by the Banking Act in order to strengthen the Polish banking system are the following:

- Bank licensing is now conditioned by a compulsory review of the abilities and fairness of the main shareholders and managers. Their honesty must be tested by the same means used by the EU (the fit and proper test). At least two members of the board of directors of the

bank should be sufficiently educated and experienced to manage a bank (four-eye principle).
- Minimum capital is set at 5 million ECU.
- In order to avoid money laundering, it is now compulsory to be able to stipulate the legal origin of funds.
- In order to limit risk exposure, connected exposure (that is, to a related group of clients) may not exceed 25 per cent of core capital, and aggregate 'large exposure' may not exceed 800 per cent of core capital. Exposure is considered 'large' if it reaches 10 per cent of the bank's core capital. The granting of such a credit must be first signalled to the Banking Supervision Office.
- The Cooke ratio (or BIS ratio) is set at 8 per cent. For newly created banks, it must not be lower than 15 per cent during the first year of activity, and 12 per cent during the second year.

Other pieces of legislation complete the present legal framework.

- The Act on Mortgage Banks, which came into effect on 1 January 1998, specifies the principles of creation, organization, activities and control of the mortgage banks, along with the rules of issuing, acquisition and guarantee of 'listy zastawne' (Mortgage bonds).[3]
- The 1997 Act on the reform of the pension system opens the way for the creation of new financial institutions, including those set up by the banks.[4]
- A special act regulates the functioning of the 'housing funds' that fall within the purview of the banks.[5] Another act on savings and buildings societies makes it possible to create banks dedicated to managing savings destined for financing housing.[6]

According to studies recently carried out in Poland (Styczek, 1999), Polish legislation already formally conforms, to a large degree, with the standards established by the European Council in Cannes in June 1995 and published in the White Paper. However, a far longer period will be necessary in order to appreciate whether or not, in practice, these new standards are truly being applied and are having an effect on the banking system. Certain elements of the new legislation are already being applied while the introduction of others is proving more complicated. It should be borne in mind that the norms used to decide on the *acquis communautaire* in the field of banking were originally established for Western countries with mature market economies. It is, therefore, only natural that their application to a transition economy in the process of building its banking infrastructure (see the following section) has brought about certain problems and calls for an adaptation process.

Among the changes that lean towards EU directives without actually following them to the letter, the Banking Guarantee Fund, which has been working since 17 February 1995, should be mentioned. It is funded by a group of banks as well as contributions from the Ministry of Finance and the central bank. All banks are obliged to participate in the Fund (including the cooperative banks). Until 1997, the Fund used to insure each depositor for 100 per cent of any deposit amounting to up to ECU 1000 and 90 per cent of amounts between ECU 1000 and ECU 3000. From July onwards, the ceiling was raised to ECU 4000 and, since January 1998, to ECU 5000 (Wyczanski and Golajewska, 1998, p. 4). Three banks – Pekao SA, PKO BP and BGZ – deserve special attention. Until 1999, they participated less actively in the Fund than other banks and enjoyed a full guarantee of the return of funds in savings accounts. Poland is still far from the 20 000 ECU sum fixed within the EU as the guaranteed ceiling.

Some of the main data

Despite considerable progress made over the last few years, the Polish banking sector remains at an early stage of development. The ratio of total banking assets to GDP is low. In 1996, it was evaluated at 44.1 per cent, while the same ratio, when calculated for the 15 members of the EU, reached 154.2 per cent. Table 2.1 illustrates the weakness of financial intermediation in Poland.

Table 2.1   Indicators of financial intermediation in Poland and in the EU-15 (1996 data)

	Poland	*EU-15*
Total financial intermediation (bank, equity, bonds) bn US$	86.4	1890.1
Bank intermediation ratio (bank assets/total intermediation)	68.7	55.3
Equity intermediation ratio (stock market cap./total interm.)	9.7	17.1
Bond intermediation ratio (bonds/total intermediation)	21.6	27.1
Bank assets (% GDP)	44.1	154.2
Total financial intermediation (% GDP)	64.3	288.1
Financial intermediation per capita (in USD)	2 238	67 208

Source: Fink et al. (1998).

In relation to GDP, financial intermediation is over four times higher in the EU than in Poland and per capita intermediation is approximately thirty times higher. Only the Bank intermediation ratio is higher in Poland, thus indicating the preponderant role of the banking sector in the Polish financial system.

The number of agencies has increased considerably over the last few years, from 1436 in 1993 to 2060 in June 1999 (NBP, September 1999). The number of clients per agency fell from 26 880 in 1993 to 19 320 in early 1999, but still remains 4 to 16 times higher than in Western European countries.[7] Even if certain statistical biases (inevitable in this sort of comparison[8]) are taken into account, the density of the Polish banking network is very different from that found in the EU.

Employment, on the other hand, is relatively high in Polish banks compared with their Western counterparts. In June 1999, Poland counted 80 banks, which employed, in all, 150 100 people, that is, on average, 1876 people per bank. In European Union countries, in 1993, the same indicator varied from 277 in Denmark to 1138 in Spain (Baka, 1998a).

Since 1995, credit activity has been dynamic, but the role of credit, expressed as the ratio of credit to GDP, is four or five times lower in Poland than in developed countries. For instance, in 1997, this ratio was only 22.9 per cent in Poland while it was 126 per cent in the UK (Zareba, 1998). The enormous needs of the Polish economy as far as capital is concerned will help make the banking sector more dynamic. Everything leads one to believe that over the next few years, banks will be able to maintain their dominant position within the Polish financial system. At the present time, banks have a quasi-monopoly as far as draining savings is concerned, they represent a high percentage of stock market capitalization (27 per cent for the first half of 1999), are increasing their participation in pension funds, and are in the process of becoming the main stockholders in insurance and leasing companies. Bank restructuring presently under way underlines this 'bancostructure' of the Polish financial system.

The changing structure of the banking system

The 1993 law on the restructuring of banks and companies,[9] which has been successfully put in place, has made it possible to recapitalize several large banks, making them more attractive in the eyes of potential clients. Foreign capital has become increasingly present in privatization and in the system's consolidation, thereby modifying its structure.

Table 2.2   The structure of the Polish banking system

Type of bank	Number of banks[a]						
	1993	*1994*	*1995*	*1996*	*1997*	*1998*	*(June 1999)*
Commercial banks, of which	87	82	81	81	83	83	80
Majority state-owned banks[b]	29	29	27	24	15	13	10
belonging directly to the State[c]	16	15	13	8	6	6	5
belonging indirectly to the State	11	11	11	13	8	7	5
belonging to the NBP	2	3	3	3	1	0	0
Banks with a majority of private capital	58	53	54	57	68	70	70
a majority of Polish capital	48	42	36	32	39[d]	39	34
a majority of foreign capital[e]	10	11	18	25	29[f]	31	36
Cooperative banks	1653	1612	1510	1394	1295	1189	902
Total	1740	1694	1591	1475	1378	1272	982

[a]   Not including banks undergoing bankruptcy or liquidation proceedings.

[b]   Banks in which the Treasury, legal state entities and the NBP hold stocks representing at least 50% +1 voice at the shareholders' AGM.

[c]   Banks in which the Treasury holds shares representing at least 50% +1 voice at the shareholders' AGM.

[d]   Including Rzeszowski Bank Regionalny SA, presently being set up.

[e]   Subsidiaries of foreign banks and banks established as limited liability companies in which foreigners (legal entities or physical persons) directly or indirectly hold shares worth at least 50% + 1 voice at the shareholders' AGM.

[f]   Including Bank of America Polska SA, presently being set up.

Source: *The Financial Situation of Banks During the First Semester 1999*. Synthesis, NBP, September 1999.

Changes since 1993

The period under consideration was marked by a fall in the total number of banks, a shrinking of the state-run banking sector to the benefit of the private sector and a growing presence of foreign capital (Table 2.2).

On the one hand, a sizeable reduction in the number of banks controlled by state capital can be observed (falling from 29 in 1993 to 10 in 1999) and, on the other hand, a large increase in the number of foreign banks within the 'private banks' group is clear. In 1993, the number of banks formed with a majority of Polish capital was 48 while in June 1999 it was only 34. During the same period, the number of banks formed with a majority of foreign capital went from 10 to 36, including 21 formed entirely (100 per cent) with foreign capital (3 subsidiaries of foreign banks and 18 joint-stock companies).

The cooperative banking sector, made up of small banks concentrating on financing agricultural activities and the food industry, has also undergone large-scale transformation. Following mergers, revivals and bankruptcies, the number of cooperative banks has fallen from 1653 in 1993 to 902 in June 1999. In 1998 alone, 285 mergers were carried out as well as the bankruptcy of two banks (one of which was taken over by a commercial bank) (NBP, September 1999).

The role of private banks in total assets has been growing continually, going from 13 per cent in 1993 to 52.1 per cent in June 1999. Within this group, the assets of banks with a majority of Polish capital represent 25.7 per cent and with a majority of foreign capital, 26.4 per cent (Table 2.3).

The weight of foreign banks is even greater as far as equity is concerned. In 1999, foreign banks in total equity reached almost 35 per cent. At the same date, the role of state-owned banks was 31.5 per cent, while banks with a majority of Polish capital represented 20.1 per cent. It should not be forgotten that equity determines a bank's potential capacity and its real activity. (It is, in particular, based on equity that the solvency ratio and the concentration limit are calculated.)

The Polish banking sector has a dual structure: on one hand, there are a dozen or so large banks, and on the other hand, there is a multitude of small banks taking up a modest part of the market. Thus, in 1998, the ten biggest banks totalled 62.1 per cent of all assets, 67.8 per cent of

Table 2.3   The structure of net assets and equity in the Polish banking sector

Type of bank	1993	1996	June 1999	1993	1996	June 1999
	Net assets (%)			*Equity (%)*		
Commercial banks, of which	93.4	95.4	95.8	92.0	95.1	95.5
Majority state-owned banks	80.4	66.5	43.7	76.8	55.9	31.5
belonging directly to the state	76.1	51.1	41.8	72.8	43.7	29.0
Banks using a majority of private capital	13.0	28.9	52.1	15.2	39.2	64.0
a majority of Polish capital	10.4	15.1	25.7	13.0	18.3	29.1
a majority of foreign capital	2.6	13.7	26.4	2.2	20.9	24.9
Cooperative banks	6.6	4.6	4.2	8.0	4.9	4.5
Total	100	100	100	100	100	100

Source: The Financial Situation of Banks During the First Semester 1999. Synthesis, NBP, September 1999.

deposits and gave out 60 per cent of all credits (see Table 2.A2 in the Appendix).

Foreign banks: the victory of pragmatism

Between 1989 and 1991, despite an attractive fiscal environment, few foreign banks established themselves in Poland. Among the pioneers were Citibank (USA), ING Bank (Netherlands), Creditanstalt and Raiffeisenbank (Austria) and Société Générale (France).

In 1992, Poland changed its policy towards foreign banks: henceforth, access to the Polish market would be restricted to banks that were ready to participate in restructuring damaged Polish banks. Thus, until September 1994, no new licence was granted to foreigners and no foreign bank was able to obtain a controlling stake in a Polish bank.

The signature of the agreement with the London Club on debt rescheduling in September 1994 constitutes the starting-point for foreign banks' expansion in Poland. On the one hand, Polish licensing policy became more liberal (the first licence was granted in September 1994 to a consortium formed by Banque Nationale de Paris and Dresdner Bank, as a reward for the active participation of the latter in the positive outcome of the London agreement). On the other, visible economic progress has made Poland increasingly attractive to foreign investors. In particular, German banks, absent at the beginning of transition, have made a massive breakthrough in the Polish market.

According to data for June 1999, German capital accounted for 35 per cent of foreign capital invested in the Polish banking system, followed by American capital (24.3 per cent), Dutch (13 per cent), French (8.4 per cent) and Austrian (6.8 per cent). The UK finds itself in 12th place with 0.7 per cent of total invested capital (NBP, September 1999).

Foreign banks have progressively changed their implantation strategy in Poland. At the beginning of transition, they tended to prefer greenfield investments. At the present time, they are trying to take over the larger Polish banks with their network of agencies (brownfield investments). The NBP made these operations possible by accepting, as early as 1996, that foreign banks could claim a controlling stake in banks (Kubielas, 1998). The same year, six Polish banks came under foreign control, three of which were very important banks: Wielkopolski Bank Kredytowy SA, Bank Slaski SA and Bank Rolno-Przemyslowy SA.

Legally, foreign banks may be universal banks as soon as the NBP gives them a business licence. For several years, foreign banks often specialized in foreign trade or followed their clients in Poland. At present, they are trying not only to finance large Polish companies, but also to offer financial services to individuals. Foreign banks no longer appear as niche-market hunters, but as direct competitors with Polish banks. In effect, they already provide 32.7 per cent of all credits and receive 21.7 per cent of deposits, as opposed to 2.6 per cent of credits and 2.1 per cent of deposits in 1993 (NBP, September 1999).

The present growth in foreign capital has brought to life new fears for those who had hoped to keep the major banks under national control. They propose to search for a strategy that would make it possible to lessen this foreign presence (Jaworski, 1999). At the other extreme, another group believes that the multiplication of foreign banks will be the main means of increasing capitalization in the sector and bringing about modernization (Bonin et al., 1998; Orlowski, 1999). Recent events seem more in line with the second option.

In virtue of its agreements with the OECD and the European Union, Poland has very little room to slow down the expansion of foreign capital in the banking sector. In any case, it is not clear that such a change would be in the country's best interest.

Privatization and the consolidation of the banking sector

Bank privatization fits into the overall general privatization process which has been taking place since the beginning of the 1990s in the transition economies. This process seems to be an indispensable element of the strategy which aims to install a market economy and free enterprise in these countries. Privatization should not, therefore, be perceived as an end in itself, but as the means which will help new economic rules to work correctly, thereby ensuring the best allocation of resources and a rise in general welfare (Lachowski, 1996).

Many authors believe that the privatization of the banking sector will ensure that banks will be governed better and will operate more efficiently. Thanks to the improved management of resources, privatized banks will be able to carry out more active credit policies, thus becoming more competitive (Baka, 1998b; Bonin et al., 1998; Orlowski, 1999).

Privatization: from a difficult start to an acceleration

In Poland, the programme for the privatization of the banking sector was adopted by the Economic Committee of the Council of Ministers in 1991. In accordance with this programme, seven banks born of the break-up of the NBP were supposed to be privatized between 1993 and

1996 after having been transformed into limited liability companies. Following this, specialized banks were to be privatized (Bank Handlowy, Pekao SA, PKO BP and BGZ).

The programme's aim was to find a strategic investor for each bank (preferably a well-known foreign bank), ready to play an active part in managing the bank. Nevertheless, the Treasury would remain the principal shareholder and the strategic investor was to hold no more than 30 per cent of total shares. The subsequent sale of a part of the shares held by the Treasury remained possible, but only if the operation could take place without allowing a private shareholder to become a majority shareholder.

The realization of this programme fell far behind schedule due to economic, technical and political problems. In the end, only four of the nine banks were privatized before the deadline date (by the end of 1996): Wielkopolski Bank Kredytowy, WBK (April 1992), Bank Slaski (late 1993), Bank Przemyslowo-Handlowy (January 1995) and Bank Gdanski (December 1995). The fifth bank, the Powszechny Bank Kredytowy SA of Warsaw (PBK), after a few misadventures, was privatized in 1997. The privatization process concerning the 'nine' was completed in 1999. Henceforth, 80 per cent of the assets of Bank Zachodni of Wroclaw are controlled by the Allied Irish Bank. The following three banks – Pomorski Bank Kredytowy SA of Szczecin, Bank Depozytowo-Kredytowy SA of Lublin and Powszechny Bank Gospodarczy SA of Lodz, which, have belonged to the Pekao SA group since 1996 – have been taken over by foreign capital (by the consortium formed by UniCredito Italiano SpA and Allianz Aktiengesellschaft (see Table 2.A7 in the Appendix).

Following their transformation into limited liability companies (in 1991), the nine banks were 'X-rayed' during audits carried out by Western agencies. It emerged that only two of these banks were in good financial condition, while the seven others could not be privatized without first being recapitalized. This was done with the help of a law dated 3 February 1993. In the space of two years (1993–94), the nine banks which participated in the financial restructuring programme (seven banks left after the break-up of the NBP as well as BGZ and PKO BP) received Treasury bonds named 'restructuring bonds', with a 15–year maturity, and worth a total value of 40 000 billion zlotys at the time.[10] These bonds served to increase the banks' equity and to create provisions for bad debts that were taken from their portfolios in late 1991. The cost of recapitalization of these banks was to be shouldered by the Polish taxpayer, and, to a great extent, by the Polish Banks Privatization

Fund, created with the agreement of Western countries, using the Zloty Stabilization Fund constituted in 1990. Until the recapitalized banks were privatized, bond servicing was to be covered by the state budget, and, following their privatization, by the Polish Banks Privatization Fund.

The two 'healthy' banks, privatized before the others, WBK and Bank Slaski, easily found minority shareholders. The EBRD expressed its interest in WBK, taking a 28.5 per cent stake, while Bank Slaski attracted the Dutch bank ING (with a 25 per cent stake). At the same time, the state remained majority owner of these banks, and later sold its remaining stakes in June 1996. In 1998 it owned a mere 5 per cent stake in each bank, while foreign banks are the major shareholders: Allied Irish Bank owns 60.14 per cent of WBK's shares and ING owns 50.08 per cent of Bank Slaski (another main shareholder, Franklin Templeton, holds a 5.63 per cent stake) (Kubielas, 1998).

As for the banks privatized in 1995, initially the state was the largest shareholder in Bank Przemyslowo-Handlowy (BPH) and Bank Gdanski (respectively 46.61 per cent and 39.94 per cent of shares). Foreign banks owned a 25 per cent stake in BPH and a 35 per cent stake in Bank Gdanski. Since January 1999, BPH is controlled by foreign capital (the State yielded 36.7 per cent of the shares to Bayerische Hypo-und Vereinsbank), while foreign Polish capital claims the main part of BIG Bank Gdanski's capital (NBP, September 1999).

In 1996, Mr Cimoszewicz's social-peasant government launched a new and ambitious programme, which anticipated the privatization of about ten banks between 1997 and 2000. But following their election defeat in October 1997, his government was only able to put into place part of the programme: the privatization of PBK, the fifth Polish bank left after the break-up of the NBP, and that of the prestigious Bank Handlowy.

The privatization of PBK was characterized by changes and about-faces. It is not clear why the outgoing government cancelled the sale by tender of PBK, won by Samsung Life Insurance against a consortium of Polish banks (Bank Przemyslowo-Handlowy, insurance company TUR Warta, Polski Bank Rozwoju and Kredyt Bank) and supported by the EBRD. In the end, PBK was privatized by IPO (Initial Public Offering) in October 1997 and has since been a great success with the Polish public. Among institutional investors, we should mention Bank Austria/Creditanstalt (now one entity), Kredyt Bank and the insurance company Warta, each with a 13 per cent stake. PBR also received a 1 per cent stake in the bank, and 10.5 per cent of shares were allotted to foreign and Polish investment funds. In 1998, Creditanstalt reinforced its position by acquiring 15 per cent of shares sold by the Treasury. However, to date, PBK remains one of the two banks that has emerged from the NBP and that is still controlled by private Polish capital (Table 2.A1 in the Appendix).

Bank Handlowy, on the other hand, was privatized using an original scheme (Szymkiewicz, 1998):

- Special convertible bonds[11] (SPOZ) were destined for the state, the sum of which was to be allocated to the financing of the pension system reform. Thanks to the special structure of the SPOZ, the Treasury is now definitively deprived of voting rights but, at the same time, earns a dividend and a possible capital gain. The state may use the SPOZ in a variety of ways, based on the solutions chosen concerning the pension system. As soon as the SPOZ are sold to other investors, the mute shares are transformed into normal stock.
- Instead of a single foreign investor, eventually three stable investors were chosen, enabling the bank to be managed by a group of active professional investors and helping it to avoid falling under the control of one single strategic investor. The partners are:
  – JP Morgan, the powerful American investment bank;
  – Zurich Insurance Company, the biggest Swiss insurance group;
  – Sparbanken Sverige AB–Swedbank, the main Swedish network bank.
- An IPO, directed at a large Polish audience (mainly individual investors) and foreign institutional investors.

At the end of privatization, the equity of Bank Handlowy (stock + SPOZ bonds) was distributed as follows:

- Stable investors: 24 per cent, of which JP Morgan held 12 per cent, Swedbank 6 per cent and Zurich Insurance Company 6 per cent.
- IPO main investors: 41.24 per cent among which individual investors represented 20.27 per cent and institutional investors 20.97 per cent. Among the latter, the presence of world known investment funds like Fleming, Templeton Group, Capital International, Mercury Asset Management, Robeco, Scudder Stevens & Clark and the International Pension Fund, Scottish Widows should be noted.
- Bank Handlowy's staff (purchasing stock under preferential conditions): 4.99 per cent.

- Polish Treasury: 29.77 per cent. Taking into account the stock (which provides voting rights), the Treasury owns 7.9 per cent. (The state kept 5 per cent of stock to provide for a restitution fund set up to reimburse Polish citizens deprived during the communist era); 2.9 per cent constitute the premium given to individual shareholders who will keep shares bought under IPO for one year. After distribution to shareholders, only 5 per cent of total stock will remain in state hands (Kawalec et al., 1997, p. 24).

The year 1998 was marked by the above-mentioned completion of the privatization of Bank Przemyslowo-Handlowy. At present, its strategic investor, Bayerische Hypo-und Vereinsbank, holds less than 50 per cent of the bank's shares, but it will probably try to become the majority shareholder by purchasing shares from the EBRD and ING.

One of the major events of 1999 was the privatization of the Pekao SA group, the second largest Polish bank (with about 20 per cent of the Polish banking system's assets) not to mention the third largest among central Europe's main banks (following the Czech Komercni Banka AS and another Polish bank, PKO BP).[12] The group, which was launched in 1996 by administrative decision by the then social-peasant government, is composed of Bank Polska Kasa Opieki SA (group leader), and three large regional banks: Bank Depozytowo-Kredytowy SA of Lublin, Powszechny Bank Gospodarczy SA of Lodz and Pomorski Bank Kredytowy SA of Szczecin. The group's privatization took place in two stages.

During the first stage, the Treasury floated 14.58 per cent of the merged bank on the Warsaw Stock Exchange (June 1998) and distributed 14.10 per cent to employees. At the same time, an increase in shareholders' equity was decided upon through a new share issue worth US$100 million destined for the EBRD. These shares were introduced onto the stock market on 31 July 1998. The EBRD holds 5.29 per cent of Pekao SA's capital (Chorylo et al., 1999).

On 23 June 1999, the most important transaction in the history of Polish privatization was signed: the alliance of UniCredito Italiano SpA and Allianz AG paid 4.24 billion zlotys (approximately $1.08 billion) for a 52.09 per cent stake in Pekao SA (Sawicka, 1999). It would appear that the price offered was not the deciding factor in the choice of this strategic investor. The latter accepted the strategy proposed by the Polish bank and made several promises concerning the bank's development. Thus the investor promised to increase the bank's capital by 1 billion zlotys within the framework of an investment programme worth 2 billion. It also promised to reinvest profits until the year 2000, introduce new technology, train personnel, and so on. Pekao SA was to keep its name, its logo and its headquarters in Warsaw, and its shares were to continue to be quoted on the Warsaw Stock Exchange.

Today, it is the country's only nationwide, universal bank. Its ambition is not simply to remain the leader on the Polish market but, soon, to become a leader on the other markets of Central and Eastern Europe. Several other banks in Poland, without actually making the same ambitious claims, are also advancing in the consolidation process.

By late 1999, only two 'problematic giants' remained to be privatized: PKO BP and BGŻ. The first (entirely state-run) is faced with the unresolved problem of old loans granted to construction cooperatives by administrative decision. The second old 'centre' of cooperative banking (in which the state holds a 60 per cent stake and the cooperative banks 40 per cent) is in the process of being restructured, as is the entire cooperative banking system.

Towards consolidation

Studies on the question of consolidation in Poland give several different definitions of this term (Solarz, 1993; Lachowski, 1996). In the present chapter, we propose a definition in line with the Polish one which differs from the generally accepted definition. Consolidation is herein understood as the action of making the Polish banking sector more solid (and thus more competitive) by means of mergers and acquisition of control. Consolidation translates into a concentration of capital and a reduction in the number of banks. Up until 1995, consolidation was mainly driven by takeovers of weak banks by bigger and healthier banks. From 1995 onwards, a new type of merger came to light, characterized by unions between sound banks wishing to improve their market share.

Between 1990 and 1995, 11 private banks (other than cooperative banks) disappeared following takeovers. At the same time, ten banks survived after selling off majority stakes to other banks. In many cases, the NBP helped this type of consolidation with its financial weight. Cooperative banks were also concerned by these developments. Between 1990 and 1995, the NBP provided aid for the recuperation of 38 banks by other financial institutions; moreover, 18 mergers without the help of the NBP were recorded.[13] This phenomenon has accelerated since 1996: a great number of mergers and acquisitions have occurred. Changes are happening so quickly that it is difficult to follow them in all their details, especially as these changes effect all levels: national banks, local banks and cooperatives.

In the 'major league', in September 1997, Kredyt Bank purchased Polski Bank Inwestycyjny and Prosper Bank.[14] These two acquisitions were added to five others previously carried out by Kredyt Bank and bear witness to its development strategy.

The same month, a merger took place between BIG and Bank Gdanski leading to the creation of BIG Bank Gdanski SA (see Table 2.A2 in the Appendix). This is the only privatized bank that does not yet have a strategic investor. Early in 1999, its retail partner, Banco Commerciale Portugues, increased its stake in the bank's capital. Among other candidates ready to assume important stakes in the capital are Deutsche Bank and BRE Bank SA. The latter, controlled by Commerzbank (Germany), is particularly dynamic. In 1998, it took control of the Polish Bank of Development (PBR), and changed its name from Bank Rozwoju Eksportu SA (Export Development Bank) to BRE Bank SA. Since July 1999, it has officially been preparing its merger with Bank Handlowy. The merger of the country's 120–year-old trade finance bank and its corporate-banking competitor was to create Poland's third biggest bank which was to retain the prestigious name, Bank Handlowy.

Some believe that in the short term, it is not reasonable to expect other mergers of this size to take place, because consolidation within the group of major banks is already finished (Kowalik, 1999). However, it is not impossible that banks quoted on the stock market (16 in all, of which 10 figure among the 15 biggest) may, in future, change their structure and shareholders.

Consolidation is also continuing within the group of mid-sized banks (between 1 and 3 billion zlotys in assets, that is $250 to 750 million) and small banks (up to 1 billion zlotys in assets, that is approximately $250 million). 'Small' banks remaining unconsolidated are now a rarity. Those that subsist are seeking foreign investors and risk falling 'prey' to larger banks (for instance, Kredyt Bank is renown for its development strategy based on buying up 'small' banks). Some small banks are trying to group together (with or without a capital merger). Thus Bank Inicjatyw Spoleczno-Ekonomicznych has already acquired an energy bank, BEN, and a sugar bank: Cukrobank (Kowalik, 1999).

Finally, consolidation is continuing in the cooperative sector. The number of cooperative banks has fallen from 1189 in late 1998 to 902 at the end of June 1999. Before the end of 2000, this number was to have further decreased because, at that point in time, minimum equity for a cooperative bank was fixed at 300 000 euros[15].

Bank activity: present problems and strategy for the future

One of the main motivations encouraging consolidation is the increase in the capitalization of Polish banks. This should help consolidated banks to participate in financing large projects and to increase profits without taking too many risks. The perspective of future membership in the European Union demands that Polish banks not only consolidate their balance sheets but also improve cost management and modernise services. What is the present situation in the sector and what are its survival perspectives in such a competitive environment?

Banks' performance (1996–99)

During the period studied, the financial results of the Polish banking sector were, overall, satisfactory with, however, a trend of gradual deterioration. The year 1996 was particularly good thanks to a favourable combination of factors. Economic growth encouraged banking activity's development (GDP grew by 6.1 per cent in 1996). Furthermore, several banks registered extra income issuing from 'restructuring bonds' while certain among them (whose reliability was in question) benefited from financial aid from the NBP and the Banking Guarantee Fund (Baka, 1998b). This explains the important growth of total assets, surpassing its 1995 level by 25.8 per cent in nominal terms and 6.2 per cent in real terms.

In 1997–98, growth of assets continued. In nominal terms they increased by 27 per cent in 1997 and by the same amount again in 1998. In real terms, their growth was 13 per cent in 1997 and 17 per cent in 1998 (Golajewska et al 1999).

At the same time, equity increased in the following manner (growth compared to the previous year):

- in nominal terms, 1996: 78.5 per cent; 1997: 58.0 per cent; 1998: 62 per cent
- in real terms, 1997: 39.6 per cent; 1998: 49 per cent.

This trend is positive and has contributed to the reinforcement of the banking system. The ratio of assets to GDP is also an improvement worth noting, increasing from 44.1 per cent in 1995 (Table 2.1) to 53 per cent in 1997 and finally to 60.7 per cent in 1998.[16]

Three stages in the evolution of credit policy can be observed since 1990: first, its growth, despite tight monetary policy (1990–91), then a strong contraction of its quantity, banks becoming more prudent

Table 2.4   Credit growth in Poland (% change over the previous year)

	1995	1996	1997	1998
Total credit in nominal terms	35.4	42.4	33.5	
Total credit in real terms	11.4	19.9	16.5	
Credit to companies (nominal value)	32.6	35.2	35.0*	28*
Credit to companies (real value)	9.1	20.6	19.0*	17*
Credit to households (nominal value)	67.4	107.8	56.2	30.0
Credit to households (real value)	37.7	73.3	35.9	18.8

*   *Sytuacja finansowa bankow w 1998*, NBP, March 1999, p. 30.

Source: 1995: *Survey Banki 1996*, published by Zwiazek Bankow Polskich, Warsaw 1997 and *Raport o bankach*, Rzeczpospolita, 23 April 1998.
1996 and 1997: *Raport o inflacji*, NBP, Warsaw, July 1998, pp. 60–1.

(1992–94), and finally a resumption of credit activity since 1995. Improvement in the capitalization of banks and sounder credit portfolios played in favour of intense credit activity. Thus, during the 1996–99 period, credit increased faster than inflation (inflation being 19.4 per cent in 1996, 14.8 per cent in 1997 and 8.6 per cent in 1998).

Thanks to the central bank's strictness aimed at getting inflation under control, by 1998, the rate of growth of credit was reduced compared to that recorded in 1996 (see Table 2.4). However, it remained high, especially in the case of consumer credit.

Attracted by the consumer society, the Polish people have grown into the habit of relying on credit to finance their buying power (especially where cars were concerned). As for banks, they have been increasingly diversifying supply of credit, launching credit cards and offering attractive deals to those consumers who already own a current or savings account in their outlet.

Despite the increasing volume of credit granted to households, the credit to companies remains dominant in banks' portfolios: 83.4 per cent in late 1996 and 81.1 per cent in 1998. It is interesting to note that, progressively, credit to state-owned companies has diminished and credit granted to the private sector has increased. In 1998, credits granted to companies could be broken down in the following way (NBP, 1999):

- state-run companies: 29.5 per cent
- private sector companies: 51.8 per cent
- individual entrepreneurs: 13.2 per cent
- agriculture: 5.5 per cent

During the 1996–98 period, the deposits market witnessed important developments (Table 2.5). It is interesting that, throughout the 1990s, demand deposits decreased while short-term investments increased. The results for 1998 confirm this tendency: company demand deposits represented 27.3 per cent of their deposits against 31.0 per cent in 1997. As far as the banks were concerned, this signified an increase in the cost of money, but, at the same time, a greater stability of deposits and, therefore, a lower level of obligatory reserves. In 1998, only 18.3 per cent of deposits were made in foreign currency (compared with 26.7 per cent in 1995).

The deposits market is the biggest financial market in Poland. At the end of 1997, total deposits were as high as 33.5 per cent of GDP,[17] while the share of credit to GDP was 24.3 per cent. Readers should be reminded that Warsaw Stock Exchange capitalization is still low: less than 9 per cent of GDP in 1997[18].

In view of the economy's enormous needs, the current savings rate in Poland is not sufficient. But, until recently, due to a state of excess liquidity, banks neglected this kind of business to a great extent. Competition in the deposits markets should intensify in the near future.

Since 1997, banks' net and gross financial results have been deteriorating. Gross income fell by 4.7 per cent in 1997 and 20.1 per cent in 1998. The fall in net income was 1.0 per cent in 1997 and 35.6 per cent in 1998 (Wyczanski et al 1998 and Golajewski et al 1999). This downward tendency, which continued in 1999, is the result of a faster rise in costs than in income.

The data presented in Table 2.6 describe, in a synthetic way, the banks' financial results:

Table 2.5   Deposit growth in Poland by type of client (in zlotys; % change over the previous year)

	1996	1997	1998
Deposits (in nominal terms)	32.0	29.1	29.8
Deposits (in real terms)	11.4	14.0	19.6
Of which			
– households (in nominal terms)	31.0	31.7	30.5
– households (in real terms)	10.5	16.3	20.1
– companies (in nominal terms)	34.8	23.0	28.3
– companies (in real terms)	13.8	8.6	18.1

Sources: 1996: *Raport o inflacji*, NBP, Warsaw, July 1998, pp. 60–1, 1997–98: Golajewski et al 1999.

Table 2.6 Main efficiency indicators of banks in Poland

	1996	1997	1998
Margin of interest	5.98	5.23	4.29
Income other than interest	1.81	2.04	1.97
Operating expenses	3.94	3.99	3.94
Net mandatory provisions	0.09	0.28	0.63
Total costs	4.03	4.27	4.57
Return on assets (ROA)*	2.56	2.11	1.06
Return on equity (ROE)**	68.06	43.18	17.29

*   ROA (return on assets), or ratio: net profit/assets.
**   ROE (return on equity), or ratio: net profit/capital.

Sources: Golajewska et al. (1999), p. 22.

In spite of a decline in 1999, interest margins (the difference between the lending rate and the rate earned on deposits) remain high compared with those in Western countries (on average 1.5 per cent in Japan and 3.3 per cent in the United States).

Among the main efficiency indicators of commercial banks, the ROE and ROA are higher in Poland than in the countries of the European Union, but the ratios decreased in 1997 and 1998. Intensifying competition and, at the same time, a need to invest in the future of the banking sector allow for a prognosis of a continuing drop in profitability. It is most probable that the intermediation margin will shrink and that the ROA will fall below 2 per cent.

Polish banks will find it necessary to make an effort to reduce operating expenses. A fall in employment, in particular, should be expected in the sector as labour constitutes a major cost (51.3 per cent of total costs in 1998).

One of the causes of the falling efficiency of banks is the result of the tight policy undertaken by the NBP in 1997, aimed at counteracting the progression of credit. In particular, the problem of the high level of provisions transferred to the Central Bank and earning no interest has arisen. Up until October 1999, banks transferred on average 12 per cent of their deposits to the NBP (the rates varied from 5 per cent for deposits in foreign currency to 20 per cent for demand deposits in zlotys). They have, apparently, lost approximately 200 million zlotys of net income per month.[19] Following intense pressure from the banking sector, the average rate was lowered to 5 per cent in October 1999 (Wilkowicz, 1999). This measure should not only improve the accounting results of banks, but also their competitive position with regard to foreign banks whose overheads are less weighty (in countries within the European Union, average provision rates run at about 2 per cent). The amounts 'frozen' in the form of provisions by the NBP[20] were to be converted into special NBP bonds (Ziolkowska, 1999).

Future perspectives

The first steps of restructuring established the foundations of a market-based banking system. The second step will be the integration of the Polish banking system into the European Union. The results of adjustments made up to now are far from negligible, as summarized in the following list:

- Banking legislation has become more consistent with European directives.
- Bank supervision is increasingly successful.
- Prudential rules are, generally, now respected. In June 1999, only seven commercial banks and 49 cooperatives had not yet reached the required solvency ratio (8 per cent). Late in 1998, they numbered, respectively, eight and 102.
- The creation of the Banking Guarantee Fund has brought the Polish banking system closer to European standards in the field of deposit insurance.
- The privatization by classic sales methods used in the West has sometimes been viewed as a waste of time and money. But the method deserves credit for having created both transparent and market-friendly structures. Foreign capital's entry into privatized banks made it possible to transfer power to foreign strategic investors and, in this way, ensure the arrival of proper management in privatized banks.
- The recorded progress as far as the concentration of banks is concerned is a positive phenomenon, especially the creation of several banking groups as well as the birth of 'bancassurance' (banking and insurance groups) (Tables 2.A3 and 2.A4).
- The quality of staff has greatly improved and computerization of the banking networks has advanced well.

The speed with which the Polish banking sector has been transformed indicates the banks' will to adapt to new conditions. The future situation of banks in Poland will depend, in part, on the evolution of the Polish economy (growth has slowed since mid-1998) and economic policy, which has a direct effect on bank activity (obligatory provisions, tax levels and so on). But, above all else, banks need a clear vision of their place within this financial system undergoing deep change.

None the less, Polish banks will have to compete severely to consolidate their market position. Besides competition from foreign banks, they will soon meet with that of other institutions wishing to drain savings: the Stock Exchange, Investment Funds and Pension Funds.[21]

Various actors on the Polish financial scene can already be observed creating closer links among themselves. In particular, banking capital has been used extensively in the insurance sector (13.6 per cent of total capital) (Witek, 1998).

Small and medium-sized banks will be forced to find a niche and improve the quality of their services. Certain among them will be able to offer their services to Western banks not yet ready to enter directly into the Polish market.

Conclusion

The second stage of bank restructuring, qualified by Gronkiewicz-Waltz as the stage of qualitative development, is characterized above all else by the increased participation of foreign banks in privatization and the consolidation of the Polish banking system. Feared by part of the Polish population and welcomed by the other, this foreign presence is now part of the Polish banking scene. It is, on the one hand, the direct result of the initial privatization programme, and on the other, the effect of the liberalization of the Polish economy.

It was obvious that due to a lack of sufficient national capital, the privatization of a dozen large Polish banks could not take place without a massive injection of foreign capital. There was no real alternative: either privatization would go ahead with the help of foreign investors, or privatization would be cancelled. The first solution held a double advantage: it would lead to the improved management of the newly privatized banks while, at the same time, providing budget revenues that could be used to finance large-scale structural reform such as healthcare reform, pension reform or education. This is why the various government teams, regardless of their political orientation, all pursued privatization. Westerners, attracted by Poland's positive results, are now willing to pay high prices to acquire stakes in Polish banks (this was not the case at the beginning of transition).

The people who defined the reform programme were initially criticized for having forgotten to establish a clear strategy concerning the banking system. Today, the strategy adopted seems well adapted to the demands facing the country in view of its future membership of the European Union. Various actors are still doing their part in order to ensure the success of this strategy: the government, which is presently pursuing the process of large-scale privatization; the legislator, who is trying to align Polish banking legislation with European norms; and Polish bankers, who are looking for new alliances in order to increase their competitiveness.

Appendix

Table 2.A1   Property structure of the regional commercial banks born of the break-up of the NBP

Name	Property structure	
	Year of privatization	*Main shareholder (1999)*
Wielkopolski Bank Kredytowy SA in Poznan	1992	Allied Irish Bank (60.14%)
Bank Slaski SA in Katowice	1993	ING Netherlands (50.08%)
Bank Przemyslowo-Handlowy SA in Krakow	1995	Bayerische Hypo- und Vereinsbank (50%)
Bank Gdanski in Gdansk	1995	Majority private Polish capital
Powszechny Bank Kredytowy SA in Warsaw	1997	Majority private Polish capital Creditanstalt Bank-verein 18.06% (1 Jan 1998)
Pomorski Bank Kredytowy SA in Szczecin	Grouped together	UniCredito Italiano SpA and Allianz Aktiengesellschaft (52.09%)
Bank Depozytowo-Kredytowy SA in Lublin	Pekao SA in 1996	
Powszechny Bank Gospodarczy SA in Lodz	Privatized in 1999(*)	
Bank Zachodni SA in Wroclaw	1999	AIB European Investments Ltd (80%)

* The Group 'Pekao SA' is composed of these 3 banks and of Bank Polske Kasa Opieki SA (group leader); see p. 69

Table 2.A2 Top Polish banks (ranked by assets)

Bank (Rank 31 July 1999) Main shareholders	Assets in millions of US$* (31 July 99)	Assets change, 1999/98 (%)	Total equity, millions of US$ 31 July 99	Solvency ration[a]	Return on equity (ROE)[b]	Return on assets (ROA)[c]
1 PKO BP The savings bank, state-owned	15 992.9	11.7	424.2	8.5	9.6	0.5
2 Pekao SA (see note Table 2.A1)	14 939.4		935.5	15.0	6.9	0.4
3 Bank Handlowy Privatized in 1997 Minority foreign capital: JP Morgan 12%, Swedbank 6%, Zurich Ins. Co. 6% IPO main institutional investors 20.97%	5 052.9	11.5	714.6	15.8	8.5	1.2
4 BGZ SA Restructuring process State owns 60%, cooperative banks own 34%	4 352.3	12.3	122.4	7.0	28.3	1.8
5 Powszechny Bank Kredytowy SA (PBK) (see Table 2.A1)	4 130.8	38.8	350.7	11.9	9.3	0.8
6 BRE Bank SA (until 23 March 1999 Bank Rozwoju Eksportu SA) see p. 71 Strategic Investor: Commerzbank 49%	3 915.1	78.0	353.7	11.6	11.5	1.0

Table 2.A2   (Cont.)

Bank (Rank 31 July 1999) Main shareholders	Assets in millions of US$* (31 July 99)	Assets change, 1999/98 (%)	Total equity, millions of US$ 31 July 99	Solvency ratio[a]	Return on equity (ROE)[b]	Return on assets (ROA)[c]
7 Bank Przemyslowo-Handlowy	3 642.2	28.3	428.4	18.4	7.9	0.9
8 Kredyt Bank – PBI SA Founded in 1997, majority foreign capital since May 1999	3 523.3	41.0	327.2	12.1	5.7	0.5
9 Bank Slaski (see Table 2.A1)	3 494.4	22.0	356.7	15.2	7.5	0.8
10 BIG –Bank Gdanski SA (see Table 2A.1)	2 948.4	20.9	374.5	15.1	8.5	1.1
11 Wielkopolski Bank Kredytowy SA (WBK) (see Table 2A.1)	2 368.0	21.7	193.7	14.3	10.3	0.8
12 BIG Bank SA (Majority private Polish capital)	2,156.1	71.6	12.7	n.a.	9.8	0.1
13 Bank Zachodni SA (see Table 2A.1)	2 078.6	7.3	177.2	12.9	14.4	1.2
14 Citibank SA (100% foreign capital)	1 928.8	60.0	249.3	13.8	4.0	0.5
15 Prosper Bank SA (Controlled by foreign capital through Kredyt Bank PBI SA)	1 148.7	78.5	20.3	n.a.	7.4	0.1

*   Converted by the author: 1US$ = 3.86 zloty
[a]   Cooke ratio (30 June 1999)
[b]   ROE: Net profit/total equity (30 June 1999)
[c]   ROA: net profit/total assets (30 June 1999)

Sources: *Gazeta Bankowa*, no. 35, 31 June 1999 and no. 41, 12–18 October 1999

Table 2.A3   Banks as shareholders of insurance companies in Poland (end 1997)

Name of insurance company	Bank shareholder	Share (%)
TU Allianz BGZ Polska*	BGZ	49
TU Alliance BGZ Polska Zycie	BGZ	49
BTUiR Heros	PBG	79
	EBRD	15
TUPBK	PBK	50
TuiR Warta	PBK	20
TU Energoasekuracjaell	BEN	13
TU Azur	EBRD	35
TU STU	Bank Wschodnio-Europejski	49
TU Commercial Union na Zycie	WBK	10
BTUiR Heros Life	Kredyt Bank PBI	88
TUK	Kredyt Bank PBI	33
Polisa Zycie	Kredyt Bank PBI	33
TU PBK Zycie	PBK	50
TU Warta Vita	PKO BP	29
Tu Azur Zycie	EBRD	35
	BIG Bank Gdanski	11
Alte Leipziger Hestia	BRE	15

*   TU Towarzystwo Ubezpieczeniowe (insurance company).

Source: Lachowski (1998), p. 46.

Table 2.A4   Insurance companies as shareholders of Polish banks (end 1997)

Name of bank	Name of insurance company	Share (%)
BIG BG	PZU SA and PZU Zycie	17.00
Kredyt Bank	PZU SA and PZU Zycie	7.50
Kredyt Bank	TUiR Warta	6.70

Source: As for Table 2.6

Notes

1   The Banking Act of 31 January 1989 (*Dziennik Ustaw* [Official Journal] 4/89 item 21) and the Act on Narodowy Bank Polski of 31 January 1989 (*Dziennik Ustaw* 4/89, item 22).

2   The Act on the National Bank of Poland of 29 August 1997 (*Dziennik Ustaw* 140/97, item 938 and the Banking Act of August 1997 (*Dziennik Ustaw* 140/97, item 939).

3   The Act on Mortgage Bonds and Mortgage Banks of 29 August 1997 (*Dziennik Ustaw*, 140/940).

4   The Act on Organization and Functioning of Pension Funds of 28 August 1997 (*Dziennik Ustaw* 139/934).
5   The Act on Several Incentives to Housing Construction of 26 October 1996 (*Dziennik Ustaw* 133/654).
6   The Act on Savings and Building Societies and the State Promotion of Housing Savings of 5 June 1997 (*Dziennik Ustaw* 85/538).
7   In 1994, this indicator stood at 4300 for Greece, 2900 for the UK (excluding building societies) and Portugal, 2500 for France, 1700 for Germany, 1300 for Belgium and 1200 for Spain. (*Credit Institutions and Banking*, European Communities, Economic Research Europe, Luxembourg, 1997).
8   Since 1996, other than the heading 'agencies', Polish statistics also cite a group called 'others', which included subsidiaries, administratorships (without representation) and so on. In June 1999, their number had reached 8112 (NBP, September 1999).
9   'The Law date February 3, 1993 on the financial restructuring of banks and companies and on the modification of certain laws', (*Dziennik Ustaw* no. 18, 1993, paragraph 82).
10   The zloty was devalued on 1 January 1995. One new zloty is worth 10 000 old zlotys.
11   That is, bonds convertible into special stock, called 'mute stock'.
12   *Central Europe's Largest Banks Ranked by Assets*. Compiled by Thomson Financial Bank Watch, *Central European Economic Review, The Wall Street Journal Europe*, October 1999, p. 19.
13   *Banking and Finance in Poland 1996–1997*, 1997.
14   B. Z., *Krajobraz po fuzjach* (The landscape after mergers), *Gazeta Bankowa*, no.3, 18 January 1998, p. 10.
15   Disposition of the Commission for Banking Supervision, Dz. U. of the NBP, 1998, no.19, position 44.
16   *Banki 1998*. Raport., Zwiazek Bankow Polskich, p. 36.
17   Stated here are total deposits, both forex and zloty deposits, held by households and companies.
18   *Raport o inflacji*, NBP, Warsaw, July, 1998, p. 64.
19   'Redukcja rezerw w styczniu?' (Fall in provisions in January?), *Prawo i Gospodarka*, 16 December 1998, p. 7.
20   Approximately 18 million zlotys, that is $4.5 million at the end of 1998 (Zaleska, 1998).
21   The creation of pension funds was written into a law dated 22 August 1997 (Dz. U, no.139, pos. 932), which came into effect on 1 April, 1999.

References

W. Baka, *Sektor finansowy – stan i perspektywy* (Financial Sector – Present State and Prospects), *Bank*, 11 (1997), 46–50.

W. Baka (ed.), *Integracja europejska a strategie bankow komercyjnych* (European Integration and Strategy of Commercial Banks), (Katowice: Miedzynarodowa Szkola Bankowosci i Finansow, 1998a), p. 179.

W. Baka, 'Polski sektor bankowy na tle bankowosci europejskiej – w kierunku podwyzszenia konkurencyjnosci' (The Polish Banking Sector at the Bottom of the European Banking System – Towards an Improvement of its Competitive Position). Paper presented at the Conference 'Influence of the Single Financial Market on the Banking Strategies and the Structural Transformation of the Banking Sector – EU Experiences, Recommendations for Polish Banks', International School of Banking and Finance, Warsaw, 28 January (1998b), p. 24.

J. Bonin, K. Mizsei, I. Szekely and P. Wachtel, *Banking in Transition Economies. Developing Market Oriented Banking Sectors in Eastern Europe* (Cheltenham, UK and Northampton, US: Edward Elgar, 1998), p. 191.

A. Bury, A. Gladysz and J. Zebrowski, *Financial Markets in Poland 1997–1998* (Warsaw: CeDeWu – Consulting and Publishing Center 'Multi Press', with the cooperation of BRE Bank SA, 1999), p. 378.

D. Chorylo, A. Mazur and D. Faszczewska, 'Przedstawiamy biuro prywatyzacji Banku Pekao SA' (Presentation of the Office of Privatisation of Pekao Bank SA), *Bankier*, Bank Pekao SA, 3 (1999), 4–5.

European Communities, Economic Research Europe *Credit Institutions and Banking*, Luxembourg, 1997, p. 424

G. Fink, P. R. Haiss, L. T. Orlowski and D. Salvatore, 'Central European Banks and Stock Exchanges: Capacity Building and Institutional Development', *European Management Journal*, 16, 4 (1998) 431–46.

G. Fink, P. R. Haiss, L. T. Orlowski, D. Salvatore, *Privileged Interfirm/Bank Relationships in Central Europe: Trigger or Trap for Corporate Governance?*, *Studies & Analyses*, CASE: Center for Social and Economic Research, Warsaw, 1999.

M. Golajewska, M. Jozefowska and P. Wyczanski, 'Sytuacja finansowa bankow w 1998' (The Financial Situation of Banks in 1998), *Materialy i Studia*, Dpt. Analiz i Badan, NBP, 86 (March 1999), p. 54.

H. Gronkiewicz-Waltz, 'Stan i perspektywy polskiego sektora bankowego' (Development Strategy of the Polish Banking System), paper presented at the Conference 'Development Strategy of the Polish Banking Sector', organized by NICOM Consulting LTD *and Gazeta Bankowa*, Warsaw, 21 September (1998), p. 3.

W. L. Jaworski, 'Kierunki reformy sektora bankowegow Polsce' (The Direction Taken by the Reform of the Polish Banking Sector), in W. L. Jaworski (ed.), *Banki polskie u progu XXI wieku* (Warsaw: Poltext, Studia finansowo-bankowe, Szkola Glowna Handlowa, 1999), pp. 79–94.

S. Kawalec, A. Nieradko and C. Stypulkowski, *Prywatyzacja banku. Doswiadczenia Banku Handlowego SA w Warszawie* (Privatization of Bank Handlowy in Warsaw), preliminary version (Warsaw: Bank Handlowy SA, 1997), p. 61.

F. Kowalik, 'Nie konczaca sie opowiesc' (The Lasting Discussion), *Gazeta Bankowa*, 35 (1999), 5–7.

B. Z. *Krajobraz po fuzjach* (The landscape after mergers), *Gazeta Bankowa*, 3, 18 January 1998, p. 19.

S. Kubielas, 'Rola bankow zagranicznych w prywatyzacji i konsolidacji polskiego sektora bankowego' (The Role of Foreign Banks in the Privatisation and the Consolidation of the Polish Banking Sector), paper presented at the Conference 'Development Strategy of the Polish Banking Sector, organized by NICOM Consulting LTD and *Gazeta Bankowa*, Warsaw, 21 September (1998), p. 15.

S. Lachowski, 'Uwagi o prywatyzacji bankow polskich' (Remarks on the Privatization of Polish Banks), in *Jak dokonczyc prywatyzacje w Polsce* (How to Complete

Privatization in Poland), *Zeszyty PBR – CASE*, Wydanie specjalne (1996), pp. 7–17.

S. Lachowski, 'Fuzje, przejecia i alianse po polsku' (Mergers, takeovers and alliances the polish way) *Bank*, no. 2 (February 1998).

Narodowy Bank Polski (NBP), *Sytuacja finansowa bankow w 1 polroczu 1999 roku. Synteza* (Financial Situation of Banks During the First Semester 1999) (Warsaw, NBP, Generalny Inspektorat Nadzoru Bankowego, September 1999), p. 52.

Narodowy Bank Polski, NBP (1998), *Raport o inflacji* (Report on Inflation), Warsaw, July, p. 98.

L. T. Orlowski, 'The Development of Financial Markets in Poland', *Working Papers CASE–CEU*, 3 (1999), p. 32.

Raport o bankach: Banki w 1997, (Report on Banks: Banks in 1997), *Rzeczpospolita*, 23 April 1998, pp. 13–20.

J. Sawicka, 'Unicredito i Allianz Inwestor strategiczny Pekao SA' (Unicredito and Allianz: a Strategic Investor for Pekao SA), *Bankier*, Bank Pekao SA, 7–8 (1999), 4–5.

K. Solarz, *Konsolidowanie systemow bankowych* (The Consolidation of Banking Systems) (Warsaw: Biblioteka FEiBB, Fundacja Edukacjii Badan Rynkowych, 1993), p. 125.

D. Styczek, 'Zaawansowany proces harmonizacji z Unia Europejska' (The Advanced Process of Harmonization with the European Union), *Bank*, 7 (1999), 30–32.

K. Szymkiewicz, 'L' émergence d' un systéme bancaire efficace en Pologne' in Le Courier des Pays de 1' Est, 430, (1998) pp. 38–51.

K. Szymkiewicz and J. Y. Moisseron, 'La restructuration du système bancaire en Pologne', *Le Courrier des Pays de l'Est*, 389 (1994), 35–50.

L. Wilkowicz, 'Zysk dla klienta' (The Client Will Profit), *Gazeta Bankowa*, 31 (1999), 10.

J. Winiecki, *Post-Soviet-Type Economies in Transition* (Aldershot, UK and Brookfield, US: Avebury, 1993), p. 199.

Z. Witek, 'Zmiany w strukturze wlascicielskiej polskiego sektora bankowego' (Changes in the Property Structure of the Polish Banking System), *Zeszyty PBR-CASE*, 37 (1998), 29–35.

Warsaw School of Banking, Finance & Management – Pekao SA Group in Association with Ministry of Finance, *Banking and Finance in Poland 1996–1997*, Warsaw, July 1997, p. 330.

P. Wyczanski and M. Golajewska, 'Sytuacja finansowa bankow w 1997 r.', (The Financial Situation of Banks in 1997), *Materialy i Studia*, NBP, Departament Analiz i Badan, April (1998), p. 47.

J. Zareba, 'Globalizacja rynkow finansowych a strategie bankow w Polsce' (Globalisation of Financial Markets and Bank Strategy in Poland), *Zeszyty PBR-CASE*, 35 (1998) p. 32.

W. Ziolkowska, 'Trudne zalozenia' (Difficult Objectives), *Gazeta Bankowa*, 42 (1999) 6–7.

Zwiazek Bankow Poskich, *Banki 1998. Raport* (The banks in 1998. Report), Warsaw, p. 71.

Zwiazek Bankow Polskich (1997), *Banki 1996 Raport* (Survey The Bank in 1996), p. 90.

3
Banking Sector Restructuring in the Baltics[1]

Alex Fleming

Introduction

For any country a banking crisis can be a costly experience, but for a country in transition it can also cause significant disruption to the transition process itself and undermine the authorities' efforts to construct a modern, market-based financial system. Although the Baltic republics of Estonia, Latvia and Lithuania have been in the vanguard of transition in the Former Soviet Union (FSU), and have made significant steps towards a market-based economy, their transition efforts were almost undermined by serious banking crises in the mid-1990s. The banking crises in the three Baltic republics shared some common roots but they manifested themselves in different ways and at slightly different times in the transition. The main similarities relate to the broad context in which they arose, specifically the environment of simultaneous transition and adjustment, which puts tremendous strain on banks and their enterprise borrowers and reveals the inherent weakness in the banks and their regulations. Another similarity relates to the factors internal to the banks: weaknesses in management and in general banking skills.

These countries' banking crisis experience provides a series of case studies from which it is possible to draw some general conclusions, concerning both the causes and the implications of serious banking crises in countries in transition. This chapter aims to extract these general conclusions. It begins by describing the efforts to construct a market-based banking system in each of the Baltic states and then considers the various factors, including errors of policy, that contributed to the banking crisis. This is followed by an analysis of the authorities' response to the crisis and the measures that were adopted to attempt to resolve it. The chapter then examines post-crisis developments in bank restructuring in the three Republics. It ends with a conclusion setting out some of the general factors that were at work in the Baltic crises.

The banking system in the early phase of transition

In common with other FSU countries, the three Baltic republics began the transition process with a monobank system that had been inherited from the old centrally planned economy, with specialized state banks servicing specific branches of the economy. The three republics had, at the outset, to decide what to do with their remnant of the FSU banking system. At the same time, they had the twin challenges of encouraging the growth of the new private banking sector while ensuring that such growth took place within the bounds of prudential norms. Furthermore, none of the three possessed a human resource base skilled in modern banking practices and none had an appropriate legal, regulatory and supervisory framework governing the banks. Their early efforts at financial sector reform involved the development of a two-tier banking system, in which the functions of a central bank were clearly delimited from those of the commercial banks. The Baltic countries also adopted a liberal licensing policy towards the formation of new banks, and this was subsequently to be a significant contributory factor to their banking crises.

In Estonia a central bank, the Bank of Estonia (BOE) was established in 1990, and its position as the central bank was affirmed when, after Estonian independence was declared in 1991, the BOE took over the Estonian branch of Gosbank. However, the core of the post-transition banking system was represented by the five specialized state banks formed by Gosbank in 1987: (i) Savings Bank; (ii) Agriculture Bank (Maapank); (iii) Social Bank; (iv) Industry and Construction Bank; and (v) Foreign Trade Bank (Vnesheconombank, later renamed the North Estonian Share Bank (NESB)). Subsequently, the Maapank was split up into 14 entities, which operated independently. The state banks were augmented by the creation of new banks; by 1992, 25 new banks had been licensed. Licensing requirements were comparatively lax and minimum capital was set at only 5 million rubles (less than $40 000 in 1992 figures). Hence, by end 1992 the Estonian banking sector comprised 43 banks; its evolving structure is summarized in Table 3.1.

The Latvian central bank, the Bank of Latvia (BOLAT), was also established in July 1990. However, rather than moving swiftly to create a two-tier banking system, the government decided to combine 45 branches of

Table 3.1   Evolving structure of the Baltic financial systems

	State banks[a,b]	*New commercial banks*[a]	*Branches/ rep. offices of foreign banks*	*Total*[a]
ESTONIA				
Number of banks (and branches)				
Sep. 92[d]	18	25	–	43
Dec. 94	3	18	3	24
Jan. 96	1	13	9	23
Aug. 99	0	5	6	11
Assets, % of total				
Sep. 92	60%	40%	–	US$427 million
Dec. 94	28%	72%	N/A	US$880 million
Jan. 96	10%	90%	N/A	US$220 million
Jul. 99		95%	5%	US$2986 million
Capital, % of total				
Sep. 92	22%	78%	–	US$16 million
Dec. 94	11%	89%	N/A	US$89 million
Dec. 95[g]	2%	98%	N/A	US$122 million
Jul. 99	–	100%	0%	US$471 million
LATVIA				
Number of banks (and branches)				
Dec. 92	2(86)[h]	50 (18)	–	52 (104)
Dec. 94	2 (56)	53 (121)	–	55 (177)
Dec. 95	2 (61)	37 (103)	1	40 (164)
Dec. 98	1 (32)	26 (162)	1	28 (194)
Assets, % of total				
Dec. 92	53%	37%	–	US$605 million
Dec. 94	15%	85%	–	US$1138 million
Dec. 95	27%	74%	N/A	US$1542 million
Dec. 98	7%	91%	2%	US$2625 million
Capital, % of total				
Dec. 92	15%	85%	–	US$22 million
Dec. 94	13%	87%	–	US$336 million
Dec. 95	18%	82%	N/A	US$262 million
Dec. 98	0.4%	99%	N/A	US$271 million

Table 3.1   Cont.

	State banks[a,b]	New commercial banks[a]	Branches/ rep. offices of foreign banks	Total[a]
LITHUANIA				
Number of banks				
(and branches)				
Dec. 92	3 (121)	N/A	–	N/A
Dec. 94	3 (121)	24 (N/A)	–	27 (N/A)
Dec. 95	3 (121)	13 (129)	–	16 (250)[c]
Dec. 98	2 (N/A)			12 (175)
Assets, % of				
total				
Dec. 92	N/A	N/A	–	N/A
Dec. 94	54%	46%	–	US$1451 million
Dec. 95	53%	47%	–	US$1777 million
Dec. 98	37%			US$3053 million
Capital, % of				
total				
Dec. 92	N/A	N/A	–	N/A
Dec. 94	51%	49%	–	US$249 million
Dec. 95	51%	49%	–	US$261 million
Dec. 98	26%	72%	2%	US$32 million

[a]   Number of branches are in parentheses.
[b]   State banks that were a remnant of the Soviet System only.
[c]   Excluding banks in liquidation or bankruptcy.
[d]   Pre-crises data. December 1992 was omitted, as the Bank of Estonia was undergoing a bank relicensing process at the time. January 1996 data are shown in lieu of December 1995.
[e]   Asset and capital data must be read with caution. Banks gradually converted to IAS standards over the period studied; hence, not all the reported figures are comparable. Many banks reported figures that did not include proper provision for loan losses, with the result of inflating both assets and capital figures.
[f]   Data for new commercial bank include the Latvian Mortgage and Land Bank (relatively new state bank) and the Latvian Investment Bank (35 per cent state-owned)
[g]   Estonian Investment Bank data were not available for inclusion in 1995/96 figures.
[h]   Figures for December 1992 represent former branches of BOLAT that were overseen by the Bank Privatization Committee. Figures beginning with December 1993 (March, December 1994 and 1995) reflect the operations of Unibank.

the former Soviet banks and to place them under the control of BOLAT. These were disposed of over the course of the next three years. Nine branches were sold to private commercial banks, while 15 further branches were consolidated into eight private banks and sold through share offerings. Finally, on 28 September 1993 the rump of 21 branches was structured into one state bank – the Universal Bank of Latvia, or Unibank – and subjected to intense institutional development support.

Although placing these branches under the control of BOLAT was intended to allow maximum flexibility in their disposal, weaknesses in their governance arrangements meant that the branch managers could operate with a high degree of independence of BOLAT. As a result, from the time the 45 branches were combined under BOLAT until the creation of Unibank, a significant amount of imprudent lending – in the order of US$50 million equivalent – took place. Although the state-owned Savings Bank was not part of this arrangement, a lack of strong management there meant that the financial condition of this bank also gradually deteriorated.

Like Estonia, Latvia also followed a liberal licensing policy towards new banks. By 1993, over 60 new commercial banks had been licensed in Latvia. Some of them were 'pocket' banks owned by state enterprises, some were purely private but were dedicated mainly to raising deposits to on-lend to the owners, and some were set up with specific functions in mind (Olympia Bank was set up to help finance the Latvian Olympic team). All of these private or quasi-private banks were allowed to develop with little initial supervision from the BOLAT.

The new commercial banking sector grew very rapidly in relation to the remainder of the state banking sector over the period 1992–94. Between December 1992 and December 1994, the new commercial banking sector share of total assets grew from 47 per cent to 85 per cent. Credits granted by the banking system also grew sharply over this period, with the new commercial banks accounting for 89 per cent of the total by the end of 1994, up from only 23 per cent two years earlier (see Table 3.1).

Among the private banks that developed very quickly in 1993 and 1994 was Bank Baltija. Its assets grew from about US$25 million in January 1993 to US$242 million in January 1994, and then to almost US$500 million by early 1995. Bank Baltija became the largest Latvian commercial bank in terms of assets, capital and deposit funding by 1994. The bank's reported capital grew from about US$1 million in early 1993 to US$20 million in January 1994 and to US$44 million in January 1995. The bank had 37 branches and 49 offices throughout Latvia with 1300 employees in total. In April 1995, when the banking crisis began, the bank had total deposits of US$392 million. Bank Baltija was at the heart of the Latvian banking crisis.

In contrast to the approach taken in Latvia, the Lithuanian government decided early on to corporatize and partially privatize the three specialized state-owned banks which were split off from Gosbank: the State Savings Bank, the State Agriculture Bank and the State Commercial Bank. Up to 49 per cent private ownership was permitted through the infusion of new capital, with the government continuing to own the rest. However, this privatization was done without appropriate disclosure of the banks' financial condition (International Accounting Standards [IAS] audits showing that the banks were insolvent were not made available to potential purchasers) and without any improvements in corporate governance or changes in management. Early attempts at restructuring the State Savings Bank were unsuccessful as they were partial in nature[2] and again were not accompanied by any improvements in corporate governance or changes in management. These weaknesses, when combined with the reluctance of the newly created central bank – the Bank of Lithuania (BOLIT) – to use its regulatory and supervisory powers,[3] meant that the financial condition of the three state banks steadily deteriorated during the period 1992–96, with an increasing number of incidents of fraud.

As in the other Baltic republics, many new commercial banks emerged in Lithuania, some as the treasury arm of their state-owned enterprise founders. Twenty-five new commercial banks were in operation by March 1995; approximately eight of these could be characterized as active banks, both in terms of asset size and activity. The remainder were foreign exchange offices or true 'pocket' banks that lent primarily to their owners. The share of the new private banks (by assets) in Lithuania's total banking system increased rapidly to reach 46 per cent by December 1993 (see Table 3.1) when it began to stabilize.

The funding of the fast-growing banks came mainly from new private sector enterprises, and was to a large extent foreign currency denominated. Lending activities were mostly focused on newly private and privatized enterprises engaged in trade, services and manufacturing, with the notable exception of Innovation Bank, which lent mainly, and often at the government's explicit urging, to the energy sector which to date is still plagued by many structural problems.

There are therefore a number of similarities in the initial approach to banking sector restructuring in the Baltic republics. The Estonian and Lithuanian approaches were similar in that both republics reconstituted the specialized Soviet banks as national state banks and gradually or partially privatized them by selling shares to the local private sector. The Latvian approach, in contrast, was to reconstitute the Savings Bank, but then privatize the branches of the remaining banks. The residual banks were merged and rehabilitated, then subject to a formal privatization process.

However, the strongest similarity was in the approach of the three Baltic republics towards the licensing of new commercial banks. A large number of banks, it was thought, would quickly generate the competition needed to drive down deposit and lending rates and provide the lending needed to support the emerging private sector. Many new private banks were established by enterprises to gain access to a preferential and much cheaper source of funding than was available from existing banking institutions. Little thought was given initially to the implications of this policy for banking safety and supervision.

Banking crises in the Baltic states

The Baltic banking crises emerged first in Estonia in 1992, followed by Latvia in early 1995 and Lithuania in late 1995. In Estonia, the crisis was triggered by liquidity difficulties brought about by the freezing of assets in Moscow of two important banks, coupled with the suspension of cheap credits from BOE, which had previously endowed Estonian banks with significant profits and liquidity. In Latvia the proximate cause was the drying up of highly profitable trade-financing opportunities and general mismanagement and corruption in the operations of banks (particularly evident in Bank Baltija). The trigger of the crisis was BOLAT's requirement that banks be properly audited using IAS principles. A liquidity squeeze ensued as doubts about the solvency of several banks grew. Banks in Lithuania, as in Latvia, suffered a compression in their profits due to the contraction of lucrative trade-financing opportunities. An additional factor in the Lithuanian case, however, was the government's role in pressing some banks (both state-owned and private) to lend to finance quasi-fiscal expenditures. The trigger in this case was leaks of the results of on-site examinations of two banks which led to runs on each bank and liquidity shortages.

In early 1992 the Moscow offices of the Vnesheconombank and the Savings Bank froze all assets belonging to non-Russian banks. This caused financial problems in banks throughout the former Soviet republics, but three banks in Estonia were particularly badly affected: the NESB and the Union Baltic Bank (UBB), which had placed assets amounting to $40 million and $36 million respectively with the Vnesheconombank, and the Savings Bank, which had placed $25 million in assets in Moscow. Since the Savings Bank held over 85 per cent of household savings at the time, the BOE took action to ensure that these savings were protected. In April 1992, it took over the ownership of the Savings Bank, swapping some of its own assets for the Savings Bank's claim on the Moscow Savings Bank. The BOE's decision to assist the Savings Bank was in part motivated by the desire to minimize disruption to public confidence during the introduction of Estonia's new currency (the kroon) planned for June 1992.

Box 3.1 Banking distress in the Social Bank and the North Estonian Bank

The Social Bank

The resolution of the 1992 crisis did not mean the end of all banking problems in Estonia. In 1994, the Social Bank, one of the former spin-offs from Gosbank, developed serious liquidity problems. The precipitating cause was the government's decision in the spring of 1994 to withdraw much of the state's budget deposits (the equivalent of about $15 million) from the Social Bank, and reallocate the deposits among several banks in the system. By August 1994, about US$26 million of other deposits had been withdrawn, the bank ran into serious liquidity problems, and was placed into moratorium. However, the root cause of the bank's problems was a combination of mismanagement and fraud. Lending procedures were not followed, and in some cases openly overruled by shareholders. Loans were made to non-existent companies, or were made to companies clearly not financially capable of repaying loans of the size they were given.

The authorities were not as strict in the handling of this bank failure. The Bank of Estonia, which several weeks before the Social Bank went into moratorium had declared that the Social Bank was financially sound, felt that it had some responsibility to the depositors, who had relied on the BOE's statements. The BOE had also, for several weeks, encouraged other commercial banks to provide interbank loans to the Social Bank. The BOE attempted to restore confidence in the bank by providing liquidity support. It also sought for several months a potential partner or buyer for the Social Bank. One small bank, the Estonian Arengupank, merged with the Social Bank, but it was unable to provide sufficient resources to help the Social Bank. The BOE also began selling off assets of the Social Bank to try to raise funds. Ultimately, however, all these efforts failed to keep the bank afloat. In March 1995, about US$12 million of the 'better' assets were transferred to the North Estonian Bank, along with accompanying liabilities, including EEK38.5 million (US$3 million) of BOE claims that were transformed into equity. The remaining assets and liabilities were left with the Social Bank, which essentially was simply transformed into a loan recovery agency. The result of all this was that the Social Bank depositors were generally made whole, but the shareholders were wiped out. Other creditors were left with claims on recovered assets.

The overall message from this bank failure was not as clear as in the 1992 crisis. Although the Social Bank had clearly been mismanaged, the BOE provided liquidity support and sought other means of saving the bank. The eventual liquidation of the bank did leave a residual 'tough' message – but the interim manoeuvres diluted this message.

The North Estonian Bank

The initial recapitalization proved to be inadequate, as many of the loans inherited by the new bank turned out to be uncollectible. Unfortunately, after the merger and recapitalization, the new management did not seem capable of running the bank well. For more than two years afterwards, the new NEB management continued their poor lending policies. In addition, the NEB was further weakened by mismanagement in other areas, such as poor treasury operations, and also by continuing to provide interbank loans to the Social Bank, when all the other banks had ceased to provide such support. The transfer of Social Bank assets and liabilities to the NEB has also proved to be only a transfer of problems from one weak bank to another. The accumulated bad loans from the NEB and Social Bank operations was considerable.

The NESB and UBB continued to operate on the assumption that the asset freeze was temporary, and therefore did not properly husband their scarce liquid funds. The liquidity problems were exacerbated by Estonia's new, tight monetary policy, which came into force with the introduction of the kroon. A currency board system was established, meaning that the central bank could not issue new base money unless there was a corresponding increase in convertible foreign currency, or in the case of a sharply defined banking crisis. As a result of these reforms, commercial banks could no longer rely on the central bank as a source of cheap credit. Up to that point, some banks had bolstered their earnings by charging high spreads on loans financed from these cheap credits. In addition, the new unified exchange rate reduced arbitrage opportunities and buy–sell spreads, reducing foreign exchange revenues.

Another large private commercial bank, the Tartu Commercial Bank (TCB), also began having liquidity problems, as the new tight money policy made it impossible to use new credits to disguise problems in its loan portfolio. Thus in November 1992, a serious liquidity crisis developed in the three largest commercial banks: TCB, UBB and NESB. Payments began slowing down; for example, the average transfer time for a UBB payment slowed from four days to almost a month. UBB finally froze all accounts of state-owned enterprises, in the hopes that this act would force the government to assist UBB, particularly with regard to some of UBB's assets that were frozen in Moscow. Instead, the BOE placed a moratorium on all three banks. Assets in these distressed banks accounted for about 40 per cent of total banking assets.

In Latvia the banking crisis came to a head towards the end of March 1995,[4] precipitated in part by the insistence of the BOLAT that all banks should prepare and present to its Banking Supervision Department financial statements that had been audited on the basis of IAS. It was the failure of Bank Baltija to present such accounts, or indeed to give its auditors full access to needed documentation for the audit of its 1994 financial statements, that set off a chain of events leading to the bank's declaration of insolvency. But Bank Baltija was not the only bank involved in the crisis at this stage. Other banks included the Latvian Deposit Bank, Centra Bank and Olimpija Bank, all middle-sized banks that were eventually declared insolvent. A number of smaller banks also experienced difficulty.[5] In all, about 40 per cent of banking system assets were compromised, totaling almost US$900 million.

Bank Baltija was, however, the central player in the growing banking crisis. Its collapse is a classic example of banking distress brought about by mismanagement on a massive scale. As it expanded aggressively,

Bank Baltija also undertook many profligate expenditures, including throwing lavish parties for clients and government officials. This activity was apparently undertaken as a means of insuring itself politically against any future difficulties it might encounter. Apart from elements of fraud and corruption, there was poor management of currency and interest rate risk, compounded by a failure to put in place adequate systems and controls.

There is also evidence that Bank Baltija – and possibly other banks as well – followed a high-risk strategy in bidding for Lat deposits at very high interest rates. Convinced that the lat would depreciate *vis-à-vis* the US dollar, Baltija repeatedly converted large volumes of lats into US dollars which it on-lent, thereby creating a large open foreign exchange position. It is possible that Bank Baltija believed that by putting itself in a position where it dominated the banking system, any doubts about its own solvency would precipitate a fall in the lat and, thereby, improve the bank's financial condition.[6] Its strategy may also have been associated with its ambition to become a major retail bank, since it could use the very profitable trade-related lending to offer very high deposit rates, as high as 90 per cent for one-year deposits. This it did with a view to siphoning off depositors from other banks, particularly the Savings Bank. Baltija management furthered this aggressive strategy by opening a significant number of branches around the country.

However, contrary to Bank Baltija's strategy, the lat appreciated considerably against the US dollar over the 1994/95 period and market interest rates fell, exposing Baltija to significant net interest margin pressures. The growing public perception that Bank Baltija was in difficulty led to a withdrawal of deposits from the bank, initially by enterprises. Households were slower to grasp the gravity of the problem and, thus, large numbers of small deposit holders were caught unawares when the bank's doors were closed.[7]

Other Latvian banks also encountered problems at the same time as Bank Baltija. Several had been instrumental in financing East–West trade, encouraged by the high returns it offered, especially in 1993/94. These profit opportunities arose on account of the fact that prices of metals and other commodities in Russia remained well below world market prices. However, once Russian prices rose to near world levels, the financing opportunities, and the associated profits, began to dry up. This put downward pressure on banks' profit margins as the banks scrambled to find equally profitable business, which they could only do by taking on higher risk. Another factor which may have pushed some banks into ill-advised lending was the ease of availability of certain foreign credit lines[8] that were guaranteed by the government. The banks approved for channelling these credit lines often did not have adequate mechanisms in place for screening borrowers.

In Lithuania the banking crisis began in early 1995 but did not reach its peak until December of that year, with the imposition of a moratorium on Innovation Bank (the largest private, and second largest bank[9] overall in terms of total assets), Vakaru Bank (the sixth largest), and Litimpex Bank (the seventh largest), which together held approximately 29 per cent of total bank deposits. All these were private banks.

As in Estonia, Lithuanian banks suffered downward pressures on their income as a result of the introduction of a currency board in April 1994. As in Latvia, they also suffered from the drying up of the initially very lucrative East–West metal trade. A further specific factor was the tendency on the part of the government to put pressure on a number of banks – in particular the State Agriculture Bank and Innovation Bank – to finance quasi-fiscal expenditures. Faced with tightening fiscal expenditure and direct lending ceilings under its successive IMF stabilization programmes, the government increasingly (and in a less concealed manner) resorted to using the banking system as a source of financing of the agricultural and energy sectors where structural imbalances persisted. The result, as loan losses mounted, was a deepening of the already existing insolvencies. In addition, as in Latvia, a large part of foreign balance of payments support was used to finance bank loans of dubious quality. A final factor may have been the almost total absence of competition from foreign banks which were actively discouraged from setting up a presence in Lithuania by the central bank (BOLIT).

In the spring of 1995, five pocket banks had their minimum reserve balances with BOLIT frozen due to reported liquidity problems and violation of their minimum reserve requirements; these have since officially been declared bankrupt either by the general prosecutor's office or by their shareholders or creditors. By the end of June 1995, ten smaller banks were officially under administration.[10] Seven of the administrators were appointed by BOLIT and three by failing banks' shareholders or creditors.

However, the failure of Innovation Bank was the most significant component of the Lithuanian banking crisis. Like Bank Baltija, this was an almost textbook case of bank mismanagement. Its assets grew rapidly from the equivalent of US$16 million at the end of 1993 to US$77 million by year-end 1994, and by June 1995 were the equivalent of US$216 million. To achieve this growth, the bank paid above market interest rates on deposits, and rapidly expanded its branch network by building expensive facilities. Lending was heavily concentrated on the energy sector, which in Lithuania is high-risk and subject to politically influenced decision-making. The bank also extended large credits to suppliers and customers of the Ignalina Nuclear Power Station and other large, state-owned energy companies. Insider influence played a substantial part in lending decisions, in that the bank's largest share-holders (together owning 15.2 per cent of the bank) were oil-trading companies. At the end of 1994, US$30 million equivalent of loans to connected parties were classified as non-performing under IAS account-ing principles. Although the bank's shrinking interest margins and growing tranche of non-performing loans were obvious to management, especially following the audits of 1993 and 1994, their response was to continue to grow the bank. Finally, the lack of timely enforcement by BOLIT, given all the clear warning signals, permitted the problem to grow.

Box 3.2   The Innovation Bank's failure

Rapid growth

Innovation Bank's assets grew from the equivalent of US$16 mil-lion at the end of 1993 to US$77 million and US$169 million at year-end 1994 and year-end 1995. By June 1995 assets had grown to the equivalent of US$216 million. To achieve this growth, the bank paid above market interest rates on deposits. In addition, the bank rapidly expanded its branch network by building expensive facil-ities. Fixed assets were in excess of 15 per cent of total assets at the end of 1995, when over 30 per cent of the bank's branches were unprofitable, but were kept open due to 'competitive factors'.

Industry concentration

The bank focused lending activities in the energy sector. The energy sector in Lithuania is highly risky, characterized by high costs, heavy expenditures, severe payment arrears, and politically influenced decision making processes.

Insider and political influences

The bank's largest shareholders (together owning 15.2 per cent of the bank) were companies involved in oil trading. The bank also extended large credits to suppliers and customers of the Ignalina Nuclear Power Station and other large, state-owned energy companies. At the end of 1994, US$30 million equivalent of loans to connected parties were classified as non-performing under IAS accounting principles. At the end of 1995, the largest credit in the bank was to LSPS, the state energy company.

Intentional disregard of prudential rules and financial warning signals

IAS audits for 1993 and 1994 revealed the bank's insolvency. The 1993 audit uncovered violations of loan covenants by the bank. The 1993 audit also reflected the bank's non-compliance with prudential rules and contained statements such as 'management believes the banking regulator will not take any action with respect to this apparent violation'. Innovation Bank took few, if any, steps to resolve violations of the prudential rules. The bank ignored the shrinking margins resulting from the general economic situation, high rates of interest paid on deposits, and lack of repayment on loans. By the end of 1995, the bank approached a negative net interest margin, yet it continued to extend funds to non-performing borrowers and rolled over interest on credits. During 1995, operating expenses exceeded net operating revenue by 20 per cent. Management's solution was to continue to increase the size of the bank, including the proposed merger with Litimpex Bank.

Insufficient supervision

While the BOLIT cannot be blamed for weak, ineffective management in commercial banks, the lack of timely enforcement in this case, given all the clear warning signals, permitted the problem to grow. Timely action on the part of the BOLIT – intended to assess the magnitude of the bank's insolvency – could perhaps have limited the cost.

An important element in the Innovation Bank's growth strategy was a proposed merger with Litimpex Bank which it had been pursuing since the summer of 1995. The two banks' operations became increasingly entangled during the latter half of 1995, notwithstanding the fact that the BOLIT had not yet given permission for either the merger or the *de facto* integration of the two banks' operations. The first BOLIT on-site examinations in the two banks were undertaken during late autumn, revealing major irregularities in financial and prudential reporting by both banks. The examination reports were leaked to the press, triggering a run on both banks and causing a liquidity squeeze which also affected Vakaru Bank, which was vulnerable due to liquidity problems it had experienced earlier. This led BOLIT to impose a temporary moratorium on the activities of Innovation Bank and Litimpex Bank on 19 December 1995. On 21 December 1995 the powers of the shareholders' council of Vakaru Bank[11] were also suspended, its management board was removed, and an administrator was appointed.

The policy response

Despite the similarities in the background to the crises in the three Baltic republics, the authorities' immediate response differed significantly. When the crisis occurred in Estonia the authorities decided – and announced very quickly – that a harsh solution was needed. The Prime Minister warned that the 1993 budget had no funds for a bailout. Although the currency board arrangement permitted the BOE to provide credit in a banking crisis, the BOE and the IMF took the stance that the large scale of the proposed bailout would be inflationary and would undermine the fixed exchange rate.

Instead, the BOE moved quickly to liquidate the Tartu Commercial Bank, taking the view that its problems stemmed primarily from its own mismanagement, and that any rescue would just lead to moral hazard problems in the future. TCB's assets were sold, and the depositors received about 60 per cent of their deposits; shareholders received nothing.

The BOE took a different approach to the other two banks. Since the primary cause of UBB and NESB's problems was the freezing of their assets by the Moscow Vnesheconombank – which was an event that the banks' managers could neither control nor anticipate – the authorities decided not to liquidate the banks. However, since the banks could not be held entirely blameless for their financial position, the shareholders did bear appreciable costs. Thus UBB and the NESB were forcibly merged into a new entity, the North Estonian Bank (NEB).[12]

The BOE and the government then created a Vnesheconombank-fund (VEB-fund) which issued certificates backed by the frozen assets held in Moscow. The shareholders were given VEB certificates in lieu of their shares; hence they received virtually nothing for their shares. The government also exchanged VEB bonds from the new bank, NEB, for government bonds. Hence the valueless frozen assets on the NEB's balance sheet were transformed into (also valueless) VEB certificates, which were then exchanged for government bonds, which did have value. The government added additional bonds to strengthen the NEB's balance sheet, and in return took 100 per cent ownership of the bank. As a result of this financial engineering: (i) the shareholders received almost nothing; (ii) the depositors were protected since the government replaced the banks' bad assets with government bonds; and (iii) the government took ownership of the bank.

After the immediate crisis was resolved, the Bank of Estonia instituted a licensing review. A number of banks were delicensed and several others were merged. By mid-1993, the number of banks in Estonia had decreased from 43 to 23. The Bank of Estonia also began to strengthen supervision. A new Law on Credit Institutions was passed in December 1994, increasing the BOE's supervision and enforcement powers. In addition, the new law required that all banks develop internal auditing departments, and that all banks be audited annually by external auditors. Starting in 1995, all banks were required to use International Accounting Standards for their financial statements.

In contrast, the authorities' initial response to the banking crisis in Latvia was more accommodating. The BOLAT initially provided a modest amount of liquidity support for Bank Baltija, as did several large corporate names such as the Latvian Shipping Company.[13] At first it was thought that Baltija's insolvency problem was of moderate size – in the order of US$50 million – but further investigation by the bank's accountants revealed that its negative net worth was much larger, about US$320 million or 7 per cent of estimated 1995 GDP. These findings resulted in a suspension of liquidity support by BOLAT, and instead central bank and government officials began protracted negotiations with the owners and management of Baltija. Such negotiations were necessary because under the banking law BOLAT lacked powers formally to intervene in a bank, but they merely gave the owners and managers the opportunity to stall for time during which they stripped the bank of many of its remaining assets. Thus, of the roughly US$500 million in assets on Baltija's books when the crisis began, some US$260 million had disappeared by the time it was declared insolvent in July 1995.

Subsequently, the BOLAT took over the management of the bank in the context of an agreement drafted between the owners and management on the one side and the BOLAT and Ministry of Finance on the other. Initially, this agreement was used by the owners and managers to try to obtain concessions from the government, on the principle that Baltija was too big to fail and that its fall would have significant political ramifications. Ultimately, as the depth of the problem became known, and following advice from the World Bank and the IMF, the agreement was redrafted to give full control of the bank to the BOLAT (Baltija's owners could regain control of the bank if they fully recapitalized it – an unlikely event given the degree of insolvency of the bank). So the agreement served to provide the BOLAT with the powers to run and dispose of Baltija.

The Latvian authorities had to deal not only with problems in specific banks but also with a crisis of confidence in the banking sector at large. Urgent changes in the legal, regulatory, supervisory and institutional framework were necessary. In response to the banking crisis, the Bank of Latvia developed three banking laws – a new commercial banking law, a law that would set up a bank rehabilitation/liquidation agency, and a law that would create a deposit insurance system. These actions were taken in an effort to rebuild shattered public confidence in the banking system and to strengthen the legal and institutional framework for banking. The new Commercial Banking Law was much more detailed and inclusive than the 1992 statute, and was enacted in October 1995. Budgetary pressures meant that the other two laws were not ultimately enacted.

BOLAT subsequently hired additional supervisory staff, moved to tighten prudential regulations, and required banks to establish internal control departments. BOLAT also arranged for external accounting firms to supplement the work of the Bank of Latvia's on-site examiners. Enforcement was improved through an amendment to the administrative code that has permitted BOLAT to impose fines on bank management for violations of prudential regulations. This more intense supervision focused on the 'core' banks that were permitted to take household deposits. As in Estonia a number of banks were forced to close, and of the remaining banks only 14 were granted full banking licences permitting them to accept household deposits.

The initial response of the Lithuanian authorities to the early signs of the pending crisis in the summer of 1995 was at the opposite end of the spectrum to that of the Estonians. BOLIT's initial response was to provide unconditional support, without removal of management or suspension of shareholders' rights, and its liquidity support for Aura Bank alone exhausted all the scope it had for this purpose under the currency board. In addition, the government moved some of its deposits in other banks to Aura.[14] In the case of Vakaru Bank, the government channelled the proceeds of a special Treasury bill issue sold exclusively to the stronger banks outside the regular auction mechanism to the bank. This sent a signal to the banking community that there would be few if any penalties for imprudent behaviour.

As the crisis reached its peak in December 1995, the policy response at first seemed more forthright. This time, however, the authorities' hands were partially tied by the passage by Parliament of a number of emergency pieces of legislation, as well as a new deposit insurance law[17] which had been pending since the summer of 1995. The emergency legislation required the government to lift the moratorium on Innovation Bank and Litimpex Bank by 1 February 1996 and to ensure that none of the depositors in the two banks lost any money. In addition, legislation was passed allowing the government to extend up to litai 300 million (US$75 million) in guarantees for interbank borrowing as a means to address liquidity problems experienced by other banks suffering from a loss of depositor confidence in the banking system. This scheme was conceived as substituting for the lender-of-last-resort function of BOLIT, which was already exhausted by support for Aura Bank. The scheme did not specify, however, which banks would be eligible for this implicit government support, again sending a signal to the banking community that government support would not distinguish between prudent and imprudent banks. Parliament also adopted a law requiring the government retroactively to provide compensation to individual depositors in all smaller banks under bankruptcy up to 2000 litai per person (US$500).

Notwithstanding these constraints, the authorities, with the assistance of the World Bank and the IMF (during January 1995–96), drew up a detailed bank restructuring plan that encompassed both the three insolvent state-owned banks and the four failed private banks. This plan envisaged full recapitalization and renationalization of the three majority state-owned banks, merger and nationalization of Innovation Bank, Litimpex Bank and Vakaru Bank, and liquidation of Aura Bank. Under growing public pressure, however, and charges of incompetence and insider information abuse, shortly after the passage of the package of emergency legislation, the Prime Minister and several other ministers – as well as the BOLIT Governor and the Head of Bank Supervision – were forced to resign.

Post-crisis trends in the Baltic banking sectors

Since the banking crises of the early and mid-1990s, the three Baltic republics have continued to be buffeted by forces that have changed the structure of their respective banking sectors. The Russian financial crisis of 1998, for instance, had economic and financial implications for all three countries. The Lithuanian real sector suffered most from the interruption in trade, but this was not reflected in a marked deterioration in the quality of loan portfolios. By contrast, some Latvian banks were forced into insolvency through having to absorb the costs associated with the loss in value of Russian GKOs. Several banks, including one of the largest, became insolvent. Increasing competition, and the impact of tighter banking regulations and supervision, have put further pressure on banks to merge or go into liquidation. In Estonia banks were not heavily invested in Russian debt instruments (accounting for only 0.1 per cent of Estonian banks' total assets at end-July 1998), and hence the direct effect of the Russian crisis was more modest, but the banks were hurt by the general economic slowdown. As a result, extensive restructuring took place in the financial sector. Out of 12 banks in existence at the beginning of 1998, three have been closed (Land Bank, ERA, EVEA) and six others merged into three larger banks.

Aside from the impact of the Russian crisis, the story of the Estonian banking sector since the mid-1990s has been one of consolidation and the growing involvement of foreign (mainly Scandinavian) banks. One factor that accelerated the process of consolidation was a mini-crisis in the summer of 1997 caused by the bursting of a stock market bubble. Domestic banks (as well as supervisors) had failed to recognize the risks involved in extending margin loans, and consequent losses resulted in the country's sixth largest bank (Land Bank) becoming technically insolvent, and the fifth (Tallinna Bank) and the third bank (Savings Bank) had accumulated large losses. To cover these balance sheet losses Tallinna Bank and Savings Bank were forced to merge with larger banks. One was taken over by the state (new Optiva) and the two largest banks have now been taken over by Swedish banks. These banks, seeking to secure a foothold in the Baltics, have invested major sums in the equity of banks in all three of the Baltic countries in recent years. In Estonia Swedbank became a majority shareholder in Hansabank and SEB (Skandinaviska Enskilda Banken) an over 33 per cent shareholder in Uhispank. One consequence of the growing number of foreign banks in the Estonian banking sector has been for the commercial banks to play an increasingly important role in intermediating foreign savings into the country (beginning in 1996, and then more markedly in 1997). Another has been for the government's role in the banking system to decline sharply. As of the beginning of 1999, the government did not have over 5 per cent ownership in any of Estonian commercial banks.[16] These events broadened the capital base of the Estonian banking system, eased access to international capital markets, and possibly improved their corporate governance.

The Latvian banking system also showed solid improvement after the 1995 banking crisis, especially in 1997 and the first half of 1998: banks' balance sheets grew and profitability increased. Since the banking crisis of 1995, several foreign banks entered the Latvian finance market directly (for example Vereins und West-bank of Germany as 75 per cent owners of Vereinsbank Riga with IFC [International Financial Corporation] holding the remaining 25 per cent of share capital) or through acquisition of shares of existing banks (like SEB in Unibank or Merita Nordbanken in Latvian Investment Bank).[17]

After the 1995 banking crisis the Bank of Latvia tightened banking supervision and the banks started to switch from commercial and consumer lending to investment business. Initially Government of Latvia Treasury bills offered very good opportunities for profit. However, later the yields decreased significantly when the government stabilized the state budget and reduced internal borrowings. The banks then switched to holding securities of other East European countries, especially Russian GKOs, that offered high profit and no capital adequacy penalty at the same time. Ultimately this led to significant losses by Latvian banks when the Russian crisis erupted.

The GKO default and the immediate closure of Kapital Bank announced by Bank of Latvia caused depositors to begin a run on the fourth largest bank – Riga Kommercbank (RKB) – which had a high proportion of assets invested in Russian securities. In early March 1999, the Bank of Latvia (which had stepped in to help the bank) did not want to support further the deteriorating liquidity position of RKB and ceased its operations, pending the formulation of a rescue package that was finally put in place in October 1999. The RKB closure caused a second wave of suspicion among depositors of other banks, and only the largest, or banks with credible foreign owners, were able to retain public confidence. The Russian GKO default caused the Bank of Latvia to change its regulations regarding investments into securities of governments of non-OECD countries. The Bank of Latvia accordingly introduced a limit on investments in such securities (no more than 25 per cent of the bank's capital into one country) and changed the risk weight in capital adequacy calculation.

The Russian crisis, despite large losses suffered by Latvian banking industry (approx. $150 millions), may also have a positive effect in precipitating further consolidation of the banking sector. The comparatively large number of small and medium-sized banks in Latvia was in part due to the profit opportunities provided by taking deposits from non-resident Russians that were in turn reinvested in Russian securities. The drying up of this business in the wake of the GKO default means that many of these banks will struggle to maintain an independent existence. Furthermore, at the end of 1999 all credit institutions in Latvia will have had to meet a minimum equity requirement of 5 million euro. This is an additional motive for market consolidation.

In response to the crisis in Lithuania, BOLIT began a programme of enhanced regulation and supervision. New rules regarding large exposures, connected lending and loan provisioning were introduced. ISA (international standards of audit) were demanded of all banks, and IAS and Basel capital rules were implemented as of 1 January 1997. In addition, BOLIT's Banking Supervision Department (BSD) has implemented an early warning system that evaluates the current status of the banking system and foresees trends. On-call audits are carried out by international audit firms at the instigation of BSD on an ongoing basis.

In addition, Parliament passed a law on deposit insurance insuring individual deposits in all banks, initially up to 5000 litai. The law has since been amended to include deposits in foreign currency and the insurance amount is to be gradually increased to bring it into line with the EU's deposit guarantee directive. The insurance coverage is 100 per cent for smaller deposits and decreases to 70 per cent at the limit for larger deposits. Deposits in foreign exchange have a somewhat lower coverage than litai deposits.

The consolidation process, which accelerated during the banking crisis, has continued. Currently there are nine banks in operation, after BOLIT revoked the licence of troubled Litimpeks Bank in September 1999. Innovation Bank was never able to reopen, despite several efforts to revive it. Its assets were transferred to be managed by Turto Bank, a government-owned workout unit, which was created on the ruins of Aura Bank. Tauro Bank, which got into severe trouble due to connected lending, was placed into liquidation in 1997, and the state was forced to decide about liquidation of State Commercial Bank, after almost two years of partial moratorium and two failed privatization efforts. Its performing assets were transferred to the Savings Bank and the problem loans were transferred to Turto Bank.

Partly as a result of the banking crisis, the Lithuanian banking sector has polarized into three segments. The sector is dominated by the two state-controlled banks (Savings Bank and Agricultural Bank) and the two large private banks (Vilniaus Bank and Hermis Bank). These two segments each control over 40 per cent of the banking system's assets. The third segment comprises five small private banks, which have all struggled to survive and are likely to be acquired or to go out of business in the next few years. Vilniaus Bank and Hermis Bank have clearly been the most successful banks and have enjoyed fast growth of assets and profitability. A large majority of their shares are by now owned by foreign investors. A strategic investor, Swedish Skandinaviska Enskilda Banken (SEB) acquired a large stake in Vilniaus Bank in 1998 and is likely to acquire a majority in the near future. In 1998 Vilniaus Bank applied to BOLIT to acquire a large stake in Hermis Bank. BOLIT for various reasons withheld approval of the application. The application was later withdrawn, but with the arrival of SEB, the idea of merging the two banks was revived, and in September 1999 BOLIT approved the merger.

The state-controlled banks have continued to struggle. These banks are characterized by heavy asset concentration of government securities, restructuring bonds and residual loans from government-directed lending. Funding has been predominantly domestically sourced, with large government-related deposits and private individual deposits. Profitability has been low due to large amounts of low-yielding government assets, large branch networks and staff, and the cost of implementing government programmes. Both banks are due to be privatized. One attempt to privatize Agricultural Bank in 1998 failed due to lack of interest. EBRD is likely to become a large shareholder in Agricultural Bank through a conversion of a convertible loan and a share swap with the government.

Conclusion: causes and implications

Banking crises can have a profound effect on the longer-term evolution of banking systems, through changing the behaviour of banks and strengthening the resolve of the supervision authorities. As a result of the crises in the three Baltic republics, there has been a major change in the structure of the banking sector, supervision and regulation have been tightened, and a more robust banking system is emerging. By way of conclusion, it is worth considering some of the common factors behind the crises and examining whether they point to any general policy recommendations for countries in transition.

The causal factors can be be divided into *systemic* and *bank-specific*. This section will give prominence to the systemic factors, since those relating to specific banks have already been discussed earlier in the chapter. Systemic factors can be categorized under five headings: poor regulation and supervision; poor accounting and excessive taxation; an inadequate legal infrastructure for bank lending; pervasive corrupt practices coupled with weak banking skills and mismanagement on a significant scale; and, finally, the stresses and strains initiated by the combination of transition and stabilization. To some extent the factors are interrelated. For instance, the transition environment has unleashed significant profit-maximizing behaviour in many segments of society, including in the banking industry. While much of it reflects entrepreneurial zest, some of it spills over into illegal and unscrupulous activities. In some instances it has been weaknesses in bank regulation and supervision that have created incentives towards corrupt practices.

Banking regulation and supervision

Failures of banking regulation and supervision contributed to all three crises. Although efforts had been made in all three Baltic republics to strengthen the legal, regulatory and supervisory frameworks of banking, weaknesses in this area contributed to both the Latvian and Lithuanian crises. In the former case it was deficiencies in the framework itself at the time of the crisis that was a contributory factor, although there were some weaknesses in implementation. In Lithuanian it was primarily deficiencies in the implementation of regulation – even when the supervisory function had identified problems they were not acted upon. In Estonia the legal, regulatory and supervisory framework was very underdeveloped at the time of the crisis but it was less significant as a cause than in the other two countries. What may be of particular importance is the signalling effect that strong supervisory implementation can have for the banking sector in an environment where non-adherence to rules and regulations is widespread.

Accounting and taxation

In all three countries, banks initially continued to use the old Gosbank chart of accounts. In Estonia, banks were required to use IAS for the first time in 1995 although the better banks began using IAS in 1993. In Latvia, the introduction of IAS accounting and reporting requirements began in 1994. As noted above, the requirement that banks present their 1994 IAS accounts to BOLAT in fact precipitated the crisis. In Lithuania, a number of changes in bank accounting rules were introduced gradually over the last three years, but the bank accounting rules still deviate from IAS in a number of important respects.

The absence of and unfamiliarity with IAS-based accounting systems and rules has made it more difficult for bank managers, shareholders and supervisors alike accurately to gauge the solvency and liquidity problems building up in individual banks. Even though most of the Baltic banks were quick to have international auditors undertake IAS audits, these audits have not served as early warning signals, and often were ignored altogether by the supervisors.

Perhaps more importantly, while all three countries moved early on to introduce loan-loss classification and provisioning rules, in practice these rules were often not really applied (that is, loan-loss provisions were not actually booked). The most important factor was the fact that the tax rules did not allow any deduction for loan-loss provision expenses. While the better banks nevertheless used profit and loss data after hypothetical provisioning to determine dividend payouts, all banks – prudent and imprudent alike – were, as a result of this deficiency in the tax regime, taxed on the basis of fictitious profits. The problem was only rectified relatively late in the transition in Estonia and in Latvia. Lithuania introduced a scheme at the end of 1994 for the phasing in of tax deductibility of loan-loss provision over a three-year period.

Legal infrastructure for bank lending

The existence of a legal framework that supported bank lending in general was largely absent from the Baltic states in the early post-transition period. Important deficiencies related to the lack of legislation on bankruptcy and collateral, and the absence of well-functioning property titles, mortgage and pledge registers.

Another important omission in the legal framework was the absence of appropriate corporate governance and accountability provisions for banks, specifying the duties and responsibilities of bank shareholders, supervising board members and managers. Rather than the supervisory board members exercising good corporate governance based on the long-term interests of shareholders and depositors alike, they were often manipulated by shareholders exclusively to serve the latter's own short-term interests.

Corrupt practices and weak management

In all three of the Baltic economies some banks were created as captive funding mechanisms by groups of enterprises and individuals. Underlying this type of activity was the fact that raising funds directly from the public was cheaper than borrowing from banks. Owners and managers recognized that significant weakness in the banking laws pertaining to insider transactions allowed them to tap a bank's resources. In other cases, owners and managers tried to achieve their short-run profit goals by taking excessive risks within the bank, often in the form of high-risk lending, or by assuming large open foreign exchange positions. In these instances, the owners and managers were undoubtedly encouraged by the knowledge that the supervisory authority was inexperienced, understaffed and lacked effective enforcement powers.[18] The lack of bank management skills, coupled with generally weak banking skills among staff, led to poor decision-making in banks.

Transition and stabilization

Transition creates a very risky environment for banks to operate in. As well as the absence of the legal infrastructure that usually safeguards bank operations (for example, property rights and collateral legislation) they must also cope with an envirnoment in which entrepreneurs, who, not used to functioning in a market context, make mistakes in the choice of projects. Both the real and banking sectors undergo rapid structural change with the result that the nature of competition is not easy to predict. Rapid structural change is not the most propitious background against which to embed sound techniques of banking. Invariably mistakes will be made by inexperienced bankers.

A further risk for banks in transition is due to the macroeconomic policy framework. In all three Baltic republics the stabilization policies pursued as part of the transition also placed pressure on the emerging banking systems. The banks and their supervisors were unable to monitor and control the risks inherent in a policy environment where a strong stabilization had been initiated. These were the inevitable costs of a necessary economic policy.

Given all these factors, it needs to be accepted that some banking distress was inevitable in the transition economies, due to the fact that the countries of the FSU had had no experience of market-based banking in the recent past. The risks associated with lending in transitional economies combine to overwhelm many banks. While to some extent banking sector fragility is due to factors which may be beyond the authorities' ability to influence, it also emanates from some of the structural features of the emerging banking systems, particularly the existence of a plethora of small, poorly capitalized banks that are vulnerable because their capital is small and they have not, because of their size, reaped the benefit of portfolio diversification. Similarly, the state-owned banks are invariably overstaffed, driving up their operating costs when banking salary levels adjust to the higher levels in the private banking segment. This has been an additional factor in driving banks to keep intermediation margins high (the high-risk nature of bank lending being another major factor). In turn, the resulting high lending rates have further added to borrowers' debt service difficulties.

Such difficulties are a common feature of the structural transition of the banking system. On the other hand, it should also be noted that banking distress has some positive features even though in specific cases it can create hardship for certain depositors. In particular, it can lead to a much-needed consolidation of frequently overly fragmented banking systems. Indeed, in the Baltic countries the banking crises have been the catalyst for much-needed consolidation. Moreover, the beneficial effects of their crises have been more apparent because although they were quick to erupt, they were equally quick to subside. This partly reflects the growing sophistication of depositors in the Baltics who have come to expect some banking distress to take place, and have accordingly spread their deposits across many banks to diversify their risk. It also reflects the underlying resilience of the banking sector, especially that each republic had a core of solvent banks that anchored the system. This resilience militates in favour of banking authorities taking a tough stance in relation to problem banks.

Banking distress is likely to be a feature of transition in the FSU for several years to come. The authorities in these countries therefore need to prepare themselves by strengthening their supervisory capacity and readying themselves for tough implementation decisions. Even if the banking crises materialize, they are unlikely to have such severe effects on the economy as a crisis of similar proportions in a Western economy might have. The banking and enterprise sectors in the FSU are not so intimately connected as they are in the West. Such crises might in any case be viewed as part of the learning component of transition. If the lessons are properly internalized by enterprises, banks and supervisors, the long-term impact of banking crises can be positive.

Notes

1   This chapter is based upon an earlier publication: Fleming, Chu and Bakker, 'The Baltics – Banking Crises Observed', *Policy Working Paper No. 1647*, World Bank, September 1996. That publication has been updated with the help of staff from the Bank Group's Regional Baltic offices: Kristjan Kitvel (Estonia), Ilze Berzina (Latvia) and Peter Modeen (Lithuania).

2   The restructuring only addressed the claim of the bank on the former all-USSR Savings Bank head office in Moscow but not the rapidly growing portfolio of new bad loans. Artificial limits on its lending to private enterprises encouraged the bank to move more aggressively into interbank lending and lending to state enterprises of equally doubtful quality.

3   For example, while BOLIT undertook on-site examinations in nearly all private banks during the last two years, it refused, until very recently, to undertake such examinations in any of the state-owned banks, claiming that the problems of these banks were the government's responsibility, and not those of the regulator.

4   Although seven smaller banks had been declared insolvent in 1994: Lotta, Latvian Bank for Reconstruction and Development, Baltic Bank for Reconstruction and Development, Kurzeme, Sigulda, Tautas and Top-banka.

5   Other banks declared insolvent in 1995 were Latintrade, Latgale Commercial Bank, Liepajas Commercial Bank, Polarzviagzne Bank and Alejas Commercial Bank, Kredo Bank, Olti-Bank and Bauskas Bank.

6   This explanation for Bank Baltija's demise is contained in a paper by Hallagan, 'Big Bang Banking Reform: the Latvian experience', July 1995.

7   The bankruptcy of Bank Baltija was first petitioned at the end of 1995 by the Bank of Latvia but the owners successfully appealed against this order of the economic court. The bank was again declared bankrupt on 3 April 1996 by Riga District Court on the grounds that no feasible plan for rehabilitating and recapitalizing the bank had been presented. The legal battles surrounding the bank continued into 1999.

8   This funding was intended originally for balance of payments financing.

9   All references to the ranking of Lithuanian banks are based on end-June 1995 data.

10   Among these banks was Aura Bank (with total assets of US$37 million), which experienced serious liquidity problems during May 1995.

11   But already in August 1995, after the discovery during the first on-site examination of deposit-taking in foreign currency from shareholders at above-market interest rates and on-lending at below-market rates, BOLIT suspended the right of Vakaru Bank to make loans and issue guarantees (but not the right to take deposits) indefinitely.

12   The initial recapitalization proved to be inadequate, as many of the loans inherited by the new bank turned out to be uncollectible. The NEB was weakened by mismanagement in both credit and treasury operations, especially by continuing to provide interbank loans to the Social Bank, when all the other banks had ceased to provide such support. The transfer of Social Bank assets and liabilities to the NEB has also proved to be only a transfer of

    problems from one weak bank to another. The accumulated bad loans from the NEB and Social Bank operations were considerable.

13   The Latvian Shipping Company and connected companies abroad have lent funds to Bank Baltija in an amount of 23 million lats (US$46 million). These loans were secured by a mortgage on Baltija's loan portfolio, real estate and vehicles.

14   Subsequently, the government did in fact negotiate a takeover of all of the bank's outstanding shares with the shareholders for a token amount, *de facto* wiping out their ownership rights.

15   This law envisages the creation of a deposit insurance fund initially capitalized by the government and subsequently to be financed by bank premia, covering individual litai deposits in qualified banks (meeting BOLIT prudential requirements) up to 5000 litai with a 20 per cent co-insurance provision. In February 1996, the law was amended to extend cover to individuals' foreign currency deposits.

16   None the less the Bank of Estonia still owns 58 per cent of the Optiva Bank, which it plans to sell to a foreign investor.

17   An SEB capital injection into Unibank played a significant role in stabilizing the situation of the bank in the wake of the Russian crisis.

18   At a deeper level there was a belief among some bankers – a result of the liberation from the era of state control – that the state had no appropriate role in banking supervision and regulation.

References

Bulletins and *Annual Reports* (Bank of Estonia/Bank of Lithuania).

S. Bereza, *Big Bang Banking Reform: The Latvian Experience* (Washington State University, July 1995).

M. Bourke, 'The Banking Crisis in Latvia and Lithuania: The Real Lessons', *The Baltic Observer*, 31 June 1996.

G. Buyske, *Estonia's Emerging Financial System: Progress and Prospects*, (Development Alternatives, Inc., 1993).

G. Caprio and D. Klingebid, *Dealing with Bank Insolvencies: Cross Country Experience* (World Bank, forthcoming).

S. Claessens, *Banking Reform in Transition Countries* (World Bank, forthcoming).

A. Fleming and S. Talley, 'The Latvian Banking Crisis: Lessons Learned', *World Bank Policy Research Paper*, March 1996.

A. Fleming, L. Chu, and M.-R. Bakker, 'The Baltics – Banking Crises Observed', *Working Paper Series*, No. 1647 (The World Bank, September 1996).

W. Hallagan, 'Big Bang Banking Reform: The Latvian Experience' (Washington State University, July 1995).

A. Hansson, *Reforming the Banking System in Estonia* (World Bank, 1995).

A. Hansson, *Banking Crises in the Baltic States: Causes, Solutions and Lessons* (Stockholm School of Economics, May 1996).

IMF, *Latvia, Economic Review* (IMF, 1994).

C. Jones, 'Message Understood', *The Banker*, December 1995.

Ministry of Finance of the Republic of Latvia. *Bulletin. Appraisals of Latvian Finances* No. 2 (1995).

E. Repse, *The Banking Crisis in Latvia: Causes and Lessons* (Bank of Latvia, 1995).

A. Sheng, *Bank Restructuring: Lessons from the 1980's* (World Bank, 1996).

The Economist Intelligence Unit, *Baltic Republics: Estonia, Latvia and Lithuania, Country Report, Third and fourth quarters* (EIU, 1995).

World Bank, *Latvia: transition to a market economy* (World Bank, March 1993), ch. 3.

Part II

Non-Bank Reforms and Development of the Financial Sector

4
Development of Capital Markets, Stock Exchanges and Securities Regulation in Transition Economies

Joseph J. Norton and Douglas W. Arner

Introduction

Since 1989, the formerly centrally planned economies of Central and Eastern Europe and the CIS ('transition economies') have made substantial progress in the process of transition from centrally planned economies to market economies. This transformation, however, has progressed at different rates and along different paths across the region. Most importantly, while the results have been impressive so far, much remains to be done before these countries are fully integrated into the international financial system.[1]

As part of the transition process, most transition economies have established, or are in the process of establishing, a basic legal framework for the operation of securities markets and stock exchanges in the context of creating functioning capital markets. Across the region, however, the financial sector remains fragile, and securities markets continue to be thin and volatile. Moreover, problems of insider dominance of companies with traded stock, corruption and even fraud, which in the mature Western economies have been largely contained, are widespread. Insider dealing, lack of transparency in shareholdings and trades, concentrated ownership, often in the hands of banks and corporate insiders, with only a small proportion of the stock actually traded, price manipulation, problems in corporate governance and ownership structures, and lack of any active market for corporate control are all endemic. Although historically many of these problems have also been prevalent in Western European equity markets, there the strength of insider lenders, that is, banks sitting on the board of enterprises, has compensated for the limited role of equity market forces. To instill the requisite confidence upon which the growth and continuing success of securities markets, and in turn capital markets, fundamentally depends, transition economies will need to address the threats of manipulation, insider dominance and securities fraud which commonly plague emerging securities markets.

Given the unique problems of transition from state-planned to market systems, the early development of functional securities markets can play a major role in the formation of efficient business structures and capital markets in the transition economies. As there is no universally accepted model for securities regulation, but rather regulatory systems tend to vary from jurisdiction to jurisdiction, each country is free to choose from a broad spectrum of policy solutions. In this context, however, the experience of the leading Western economies can provide invaluable insights into the implications of different regulatory options and suggest practical ways of dealing with specific problems, especially securities fraud and insider dominance.

Thus transition economies might choose to rely more on 'self-regulation' (following the tradition, for example, of the United Kingdom) or to adopt formal layers of statutory and administrative regulation (in the mould, for example, of the United States). In practice, however, most transition economies may be expected to follow the example of other continental countries by placing particular emphasis on the role of the stock exchange and its internal 'rulemaking'.

Further, as most of the transition economies desire to join, or otherwise to become economically associated with, the EU, EC law, to the extent that it regulates financial-service-related matters, unavoidably presents the transition economies with a framework of minimum standards for securities regulation and the establishment of stock exchanges. In addition, the International Organization of Securities Commissions (IOSCO) has developed *Objectives and Principles of Securities Regulation*,[2] which provide significant guidance to any country seeking to establish an effective system of capital market, stock exchange and securities regulation.

None the less, the mere adoption of IOSCO or EC-inspired legal rules will not of itself be sufficient, since the transition economies are still in many cases experiencing difficulties with the practical operation of a market economy. This means that the formidable difficulties that are bound to be faced in the attempt to increase market width and depth and to introduce effective administrative and enforcement processes must also be taken into account.

Overall, the development of securities markets in the transition economies should respond to three overriding requirements: (i) the need to expand the size and increase the depth and liquidity of securities markets; (ii) the desire of many of these countries to join or be associated with the EU and the necessity of revising domestic financial legislation as a means of achieving consistency with EC standards; and (iii) the aspiration of these countries to become more integrated into the international financial system. More fundamentally, legislation and implementation must ensure stability and confidence, since these are the primary factors upon which the success of every financial system depends.

After offering a brief overview of the current position regarding the attempts of the transition economies to develop functioning securities markets and of the importance of the role of developed capital markets for their future economic development, this chapter suggests that, in view of the economic and political situation of these countries and their regional context, the EC corpus of securities and stock exchange regulation provides a suitable, but incomplete, framework that could be utilized in the creation of viable domestic securities market systems compatible with international practices and expectations (although, as to certain aspects of this developmental process the US model, especially in the areas of remedies and self-enforcing mechanisms, might be preferable as a point of reference[3]). In pursuing this thesis, the substantive content of the EC model, as well as potential policy dilemmas and perceived difficulties that may face the transition economies in their attempt to implement this model in stages, in accordance with the suggestions of the European Commission, will be discussed.

As a heuristic analytical device, the transition economies can loosely be categorized into three 'tiers' of financial system development, with Russia in a fourth category by itself.[4] Under this analysis, a 'first tier' would comprise those states that have progressed furthest in all aspects of the transition to a market economy, including the establishment of functioning securities markets, namely, the Czech Republic, Poland and Hungary. Significantly, each of these countries has signed detailed agreements of association with the EU (Europe Agreements) (EAs) as a first step towards possible accession in the future.[5] A 'second tier' would comprise the remaining transition economies which have signed EAs with the EU and are candidates for eventual accession,[6] have made considerable progress in the transition from a state-owned, centralized economy towards a functioning market economy, and have initiated the development of securities markets and/or stock exchanges. On the basis of these general criteria, the Second Tier would include: Bulgaria, the three Baltic republics (Estonia, Latvia and Lithuania), Romania, the Slovak Republic and Slovenia. A 'Third Tier' would comprise states which are not presently candidates for EU membership, suffer from chronic political instability, face particularly severe adjustment problems, and/or either experience serious dysfunction in their capital markets or are lacking operational capital markets, namely: Albania, Belarus, Bosnia–Herzegovina, Croatia, the Former Yugoslavian Republic (FYR) of Macedonia, Moldova, Serbia and Ukraine.

While in terms of its economic development Russia might properly be categorized somewhere in the second tier, it is singled out due to the immense amount of financial activity taking place in the country, the idiosyncratic nature of its transition and the unique 'systemic-type' problems which plague it (as demonstrated by its near financial collapse in 1998), and also to the fact that it has neither entered into any agreement directed towards accession to the EU, nor is it expected to do so in the foreseeable future.[7] In particular, inherent problems with corruption and crime and the extensive inefficiencies of its legal and financial infrastructure militate against including Russia within one of the three general categories of transitional development.

Within this analytical framework, some of the significant systemic problems facing individual transition economies include: securities fraud and corruption; the banking system generally; problems with investment funds; and bureaucratic/insider dominance.

Russia, Belarus and Ukraine suffer from severe political instability, accompanied by what appears to be deeply embedded corruption and criminality. Beyond posing a direct threat to the economies and societies of these nations, this situation raises transnational questions, since it is feared that the problems may be exported to other transition economies, and perhaps to Western Europe as well, as the domestically grown criminal syndicates become more sophisticated and expand their predations into other potentially vulnerable financial systems.

Russia, the Czech Republic, Estonia, Latvia and Lithuania have all suffered serious bank collapses, due not only to the 'bad loan' problems resulting from the traditional 'monobank' practices (in particular, the funding of state enterprises' current expenditure and losses in the form of bank 'loans', which, although carried on the books, were extremely unlikely ever to be repaid), but also to the rapid creation of new banks, followed by subsequent restructuring.[8] Several other transition economies, especially those of the second and third tiers, could face similar banking disturbances in the near future, and even fully fledged banking crises, such as that experienced by Russia in 1998.

The capital markets in the Czech Republic are dominated by a few large mutual funds created as part of the privatization process. These funds are, in turn, dominated by a few large banks. The same banks are the principal creditors of the underlying enterprises. This has posed a corporate governance problem.[9] In addition, the situation has raised questions of confidence in the capital market system as it presently operates in the Czech Republic.

Throughout the transition economies, the old power structures set in place under the previous regime of central planning and Communist Party dominance have often remained in place, albeit under slightly different guises. For example, businesses have often been acquired by former state enterprise managers or former or present bureaucrats, in many cases at prices which do not reflect their true value. This situation undermines confidence (both domestic and international) in the entire process of transition, but most especially in the legitimacy of the privatization process.

Role of the financial system and capital markets in transition economies

Capital markets are one of the most significant sources of long-term funding for enterprises and government within any capitalist system. Capital markets (that is, markets for longer maturity financial assets, including equity and debt) can be subdivided on the basis of the different legal relationships and forms of legal claims represented by the traded securities. At the most basic level, one could distinguish between equity markets, which focus on the issuance of, and trading in, instruments representing ownership participations in business enterprises and creating residual claims on their assets, and long-term debt markets, which deal in instruments documenting fixed nominal-value, interest-bearing claims on such enterprises.

In general terms, a capital market is composed of the interactions of two elements: the supply of capital and the demand for capital.[10] As a subset of capital markets, then, equity markets are composed of the supply of equities and demand for equity ownership. The supply of equity can be viewed as a portion of the demand for capital, while the demand for equity can be viewed as related to the supply of capital. In the context of the transition economies, a strong demand for capital, and thus a large untapped supply of securities, is guaranteed by the financing needs of commercial enterprises and the privatization efforts of governments. Supply of capital can be seen as potentially coming from two sources: domestic and foreign. Domestic capital formation is a function of domestic savings, whether privately motivated or government mandated (that is, through mandatory pension schemes). Foreign capital comes from a number of potential sources, including institutional and private investment, whether for portfolio or speculative purposes, direct financing by international financial institutions or by venture capitalists and strategic investors, and (potentially quite important in some cases) repatriation of flight capital. Developing market capitalization requires an expansion of both the supply of and the demand for securities. In the transition economies, the availability of funds for long-term investment in the region is very limited and their allocation not always efficient. Accordingly, the primary policy concern is the rationalization of securities markets with a view to encouraging participation by foreign and domestic investors and increasing the overall demand for securities, and in particular equity instruments.

The promotion of liquidity and more effective corporate governance should guide policy choices relating to the development of the financial systems in the various transition economies. As factors determining policy, liquidity and corporate governance, while both valuable for different reasons, may point to divergent solutions:[11] in highly liquid markets, control tends to be dispersed, thus reducing the governance functions of the equity market.[12] On the other hand, when control is concentrated, thus facilitating corporate governance by larger stockholders, conflicts of interest between different types of shareholders may arise and liquidity tends to be lacking.[13] To some extent, however, with the globally growing significance of institutional investors, such as pension and mutual funds, as major shareholders of corporations and users of the equity markets, this traditional dichotomy of market forms may be gradually losing some of its importance, to the extent that these institutional investors desire not only liquidity, but also some measure of control over management and some impact on enterprise decisions.[14] None the less, the choice of a model of corporate governance and its relationship to corporate finance in a given country is very important from the standpoint of policy-makers.

While specific market and corporate governance structures have become entrenched in each developed Western economy as a result of its particular historical experience, the transition economies were (and in some cases remain) in a position to select their developmental path relatively unconcerned about established structures and to learn from the experiences and mistakes of both developed and developing economies.

It is worth noting in this context that during almost two decades of rapid growth and modernization after the Second World War, two successful capitalist nations, France and Japan, relied on financial systems that did not allocate capital in an open market simply or even essentially by price.[15] This may indicate that a system based on valuation and resource allocation through open capital markets is possibly not a *conditio sine qua non* of development. On the other hand, the role of capital and securities markets in the developmental process, while traditionally ignored, has recently become the focus of attention of governments and intergovernmental organizations, and is now thought to be of considerable importance as an instrument of development.[16] Moreover, for the transitional economies the creation of a formal capital market system, including equity markets and stock exchanges, can serve several important economic roles in addition to the basic functions already described.

In particular, the creation of capital markets, especially in the form of equity markets, in these countries has served and can continue to serve as a facilitation device for privatization, as a vehicle for foreign investment, and as a possible method of 'outflanking' inherited problems in the banking system (as discussed elsewhere in this volume).

The privatization of state-owned enterprises is intimately linked to the development of supportive regulatory-based infrastructures, such as stock markets.[17] According to at least one commentator, the governments of the formerly centrally planned economies have been dependent on their respective 'voucher' and mass privatization programmes for the creation of capital markets.[18] While this is perhaps an overstatement, privatization was certainly the central force underlying the development of equity markets in Central and Eastern Europe in the 1990s. A key element in the economic success of these privatization programmes and in the growth of market-oriented economies in these countries is the involvement of the domestic population as the primary investors in privatized enterprises.[19] In this context, it is evident that an equity market, probably centred on a formal stock exchange, facilitates this process by providing citizens with a forum in which to buy and sell the portions of the accumulated state wealth transferred to them, either directly or for cash, as part of the privatization process. Overall, without the establishment of sound securities markets, privatization efforts have been significantly retarded.[20]

Several problems, however, have arisen in connection with the privatization programmes and the related attempts to increase domestic investor participation. In particular, reliable material information about privatized enterprises even today is often not available to potential investors, even though the latter need such information as a basis for their investment decisions.[21] Financial data concerning the profits, losses and outstanding indebtedness of enterprises were simply unavailable in the days of central planning, and the existing data continue in many cases to be unreliable.[22] In addition, under central planning, enterprises did not face hard budget constraints but were allowed to continue in existence even if they were accumulating losses. As a result, they were neither efficient nor profitable in any normal economic sense. Most of these firms, whether state-owned or privatized, still remain unprofitable, especially in Russia: this makes generating investor interest and confidence much more difficult. Moreover, the lack of liquidity that characterizes the stock of privatized enterprises discourages those investors, such as venture capital providers and portfolio-type investors, whether domestic or foreign, who place a premium on the existence of an economic escape route such as an organized and liquid market, which makes exit from the market feasible.[23]

While there is no question that capital is essential for the economic development of the transition economies, the volume of capital required for this purpose vastly exceeds the supply of domestic savings and retained profits available in their economies.[24] In this context, domestic equity markets are thought to provide an alternative point of entry for foreign capital into the transitional economies, and in this capacity perform a function of growing significance, as external commercial lending to these economies becomes more limited. While generally commercial lending has declined in importance as a source of capital for emerging economies, equity investment from foreign investors, whether in the form of foreign direct investment (FDI) or of portfolio investment, continues to increase, even despite the string of financial crises around the world of the past several years. While an analysis of FDI in the transition economies would be beyond the scope of this chapter, it should be emphasized that the existence of functioning domestic equity markets can encourage foreign investment in a number of ways. Such markets provide a channel for external portfolio investment. Foreign investors, especially institutional investors,[25] are much more likely to invest in countries where effective securities laws and well-disciplined stock exchanges provide them with the infrastructure and the information necessary to analyse and implement prospective investments. Evidently, this ensures additional capital for domestic enterprises. Given the volatility of portfolio-type investment, however, this may not be so important a benefit as once thought.[26] In addition, securities markets permit the eventual 'exit' of foreign venture capital, since venture capital providers typically do not wish to stay involved with an enterprise for the long term, but prefer to exit and take their profits. Even in the case of 'strategic investors', who are brought in for the purpose of exercising permanent, or at least longer-term, control of an enterprise, the possibility of potential disengagement can make involvement more attractive. Accordingly, such investors require a mechanism which makes possible the eventual liquidation of their holdings. This mechanism can be provided through the creation of functioning equity markets and stock exchanges, which for this reason encourage primary capital investment by private investors, and possibly even by international financial institutions (IFIs, such as the IFC and the EBRD).

In order to appreciate the decisions made about the regulation of stock exchanges in the transition economies, one must first have an understanding of the role of the stock exchange in a market economy.[27] A 'stock exchange' may be defined as 'a body that provides a centralised forum in which stock trades are undertaken'.[28] As such, a stock exchange provides the means by which the market prices of stocks can be openly established and through which price information can be produced and disseminated to users of the market.[29] Over-the-counter (OTC) markets are traditionally distinguished from organized stock exchanges. An OTC market traditionally refers to trading done off the floor of an organized stock exchange; however, as technology has developed, the distinction between stock exchanges and OTC securities markets has become blurred.[30] While historically observers have often viewed stock exchanges as philanthropic institutions organized to act in the public interest, this is not in fact the case.[31] Instead, stock exchanges are self-interested economic organizations which supply services to companies listing their securities in exchange for fees, which typically come in the form of an initial listing fee and an annual fee.[32] Firms are not required to have their shares listed on an exchange, but those with publicly traded stock have shown a strong interest in having their shares traded on an exchange, thus indicating that exchanges offer something of value to listing firms in exchange for the fees charged.[33]

As a concept, 'listing' may be 'unbundled' into four component services that organized exchanges provide: liquidity; monitoring of exchange trading; standard form, off-the-rack rules to reduce transactions costs; and a signalling function that serves to inform investors that the issuing companies' stock is of high quality.[34]

Liquidity is a market characteristic that assures investors that they can promptly purchase or dispose of stock at a price closely related to the market best estimate of the present value of the future income stream that the stock will generate for investors.[35] Discussions of liquidity are often based on the efficient capital markets hypothesis (ECMH). Under the ECMH, current price movements are said to reflect fully all publicly available information about the underlying companies.[36] Investors value liquidity for two reasons. First, market liquidity implies that investors can dispose of shares quickly. This also implies that the transactions costs related to holding such shares are low, thereby increasing the value of liquid assets to investors. Second, liquidity reduces information costs for market participants because competition among market professionals under the ECMH assures investors that prices reflect all the publicly available information about a given security.[37]

For these reasons, investors will generally select the secondary trading market that is most likely to provide liquidity for their shares. The actual liquidity of a given security, however, is determined by exogenous factors such as information available, number of shares outstanding, and investor preferences in a number of different areas.[38] Overall, the result is that 'undeveloped, illiquid, thinly traded securities markets tend to be inefficient, while highly developed, liquid, thickly traded markets tend to be efficient'.[39] Two by-products result from the continuous competition among market professionals for information: such activities under the ECMH tend to drive share prices to their efficient levels, and these activities provide liquidity by providing a continuous stream of purchasers and sellers for a firm's stock.[40] Besides the activities of market professionals, certain investment firms provide liquidity for many firms, especially when there is little volume or interest or, on the other hand, in the case of extremely large orders. In both cases, issuers and investors are willing to pay for the liquidity services provided by the investment firm.

Interestingly, an organized stock exchange is not necessary for the provision of liquidity, but rather depends for its existence on the benefits to the investment firms involved in the organized exchange. As such, exchanges provide a central forum for the production and distribution of information, especially in listed securities, because they generally prohibit trading in exchange-listed securities outside of the exchange.[41] As providers of a centralized location for secondary market trading, organized exchanges are well suited to provide information about recent trades, and this provision of accurate, up-to-date information about trading activity may be the single most important function of an exchange.[42] The result of the existence of a single centralized forum for trading is then both a reduction in information search costs and an increase in liquidity. Overall, the important realization is that the liquidity benefits of stock exchanges result solely from their provision of a centralized trading location – historically a necessary reality. With the rapid advance in computer and telecommunications technology, these benefits are increasingly declining.[43]

Stock exchanges also traditionally provide a monitoring function for investors through the various rules and regulations imposed and enforced by the exchanges themselves,[44] as well as reducing the agency costs associated with the separation of ownership and control within large, publicly held firms by lowering the costs of monitoring certain breaches of fiduciary duty by corporate insiders.[45] This monitoring function is especially important in the context of providing an effective forum for the monitoring of insider trading and price manipulation by market professionals.[46] Beyond increasing investor confidence and company share prices through the monitoring function, there are also significant economies of scale associated with centralized monitoring of stock trading through specialized stock-watch programmes, rather than having individual firms acquire the technology and the expertise necessary to monitor stock trading.[47]

Further, stock exchanges provide off-the-rack rules for contracting, including matters seemingly unrelated to secondary market trading, such as requirements concerning auditing and composition of directors. These requirements both reduce search costs for investors and serve to increase confidence in the value of the listing itself, and hence increase listing company share prices.

Finally, stock exchanges provide a source of reputational capital to listing firms, informing investors that listed securities are of a certain quality.[48] Beyond purely reputational implications, stock exchanges also require that listed firms meet both initial and ongoing listing requirements, including a minimum aggregate net market value and minimum numbers of shareholders, which provide investors with certain minimum levels of information regarding listed firms.[49]

In the overall process of capital market development, the establishment of the basic legal and financial infrastructure necessary for the functioning of a market economy should precede attempts to create capital and equities markets. As one commentator has observed:[50]

[C]apital markets are sophisticated institutions, sometimes fragile and always crucially dependent upon the general economic and political climate. The transition countries rightly want to set up these institutions as quickly as possible. However, it is essential first to create all the institutional conditions necessary for them to operate efficiently and transparently and to put in place the macroeconomic framework without which they cannot thrive.

The basic institutional and technical conditions necessary for the development of capital markets should respond to three requirements. First, as a fundamental and evident precondition, the basic development of capital markets in the transition economies requires a macroeconomic framework that promotes fiscal and monetary stability.[51] Second, a legal and institutional framework that promotes permanence, transparency, simplicity, ease of enforcement and respect for the 'rule of law' is essential.[52] Third, this legal and institutional framework must be generally understood and effectively enforced; without enforcement, even the best legal infrastructure is non-credible and practically useless.[53]

As part of the second requirement, the development of capital markets depends on the existence of a body of effective company law covering, at the very least, the regulation of corporate structures, protection of minority shareholders, and sound policies of corporate governance. At a more detailed level, the creation of stock markets necessarily requires limited liability of shareholders, free transferability of shares and accountable structures of corporate governance.[54] Beyond formal rules of company law, some form of functioning, reliable and transparent accounting system is critical, not only for the operation of capital markets, but also as a fundamental aspect of any meaningful corporate business structure. Moreover, well-trained management capable of adequately understanding and fulfilling its responsibilities is essential.

Beyond the mere legal infrastructure, the creation of a viable, if not fully efficient, banking system could greatly facilitate attempts to create securities markets. Capital markets require a functional banking system to provide basic payment and settlement services and financial intermediation.[55]

In order to foster properly functioning financial intermediaries, regulation and 'codes of conduct' will be needed, whether they are effected through self-regulation or through state mechanisms. This is one area where EC financial services-related legislation can be especially helpful for developing a comprehensive and coherent framework.

In view of these necessary preconditions for the development of functioning capital markets, the policy discussion should focus on the determination of the most appropriate path for their achievement.

The search for international standards: the EC System of Securities Regulation as an appropriate model

The developmental status of financial markets in the transition econom-ies as a whole is viewed favourably by some analysts.[56] The markets in at least some states have the basic legal and organizational structure necessary for the creation of viable securities markets, and most markets certainly have the potential to expand their activities.[57] Even with basic macroeconomic and legal infrastructure in place, securities market development will need to focus on two overall goals: first, maintaining and increasing confidence in the capital markets and the financial system as a whole; and second, on increasing market capitalization and participation through expanding the savings base and broadening and deepening the investment opportunities available. Further, given the aspirations of many transition economies to become Member States of the EU, these goals are also interrelated aspects in the process of bringing the capital markets of the transition economies into the Euro-pean and international financial systems. As part of this overall conver-gence process, a critical understanding of and receptivity to the minimum framework for the international market in investment ser-vices provided by the EU (to which many of the transition economies have already contracted to become aligned) and to broader interna-tional standards being promoted through the International Organiza-tion of Securities Commissions (IOSCO) and the relevant international accounting bodies (for example the IASC [International Accounting Standards Committee]).

This understanding and receptivity will need to focus on the follow-ing dimensions: (i) expansion of investment opportunities through development of the legal and financial infrastructure necessary to sup-port businesses and new investment vehicles; (ii) increasing the quality and availability of information ('transparency'); (iii) minimization of conflicts of interest in and insider dominance of securities and corporate governance markets; (iv) regulation of institutional investors, most especially the privatization funds and investment funds now existing in many transition economies; and (iv) prevention and punishment of economic fraud and corruption.

The EU framework for investment services provides minimum stand-ards for securities regulation, stock exchange regulation, company law and regulation of institutional investors. It should be borne in mind, however, that this framework is not complete: since its purpose is to ensure the harmonization of the laws of the Member States in so far as this is necessary for the achievement of a single market and to fill gaps relating to cross-border activities, it builds on the existing national systems of company and securities laws rather than trying to replace them by a complete new system. The purpose of this chapter is not to evaluate the specific provisions of the laws of individual transition economies against the EU framework; however, a general appreciation of the key elements of that framework may be most important for the transition economies to make their own initial and subsequent evaluations respecting an eventual alignment with it.

The transition economies as signatories of the various Europe Agreements desire to become full Member States of the EU. In the context of the various Europe Agreements the ultimate objective for the transition economies is eventually to obtain full EU membership, and attainment of this goal imposes various obligations on the aspiring states.[58] Under the existing Europe Agreements aimed towards eventual accession a primary obligation of the aspiring state is the approximation of existing and future state legislation in the financial services sector to that of the EU. Moreover, under the existing Europe Agreements with the various transition economies, it is agreed that EU financial companies shall have the right to set up operations in the territory of the respective Central and East European Countries (CEEC) by the end of the transition period at the latest.[59] Such a situation implies that by the end of the relevant transition period, the aspiring transition economies will need to have in place a fully EU-compatible system of banking and financial services regulation.

As an aid to this process of approximation and alignment, in April 1995 the European Commission issued a White Paper addressing the key measures in each sector of the internal market. This 1995 White Paper suggested a sequence under which the transition economies should seek to approximate their domestic legislation to that of the EU.[60] The Paper proposes that the Community legislation in, *inter alia*, the financial services area should be adopted in two stages: the first involves the introduction of the basic principles for the establishment of financial institutions, and the second (although some elements are important for the first stage) aims to strengthen prudential supervision of investment firms in order to bring them up to international standards.[61] Under this 1995 White Paper, which is addressed to the ten transition economies which already had association agreements with the EU,[62] each such country is directed to establish its own priorities and to determine its own timetable in the light of its own domestic conditions.

In the investment services (securities) field,[63] the following directives would have to be transposed or substantially implemented in the internal law of the transition economies as part of the suggested first stage: (i) the Public Offer Prospectus Directive;[64] (ii) the Stock Exchange Listing Particulars Directive;[65] (iii) the Directive on Notification of Major Holdings;[66] (iv) the Insider Dealing Directive;[67] (v) the UCITS Directive;[68] and (vi) the Money Laundering Directive.[69]

The second stage of the Commission framework for the transition economies focuses on the various EU provisions for freedom of capital and services in the financial sphere. The following directives, therefore, would be relevant to the second stage in the securities area:[70] (i) the Investment Services Directive;[71] and (ii) the Capital Adequacy Directive.[72]

The EU legislative framework for financial markets seems to be grounded in a concept that can be thought of as a search for equivalence among disparate regulatory and legal systems, while taking into account the continuing reality of separate and distinct national legal and regulatory regimes as the basis of any overall EU initiatives.[73] The key principle outlined in the Commission's 1985 White Paper[74] implementing the common internal market supporting competition among rules is that of 'mutual recognition'. According to this principle, all Member States agree to recognize the validity of one another's laws, regulations and standards, thereby facilitating free trade in goods and services without the need for prior harmonization.[75] A second major principle enshrined in the 1985 White Paper is 'harmonisation of essential minimum standards'. This principle acts to limit the scope for competition among rules by mandating Member State conformity with a 'floor' of essential minimum EU-wide requirements. As such, investment services regulation in the EU seeks to avoid the problem of competitive deregulation and regulatory arbitrage that may undermine the legitimacy and efficiency of financial markets.[76]

As a general matter, the EU system of securities regulation rests on the EU Company Law Directives. Securities law and company law are intimately interrelated; without company law, securities law is probably meaningless. Further, many areas traditionally considered in the US as matters of securities law rather than corporate law are covered under the company law framework in Europe and elsewhere.

EU company law is based on the prohibition of discrimination within the EU based on the nationality of an entity organized within a Member State under Article 7 of the Treaty of Rome.[77] Companies organized under the laws of one Member State have the right to establish branches in other Member States.[78] Further, regulation for the protection of share-holders, employees and creditors must be equivalent throughout the EU.[79] As a result of the political impossibility of achieving strict harmonization in this very diverse area,[80] the EC began to propose directives which prescribed only basic, essential principles, with a requirement of mutual recognition among the Member States.[81]

Companies are organizations which are created and administered according to legal requirements, and involve different categories of persons – shareholders, employees, creditors and third parties – who are all concerned in some way with the activity of the undertaking.[82] The first objective of the approximation or harmonization of company law at the Community level is to ensure an equivalent degree of protection for the interests of these various constituencies.[83] While the White Paper does not require the establishment of regulatory structures such as private or public sector bodies or other administrative agencies for the approximation of company, it does presuppose the existence of certain requirements as prerequisites.[84]

Given the adequate provision of these prerequisites, the White Paper creates a two-stage framework for the harmonization of company law, with no additional infrastructure necessary for the implementation of the second stage.[85] The first stage includes the First Company Law Directive[86] and the Second Company Law Directive.[87] Stage two includes the following measures: (i) the Third Company Law Directive,[88] introducing a common procedure for mergers; (ii) the Eleventh Company Law Directive,[89] providing for consolidated reporting; (iii) the Twelfth Company Law Directive,[90] dealing with single-member limited liability companies; and (iv) the Regulation on the European Economic Interest Grouping (EEIG),[91] creating a Community-level instrument permitting cooperation of undertakings from different Member State jurisdictions. The remaining non-key measures are in general proposed measures, and not presently part of the actual EU corpus.[92]

Overall, the impact of policy choices in the area of company law must be viewed as absolutely fundamental to the development of equity markets. The basic choices in the company law area to a large extent determine the ultimate nature of a given country's corporate governance structure, thereby determining the nature and role that equity markets will play in both the corporate governance process and in the capital allocation process.[93]

The EU has undertaken a number of initiatives to improve financial reporting among the Member States from both a qualitative and a quantitative standpoint. Accounting harmonization is part of the company law harmonization programme aimed at furthering freedom of establishment, and as such, is aimed not only toward the equivalent protection of all investors, but of all third parties dealing with Member States' companies.[94] While the Accounting Directives contain options for both Member States and companies, an analysis of the implications of these choices is beyond the scope of this chapter.

Under the 1995 White Paper, legislative harmonization in the accounting field presupposes the existence of a national accounting system[95] – historically, at least, a significant problem for any of the transition economies. Because the transition economies in general have instituted accounting legislation modelled on the EU accounting directives, this is no longer a barrier; however, given the general lack of accounting training and experience in the transition economies, such training is absolutely essential for implementation of the legislation.[96] Moreover, such training is a prerequisite to any meaningful financial disclosure necessary for investment decisions in the securities markets.

As in other areas, the White Paper lays down a two-stage framework for the implementation of the accounting directives.[97] Beyond the prerequisites discussed above, implementation of the accounting directives requires the implementation of the First Company Law Directive, discussed above.[98] Stage one requires the implementation of legislation consistent with three directives: (i) the Fourth Company Law Directive;[99] (ii) the Eighth Company Law Directive;[100] and (iii) the Insurance Accounting Directive.[101] The second stage then requires the implementation of two directives: the Seventh Company Law Directive[102] and the Bank Accounting Directive.[103]

The basic EU framework for disclosure and listing requirements is fairly straightforward, although not as comprehensive as the US system. Overall, it provides an appropriate basis for the establishment of minimum disclosure standards necessary for creating investor confidence in and providing sufficient information for the effective operation of equity markets in the transition economies. In fact, the recent growth of domestic Western European exchanges and securities markets suggests that such efforts are directly beneficial for the developmental of such markets.[104]

The basic framework for the EU securities regulatory regime is founded upon a series of directives known as the Stock Exchange Directives[105] (enacted before to the 1986 Single European Act), as well as directives dealing with collective investment schemes (or mutual funds in American parlance), prospectuses and insider dealing. Further, money-laundering legislation, while not strictly speaking covered under the general view of securities regulation, has become very important in the EU financial services framework. As with the company law directives, these securities law directives reflect the EU's general philosophy of mandatory disclosure as promulgated in various Commission Recommendations.[106]

The overall objective of these directives is to provide a set of minimum standards capable of operating on a uniform basis throughout the EU and in a way that removes some of the barriers which would otherwise result from the existence of conflicting requirements in a number of different markets, so as to permit greater flexibility of access to the EU capital markets.

The second level of EU investment services regulation deals with the establishment of a single market in financial services, based on the common minimum framework provided by the earlier directives. This level centres principally around the Investment Services Directive and the Capital Adequacy Directive. To put this in a broader perspective, the single market is rooted in basic tenets of the Treaty of Rome respecting the free movement of capital, establishment and services, and is manifested in the various 'single passport' directives.[107] Under the concept of the single passport, an EU firm authorized in one Member State (its 'home state') and wishing to operate in other Member States ('host states') will generally be able to choose to supply services through branches or to supply services on a cross-border basis without having a permanent physical presence in the host state.[108] The intended benefit of the passport is that it should increase competition by opening markets to a wider range of participants and by allowing firms to choose the most cost-effective means of supplying services to a particular market.[109]

The most relevant of the passport directives (for present purposes) is the Investment Services Directive (ISD),[110] adopted in 1993. The ISD is intended to provide a single passport for EU securities firms to conduct cross-border operations anywhere in the EU based on a licence issued by their respective home states.[111] As originally proposed, the ISD was designed to achieve the goal of breaking down the various EU Member States' protectionist, non-tariff barriers to domestic market entry.

Beyond its impact on bank regulation, the major provisions of the ISD are intended to be: (i) common minimum authorization or licensing requirements among the EU Member States;[112] (ii) mutual recognition of the licence granted in the home state by all other Member States or 'host states';[113] (iii) prudential rules establishing common minimum financial soundness standards among the Member States;[114] (iv) certain guiding principles for adoption of conduct-of-business rules by the host states;[115] (v) direct access to each Member State's domestic stock exchange for both outside investment firms and banks;[116] (vi) requirements for concentration of securities trading in regulated markets which preserve investor choice to trade in less regulated markets;[117] (vii) minimum transparency rules for regulated markets; and (viii) reciprocity for non-EU firms to participate in the newly integrated marketplace.[118]

Combined with the basic framework established in the company law and securities directives and the capital standards of the Capital Adequacy Directive (CAD), the ISD establishes the framework for a comprehensive European system of securities regulation.

Strong arguments exist that the transition economies should adopt the EU investment services regulatory framework in a step-by-step implementation process, with the initial requirements necessary to ensure investor protection and market confidence being adopted first. Only once the basic structures necessary to the proper functioning of the securities markets are in place should the transition economies move on to adopt the deregulatory programme of the EU system. This sequenced formulation has been suggested by the Commission in its 1995 White Paper.

While the EU contains both the oldest stock exchange[119] and the world's largest international financial centre,[120] widespread individual ownership of securities is a relatively recent phenomenon in Western Europe.[121] Several explanations have been advanced for this historic phenomenon including: the major economic dislocations resulting from two world wars and other armed conflicts; exchange and capital market controls imposed by European governments; the predominance of bank lending over securities offerings in corporate finance; the relatively small number of listed companies in Continental Europe, each with only a minority of shares available in the open market; relatively high transaction costs; insufficient or non-existent transparency and liquidity in European securities markets; the absence of regulation affording investor protection; lack of public confidence in and understanding of securities markets; and popular aversion to the risks of securities investment.[122] Importantly for the purposes of application of the EU framework to the transition economies, wider individual participation in securities markets in Europe has become an objective of national policy in a number of EU Member States, due in large part to the privatization of many state-owned enterprises.

In order to encourage broad-based securities ownership, strategic considerations mandate an effective investor protection scheme in order to maintain public confidence in any retail securities market.[123] As a result of practical governmental needs (combined with the forces of harmonization, access deregulation, and prudential re-regulation inherent in the process of opening developing the Maastricht principal of free movement of capital), national securities regulation in Western Europe has begun to expand in recent years.[124] Historically, however, securities regulation in Western Europe had been virtually non-existent outside of the United Kingdom. Although company law was well developed across Western Europe, European stock exchanges have been historically self-regulating, with little or no direct oversight by national governments. Moreover, European states have not historically mandated full disclosure systems for the distribution or trading of securities,[125] nor have they prohibited insider trading or other market manipulative practices long prohibited by the United States.[126]

In sum, the transition economies have committed politically and economically to draw closer to the EU, and (as such) to more closely converge their financial markets. In addition, with the transition economies still in the early stages of capital market development, so also most of the EU Member States (apart from the UK) have only in the past decade moved to develop broad-based equity markets. In all events, the present state of EU financial services markets is still without any comprehensive and consistent regulation and enforcement as in the US. While the envisioned EU system will be complex, it is still not as complex as that of the US (though the EU system is designed as a comprehensive and coherent regulatory system). For all these reasons, the transition economies' approximation of the EU model (given necessary national differences) should prove an appropriate, and in some cases necessary, strategy and, moreover, an effective course of action.

Conclusion

At least eight interrelated problems inherited from the previous system of central planning continue to plague the financial systems of transition economies, impeding the transition to a market economy: (i) general entrepreneurial inexperience, brought about by four decades of Communist rule; (ii) a general shortage of companies able to survive the competitive pressures of a market economy, due to the distorted incentives and productive inefficiencies of the old system; (iii) a deficiency in the mobilization of domestic capital resources, due to a lack of domestic savings and the inherited 'bad loan' problems of the banking system; (iv) political instability, resulting in an uncertain business environment which discourages investment; (v) a lack of a market-oriented culture in the relationships between labour, suppliers, manufacturers and consumers; (vi) a lack of meaningful and reliable accounting or valuation systems; (vii) low productivity, due to the inefficient allocation of resources and poor working habits developed under state planning; and (vii) small national markets and broken international linkages.[127]

Leaving aside the massive confusion prevalent in the financial markets of Russia and the threat of continued problems there, which could spill over to other countries in the region (and potentially to Western Europe as well), overall problems likely to continue to affect the financial systems in the transition economies for the near future include: the weakness of banking institutions; the prevalence of corruption and securities fraud; the lack of effective and consistent regulatory enforcement; the lack of sophisticated and efficient judicial mechanisms for the resolution of financial disputes; the inexperience of market participants; and the shortage of domestic savings. At a more fundamental level, the inefficiencies of general corporate law and of investment firm regulation, and in particular the absence of appropriate solutions to questions of conflicts of interests and insider dominance in corporate governance and securities activities, are likely to impede the smooth and rapid maturation of financial systems.

Overall, it appears that the transition economies must accomplish three steps simultaneously which the developed, Western, democracies have achieved in consecutive steps involving more than a century or more of development, namely: the generation of a market economy; the establishment of the rule of law; and the institutionalization of democratic rule.[128] Beyond these three essential steps, the transition economies will need to strengthen their financial systems in general, and given the particular characteristics of the transition economies, their capital markets, and especially their equity markets. In thinking to the future, three predominant characteristics will likely predominate in these capital markets in the next few years.[129] First, weak financial infrastructures will lag behind dynamic market forces, as the emerging markets in these countries attempt to meet the demands of investors and companies. Second, in the medium term, the strengthening of financial intermediaries, both banks and securities firms, should do much to improve the functioning of the respective capital markets. Third, in the longer term, the successful mobilization (or failure thereof) of capital should have the greatest influence on stabilization and the development of markets.

With these predictions in mind, and to solve the sorts of problems outlined herein, different nations need to adopt solutions corresponding to their different levels of development, especially in the area of stock exchange and equity market development. In this context, according to Dr Paolo Clarotti, then Head of Banking and Financial Institutions at the Commission, three elements are necessary in order to develop a properly functioning financial sector: (i) trained and reputable personnel; (ii) appropriate legislation; and (iii) effective supervisory bodies to ensure that the financial institutions respect the laws and regulations under which they work.[130] While these are indeed the goals to place at the forefront, the needs of individual nations must be paid close attention.

The nations of the first tier generally have the basic infrastructure in place and are beginning to focus on compatibility with EU legislation and more advanced concerns such as increasing liquidity, regulation of institutional investors, and matters of specific concern which develop as the system develops (for example insider trading, securities fraud and speculative pressures). In this vein, it must be noted that the developed capital markets of the US, the UK and the EU have developed through a gradual process of regulatory development to fit individual needs of the countries involved. While the first tier countries have done much to encourage the process of equity market development, these nations must re-evaluate their efforts as development and consequent needs change over time.

The nations of the second tier are generally still in the process of putting their infrastructure in place. Their needs focus on design of the stock exchange as well as more general but probably more important areas such as company law and corporate governance. Like the first tier, however, the second tier needs to increase capitalization and participation, and to deal with possible abuses by institutional investors.

The nations of the third tier are still generally in the first phase of development (that is, designing the general financial and regulatory framework necessary to create capital markets and stock exchanges). These countries are attempting to put in place the necessary infrastructure for market development and in all likelihood, their needs will grow as the transition process continues. Russia stands alone in this area: it is by far the largest market, but also by far the most chaotic. This may be inherent in the development of capital markets in a large market, has been the case in the US and seems to be the situation in China at the present time.[131]

The state of capital markets in the formerly centrally planned economies warrants specific comprehensive regulation of securities and stock exchanges in order to prevent fraud and to discourage market manipulation and insider dealing. Yet these nations also need to attract foreign investment capital. Overly restrictive regulations will most likely undermine the attraction of these new markets if investors find restrictions burdensome from a cost–benefit point of view. Of course, investors will also be searching for environments that afford adequate investor protection. Consequently, strictly enforced comprehensive disclosure obligations will most likely attract investment capital and build confidence in the emerging markets of the transition economies.

As can clearly be seen from the preceding pages, law reform cannot be looked at solely in terms of the municipal situation and needs of any given state, whether in the countries in transition of Central and Eastern Europe and the CIS or in the 'developed' economies of the West and East Asia. Today, investment flows to and from all corners of the world with amazing speed and with sometimes dangerous results.[132] In order to acquire the capital necessary for development, countries must look to what can only be described as an international market for capital.

On a general level, law reform efforts in the transition economies and elsewhere must now be seen in terms of a large number of interconnected factors, loosely broken down into national, regional and international factors.[133] On a domestic level, countries must look to lessons from a large number of policy choices and experiences elsewhere in attempting to find the path that best suits their particular situation and needs. Experience shows that no one single 'model' or piece of legislation is appropriate for every situation or every individual state.

On a regional level, efforts such as those of the EU, the NAFTA countries, Mercosur and APEC now have an increasing significance for those countries wishing to become involved with these various sorts of regional efforts. For the transition economies especially, the regional models promulgated by the European Commission are of increasing importance, given the strong desires of many of these countries to become associated with the EU and perhaps even eventually Member States. These sorts of regional factors, then, cannot be ignored in the process of domestic law reform.

On an international level, the efforts of organizations such as the Basel Committee on Banking Supervision, IOSCO and the IASC are increasingly active and interactive in the study and promulgation of 'international standards' in the area of financial market regulation and disclosure. These efforts, although technically a form of 'soft law',[134] are becoming ingrained into both domestic and regional financial market law reform efforts in developed and developing countries alike. While these standards do not necessarily represent the 'final word' on international best practices for financial market law reform, they are certainly of great importance in encouraging international standards in the transition economies and in the overall process of integrating the financial systems of these countries into the international financial system.

Notes

1   This chapter addresses the following countries: Albania, Belarus, Bosnia–Herzegovina, Bulgaria, Croatia, the Czech Republic, Estonia, FYR Macedonia, Hungary, Latvia, Lithuania, Poland, Romania, Russia, Slovenia, the Slovak Republic and Ukraine.

2   IOSCO, *Objectives and Principles of Securities Regulation* (Sept. 1998).

3   See generally Marc I. Steinberg, 'Emerging Securities Markets – A View of Internationalization from the U.S.', in Joseph J. Norton and Mads Andenas (eds), *Emerging Financial Markets and the Role of International Financial Organizations* (1996), pp. 429–50.

4   For detailed development of this analysis, see Joseph Norton, 'Reflections on the development of capital markets, stock exchanges and securities regulations in central and eastern Europe', in U. Drobnig, K. Hopt, K. Kötz and E.-J. Mestmäcker (eds), *Systemtransformation In Mittel-und Osteuropa und ihre Folgen für Banken, Börsen und Kreditsicherheiten* (1998).

5   Agreements with Hungary, Poland, and Czechoslovakia were signed on 16 December 1991. For texts of the Europe Agreements with Hungary and Poland, see *Official Journal* (henceforth *OJ*) L 347/2 and L 348/2 (1993). The agreement originally signed with Czechoslovakia was subsequently renegotiated separately with the Czech Republic and the Slovak Republic, and EAs were signed with these two countries on 4 October 1993; see *OJ* L 360/2 and L 359/2 (1994).

6   In 1993, the Community signed EAs with Romania and Bulgaria; see *OJ* L 357/2 and 358/3 (1994). Agreements with the three Baltic Republics were signed on 12 June 1995; see 'EU: Signing of the Europe Association Agreements with Estonia, Latvia and Lithuania' (95 June 12), Reuter Textline RAPID, 13 July 1995. Finally, an EA was signed between the EU and Slovenia on 10 June 1996; see 'EU: EP/Slovenia – Parliament's Assent for the Europe Agreement', Agence Europe, 25 October 1996.

7   In December 1989, the EC signed a trade and cooperation agreement with the USSR. See *OJ* L 68/3 (1990). Due to the rapid and dramatic changes which occurred soon thereafter in the USSR, namely the break-up into the CIS, a new agreement was subsequently signed with Russia on 17 July 1995. See *OJ* L 247/1 (1995). This agreement and similar agreements signed with Ukraine, Moldova, Belarus, and the non-European former republics of the USSR can be more generally classified as a 'Partnership and Cooperation Agreement' (PCA).

8   See generally Jacek Rostowski (ed.), *Banking Reform in Central Europe and the Former Soviet Union* (1995).

 9 See Benn Steil, *The European Markets* (1996), pp. 147–84.
10 See William C. Philbrick, 'The Paving of Wall Street in Eastern Europe: Establishing the Infrastructure for Stock Markets in the Formerly Centrally Planned Economies', *Law and Policy in International Business*, 25 (1994) 565, p. 576.
11 See Steil, *European Markets*, pp. 147–84.
12 This has traditionally been the case in markets characterized by broad-based equity ownership, namely the US and the UK See ibid., pp. 1–58.
13 This situation has traditionally been the case in markets characterized by dominant financial institutions, such as banks, with a large role in both enterprise funding and control. See ibid., pp. 147–84.
14 See ibid.
15 See generally Stephen S. Cohen et al., 'Congress of the United States, Credit Policy and Industrial Policy in France, Monetary Policy, Selective Credit Policy, and Industrial Policy in France, Britain, West Germany, and Sweden', Staff Paper prepared for the use of the Joint Economic Committee, Congress of the United States, US GPO No. 77–744 O (1981); see also John Zysman, *Governments, Markets, and Growth* (1983).
16 R. Levine and S. Zevros, 'Policy, Stock Market Development and Long-Run Growth' (World Bank, Feb. 1995); R. King and R. Levine, 'Finance, Entrepreneurship, and Growth: Theory and Evidence', *Journal of Monetary Economics*, 32 (Dec. 1993).
17 See Manning Gilbert Warren III, 'Global Harmonization of Securities Laws: The Achievements of the European Communities', *Harvard International Law Journal*, 31 (1990) 185, p. 194, n. 50.
18 See William C. Philbrick, 'The Task of Regulating Investment Funds in the Formerly Centrally Planned Economies', *Emory International Law Review*, 8 (1994) 539, p. 557.
19 See generally ibid.
20 See P. Guislain, 'Divestiture of State Enterprises: An Overview of the Legal Framework', World Bank Technical Paper No. 186 (1992), pp. 26–7.
21 Philbrick, 'Regulating Investment Funds', p. 557.
22 Ibid.
23 See Patrick Mordacq, 'Capital Markets in the Transition Countries and the EBRD's Experience: Address to the IOSCO Round Table on Emerging Markets', in Materials from IOSCO XX Annual Conference (11 July 1995).
24 Figures from the 1993 EBRD *Annual Economic Review* are instructive in this regard. See EBRD, *EBRD Economic Review: Annual Economic Outlook* (Sept. 1993), pp. 6–30.
25 For a discussion of the increasing role of institutional investors in the international financial system, see Steil, *European Markets*, pp. 147–84.
26 See Douglas W. Arner, 'The Implications of the Mexican Peso Crisis for Regulation of Financial Markets', *NAFTA: Journal of Law & Business in the Americas*, 4 (Fall 1996) 28.
27 See Jonathan R. Macey and Hideki Kanda, 'The Stock Exchange as a Firm: The Emergence of Close Substitutes for the New York and Tokyo Stock Exchanges', *Cornell Law Review*, 75 (1990) 1007, p. 1008.
28 Ibid., p. 1008 n. 5.
29 Ibid.

30   Ibid. In the US, the OTC markets have increasingly come to resemble the securities exchanges, especially as prices of securities are increasingly quoted and traded on various electronic exchanges, such as NASDAQ – the 'National Association of Securities Dealers Automated Quotations'. This is also an increasingly important development in the EU.
31   Ibid., p. 1009.
32   Ibid., *Id*
33   Ibid., *Id.*
34   Ibid., pp. 1009–10.
35   Ibid., p. 1012.
36   See generally Ronald Gilson and Reinier Kraakman, 'Note, The Efficient Capital Market Hypothesis, Economic Theory and the Regulation of the Securities Industry', *Stanford Law Review*, 29 (1977) 1031.
37   Macey and Kanda, 'The Stock Exchange as a Firm', p. 1013; Jonathan Macey and David Haddock, 'Shirking at the SEC: The Failure of the National Market System', *University of Illinois Law Review* (1985) 315, p. 325.
38   See Homer Kripke, 'A Search for a Meaningful Disclosure Policy', *Business Law*, 31 (1975) 293, p. 301; Jeffrey N. Gordon and Lewis A. Kornhauser, 'Efficient Markets, Costly Information, and Securities Research', *New York University Law Review*, 60 (1985) 761, p. 787.
39   Macey and Kanda, 'The Stock Exchange as a Firm', p. 1014; Myron S. Scholes, 'The Market for Securities: Substitution versus Prices, Pressure and the Effects of Information on Share Prices', *Journal of Business*, 45 (1972) 179, p. 183.
40   Macey and Kanda, 'The Stock Exchange as a Firm', p. 1016.
41   See Macey and Haddock, 'Shirking at the SEC', pp. 332–7.
42   See Macey and Kanda, 'The Stock Exchange as a Firm', pp. 1018–19. See Daniel R. Fischel, 'Organized Exchanges and the Regulation of Dual Class Common Stock', *University of Chicago Law Review*, 54 (1987), 119, p. 121.
43   See Macey and Kanda 'The Stock Exchange as a Firm', pp. 1020; see also Steil, *European Markets*, pp. 1–59.
44   Jonathan R. Macey, 'From Fairness to Contract: The New Direction of the Rules Against Insider Trading', *Hofstra Law Review*, 13 (1984) 9, pp. 58–63.
45   See Michael C. Jensen and William H. Meckling, 'Theory of the Firm: Managerial Behavior, Agency Costs and Ownership Structure', *Journal of Financial Economics*, 3 (1976) p. 305.
46   See Macey, 'From Fairness to Contract', pp. 58–63. See also Macey and Kanda, 'The Stock Exchange as a Firm', pp. 1021–2.
47   Macey, 'From Fairness to Contract', p. 59.
48   In this context, the NYSE was formed in 1792 and has developed since that time a certain cache as well as served as a certain guarantee of minimum standards of quality of listed firms. Macey and Kanda, 'The Stock Exchange as a Firm', p. 1023.
49   See ibid.
50   Mordacq, 'Capital Markets', p. 1.
51   See IMF, *World Economic Outlook* (May 1996), ch. V.
52   See Mordacq, 'Capital Markets', p. 3.
53   See Joseph J. Norton and Hani Sarie-Eldin, 'Securities Law Models in Emerging Economies', in Norton and Andenas, *Emerging Financial Markets*, pp. 335–50.

54 See C. A. Cooke, *Corporation, Trust and Company: An Essay in Legal History* (1950).
55 See, generally, Christos Hadjiemmanuil, 'Central Bankers' "Club" Law and Transitional Economies: Banking Reform and the Reception of the Basle Standards of Prudential Supervision in Eastern Europe and the Former Soviet Union', in Norton and Andenas, *Emerging Financial Markets*, p. 180.
56 Dariusz M. Budzen and Ania M. Frankowska, 'Prohibitions Against Insider Trading in the United States and the European Community: Providing Guidance for Legislatures of Eastern Europe', *Boston University International Law Journal*, 12 (1994) 92, n. 283.
57 In some of the transition economies, the level of market development may even compare favourably with certain countries traditionally viewed as 'developed'.
58 See, for example, Europe Agreement with Poland, *OJ* L 114 (1992); Ania M. Frankowska, 'The Association Agreement Between the Republic of Poland and the European Community: An Economic and Political Analysis', *University of Miami: Yearbook of International Law* (Winter 1994).
59 Paolo Clarotti, 'The E.U. as a Model for Financial Market Reform', in Norton and Andenas, *Emerging Financial Markets*, p. 25.
60 'White Paper on the Preparation of the Associated Countries of Central and Eastern Europe for Integration into the Internal Market of the Union', COM(95) 163 final 2.
61 Clarotti, 'The EU as a Model', pp. 24–6.
62 Poland, Hungary, the Czech Republic, Slovakia, Bulgaria, Romania, the Baltic republics and Slovenia.
63 In the area credit institutions, four directives should be adopted as part of the first stage: (i) the First Banking Directive, First Council Directive 77/780/EEC of 12 December 1977 on the coordination of laws, regulations and administrative provisions relating to the taking up and pursuit of the business of credit institutions, *OJ* L 322 (1977); (ii) the Own Funds Directive, Council Directive 89/299/EEC of 17 April 1989 on the own funds of credit institutions, *OJ* L 124 (1989); (iii) the Solvency Ratio Directive, Council Directive 89/647/EEC of 18 December 1989 on a solvency ratio for credit institutions, *OJ* L 386 (1989); and (iv) the Deposit Guarantee Directive, Directive of the European Parliament and of the Council 94/19/EC of 30 May 1994 on deposit guarantee schemes, *OJ* L 135 (1994).
64 Council Directive 89/298/EEC of 17 April 1989 coordinating the requirements for the drawing up, scrutiny and distribution of the prospectus to be published when transferable securities are offered to the public, *OJ* L 124 (1989).
65 Council Directive 79/279/EEC of 17 March 1979 coordinating the conditions for admission of securities to official stock exchange listing, *OJ* L 66 (1979).
66 Council Directive 88/627/EEC of 12 December 1988 on the information to be published when a major holding in a listed company is acquired or disposed of, *OJ* L 348 (1988).
67 Council Directive 89/592/EEC of 13 November 1989 coordinating regulations on insider dealing, *OJ* L 334 (1989).
68 Council Directive 85/611/EEC of 20 December 1985 on the coordination of laws, regulations and administrative provisions relating to undertakings for collective investment in transferable securities, *OJ* L 375 (1985).

69 Council Directive 91/308/EEC of 10 June 1991 on prevention of the use of the financial system for the purpose of money laundering.

70 Five directives dealing with credit institutions should be implemented during the second stage: (i) the Second Banking Directive, Second Council Directive 89/646/EEC of 15 December 1989 on the coordination of laws, regulations and administrative provisions relating to the taking up and pursuit of the business of credit institutions, *OJ* L 386 (1989) ('2BCD'), amending Directive 77/780/EEC; (ii) the Annual Accounts and Consolidated Accounts Directive, Council Directive 86/635/EEC of 8 December 1986 on the annual accounts and consolidated accounts of banks and other financial institutions, *OJ* L 372 (1986), which must be read together with the Fourth and Seventh Company Law Directives; (iii) the Capital Adequacy Directive, discussed below; (iv) the Large Exposures Directive, Council Directive 92/121/EEC of 21 December 1992 on the monitoring and control of large exposures of credit institutions, *OJ* L 29 (1993); and (v) the Consolidated Accounts Directive, Council Directive 92/30/EEC of 6 April 1992 on the supervision of credit institutions on a consolidated basis, *OJ* L 110 (1992).

71 Council Directive 93/22/EEC of 10 May 1993 on investment services in the securities field, *OJ* L 141 (1993).

72 Council Directive 93/6/EEC of 15 March 1993 on the capital adequacy of investment firms and credit institutions, *OJ* L 141 (1993).

73 Steil, *European Markets*, p. 113.

74 'Completing the Internal Market' (White Paper from the Commission to the European Council, Milan, 28–29 June 1985), COM (85) 310 final (Brussels, 14 June 1985) (the '1985 White Paper').

75 Ibid. This principle underlies the 2BCD as well as the ISD.

76 See Roberta S. Karmel, 'Can Regulators of International Capital Markets Strike a Balance Between Competing Interests?', *Boston University International Law Journal*, 4 (1986) 105.

77 Treaty Establishing the European Economic Community, 25 March ch 1957, 298 U.N.T.S. 11 [Treaty of Rome], Art. 7.

78 Ibid., Art. 58.

79 Ibid., Art. 54(3)(g).

80 See Warren, 'Global Harmonization', pp. 197–8.

81 *Id.*

82 White Paper, as note 60, Annex, p. 308.

83 Ibid.

84 These requirements include: (i) designation of a register for undertakings and a national gazette for the publication of certain information, such as the company's organization, financial details and system of publicity to third parties; (ii) designation of an administrative or judicial authority which will ensure the control of incorporation and the legality of certain acts; (iii) designation of independent experts who will evaluate the financial situation of the company in different stages of its existence; and (iv) training of modern business administrators. Ibid., Annex, p. 309.

85 Ibid., Annex, p. 312.

86 First Council Directive of 9 March 1968 on coordination of safeguards which, for the protection of the interests of members and others, are required by Member States companies within the meaning of the second paragraph of

Article 58 of the Treaty, with a view to making such safeguards equivalent throughout the Community, 68/151/EEC, *OJ* L 65 (1968).

87 Second Council Directive of 13 December 1976 on coordination of safeguards which, for the protection of the interests of members and others, are required by Member States of companies within the meaning of the second paragraph of Article 58 of the Treaty, in respect of the formation of public limited liablity companies and the maintainence and alteration of their capital, with a view to making such safeguards equivalent, 77/91/EEC, *OJ* L 26 (1977), as amended by 92/101/EEC, *OJ* L 347 (1992).

88 Third Council Directive of 9 October 1978 based on Article 54(3)(g) of the Treaty concerning mergers of public limited liablity companies, 78/885/EEC, *OJ* L 295 (1978).

89 Eleventh Council Directive of 21 December 1989 concerning disclosure requirements in respect of branches opened in a Member State by certain types of companies governed by the law of another Member State, 89/666/EEC, *OJ* L 395 (1989).

90 Twelfth Council Directive of 21 December 1989 concerning single member private limited companies, 89/667/EEC, *OJ* L 395 (1989).

91 Council Regulation (EEC) on the European Economic Interest Grouping (EEIG), Reg. 2137/85, *OJ* L 199 (1985).

92 The Sixth Company Law Directive, Sixth Council Directive (82/891/EEC) of 17 December 1982 based on Article 54 (3) of the Treaty, concerning the division of public limited liability companies, *OJ* L 378 (1982), is the only exception. The other measures are: (i) the proposed Fifth Company Law Directive, Amended proposal for a Fifth Council Directive founded on Article 54(3)(g) of the EEC Treaty concerning the structure of public limited liability companies, *OJ* C 240 (1983); (ii) the proposed Tenth Company Law Directive, Proposal for a Tenth Council Directive based on Article 54(3)(g) of the Treaty concerning cross-border mergers of public limited companies, *OJ* C 23 (1985); (iii) the proposed Thirteenth Company Law Directive, Amended proposal for a Thirteenth Council Directive on company law concerning takeover and other general bids, *OJ* C 240 (1990); and (iv) the proposed European Company Statute, Amended proposal for a Council Regulation (EEC) on the Statute for a European Company, *OJ* C 176 (1991). See White Paper, as note 60, Annex, p. 314.

93 See Steil, *European Markets*, pp. 147–84.

94 White Paper, as note 60, Annex, p. 315.

95 Ibid. These include: a register for undertakings and the scope of undertakings concerned; and rules of accounting, auditing and publication.

96 Ibid.

97 See ibid., pp. 316–24.

98 Ibid., p. 317.

99 Fourth Council Directive (78/660/EEC) of 25 July 1978 based on Article 54(3)(g) of the Treaty on the annual accounts of certain types of companies, *OJ* L 222 (1978), as amended by Directive 84/569/EEC, *OJ* L 314 (1984), Directive 90/604/EEC, *OJ* L 317 (1990), Directive 90/605/EEC, *OJ* L 317 (1990), and Directive 94/8/EC, *OJ* L 82 (1994).

100 Eighth Council Directive (84/253/EEC) of 10 April 1984 based on Article 54(3)(g) of the Treaty on the approval of persons responsible for carrying out the statutory audits of accounting documents, *OJ* L 126 (1984).

101   Council Directive (91/674/EEC) of 19 December 1991 on the annual accounts and consolidated accounts of insurance undertakings, *OJ* L 374 (1991).
102   Seventh Council Directive (83/349/EEC) of 13 June 1983 based on Article 54(3)(g) of the Treaty on consolidated accounts, *OJ* L 193 (1993).
103   Council Directive (86/635/EEC) of 8 December 1986 on the annual accounts and consolidated accounts of banks and other financial institutions, *OJ* L 372 (1986).
104   See Steil, *European Markets*, pp. 1–58.
105   The Stock Exchange Directives include: the Admission Directive, the Listing Particulars Directive, and the Interim Reports Directive. Interestingly, only the Listing Particulars Directive is addressed in the 1995 White Paper.
106   See European Code of Conduct Relating to Transactions in Transferable Securities, 20 *OJ* L 212, p. 37 (1977).
107   The passport directives in the financial services area include: (i) the First and Second Banking Coordination Directives (1BCD and 2BCD) (banking); (ii) the Investment Services Directive (ISD) (investment firms and securities markets); (iii) the UCITS Directive (collective investment schemes); (iv) the First, Second and Third Life Assurance Directives (life assurance); (v) the First, Second and Third Non-Life Insurance Directives (non-life insurance); and (vi) the proposed First Pension Funds Directive (pension funds).
108   See 'The EC single market in financial services', *Bank of England Quarterly Bulletin* 92 (Feb. 1993).
109   Ibid.
110   Council Directive 93//22 on Investment Services in the Securities Field, 1993 *OJ* L 141, 27, corr. at 1993 *OJ* L 170, 32 and L 194, 27.
111   Manning Gilbert Warren III, 'The European Union's Investment Services Directive', *University of Pennsylvania Journal of International Business Law*, 15 (1994) p. 181.
112   Investment Services Directive, Art. 3.
113   Ibid., Art. 14(1), (2).
114   Ibid., Art. 10.
115   Ibid., Art. 11.
116   Ibid., Art. 15.
117   Ibid., Art. 14(3), (4).
118   Ibid., Art. 7.
119   Amsterdam Stock Exchange, *Euromoney* (Supp.), May 1985, p. 16.
120   Namely London. See Steil, *European Markets*, p. 2.
121   See ibid., pp. 1–58.
122   Warren, 'Global Harmonization', p. 194.
123   Ibid.
124   Ibid., p. 194.
125   When the Public Offers Prospectus Directive was proposed in 1981, only five members of the EC required prospectus disclosure to investors in public offerings of securities, namely: Belgium, France, Ireland, Luxembourg and the United Kingdom, 1980–1981 Eur. Parl. Doc. (COM. No. 893) (1980), *OJ* C 355, explanatory memorandum, para. 6 (1981). As of 1990, West Germany still imposed no prospectus upon issuers in connection with public

offers of securities not listed on an exchange. Warren, 'Global Harmonization', p. 195 n. 54.

126 See Lynda M. Ruiz, 'European Community on Insider Dealing: A Model for Effective Enforcement of Prohibitions on Insider Trading in International Securities Markets', *Columbia Journal of Transnational Law*, 1 (1995) 217.

127 See, generally Stephen S. Cohen and Andrew Schwartz, 'The Tunnel at the End of the Light: Privatization in Eastern Europe', *Transnational Law*, 7 (1994).

128 Ulrich K. Reuss, 'The Politics of Constitution-Making', *Law and Policy*, 13 (1991) 107, pp. 111–12.

129 Mordacq, 'Capital Markets', p. 5.

130 Clarotti, 'The EU as a Model', p. 22.

131 See, generally Stanley Siegel, 'The Long Walk to a Market Economy: An Examination of the New Company and Securities Laws of the People's Republic of China', in Norton and Andenas, *Emerging Financial Markets*, pp. 497–512.

132 See, generally, Arner, 'Implications of the Mexica Reso Crisis'.

133 For analysis of the development of banking supervision in terms of this sort of developmental model, See Joseph Norton, *Devising International Bank Supervisory Standards* (1995).

134 See ibid., pp. 255–62.

5
The Recent Romanian Accounting Reforms: Another Case of Cultural Intrusion?

Alan Roberts

Introduction

The fall of communism in Romania was marked by a bloody uprising against the Ceauşescu regime at the end of 1989. The new governmental authorities then embarked rapidly upon a series of legislative reforms designed to develop a more market-based economy. By the end of 1991 the central accounting reform – in the shape of Accounting Law 82/1991 – was in place, although implementation of this Law took rather longer (the Implementation Decree (HG) 704/1993 required Romanian enterprises to operate under the Law from 1 April 1994). In common with other countries in Central and Eastern Europe, these reforms transformed the nature of accounting and financial reporting from one whose principal aim was 'of providing financial statistics by enterprises for use in higher level budgets' (Garrod and McLeay, 1996, p. 1) to one with a more complex set of objectives involving the provision of financial information to the various stakeholders in enterprises and to government for the purposes of tax assessment and the formulation of economic policy.

Again in common with other countries in transition, Romania had to make a deliberate choice from the various 'models' of accounting and financial reporting which exist in Western Europe and, more generally, across the world.

It is a commonplace that, despite the attempts at harmonization and standardization undertaken by the EU and the IASC, there is still a diversity of accounting regulation and practice between different countries in the world, a diversity which has spawned over the last 30 years a

146

variety of classifications of accounting. These classifications have been of various types (Roberts, 1995) and have employed various kinds of language to refer to difference, for example 'accounting development patterns' (Mueller, 1967), 'systems' and 'classes' (Nobes, 1998), 'traditions' (Krzywda et al., 1995). But perhaps the most enduring outcome of this research has been the recognition that, in the developed world, countries can be divided into two main groups for the purposes of individual company accounting and financial reporting: a group comprising the Anglo-Saxon countries and the Netherlands and a group which contains Continental European countries together with Japan and Korea. The countries in each group exhibit what Nobes (1998) calls Class A and Class B accounting respectively or what Richard (1996) terms dynamic and static accounting. Within each group there are, of course, differences between countries and, indeed, differences within countries (notably because of the adoption of IAS for consolidated accounts of listed companies in countries like France, Belgium, Germany and Italy), but the groupings do seem to be relatively robust despite international pressures for change.

The issue facing Romania at the turn of the 1990s was which model of accounting it should follow. Should it adopt an 'Anglo Saxon or continental type of accounting system' (Feleagă and Ionaşcu, 1993)? If the latter, which continental country would offer the most useful features for a country like Romania with its particular cultural and political traditions and its needs for economic modernization?

The answers to these questions were clearly set out in the detail of the 1991 Accounting Law and the Implementation Decree which, among other things, promulgated Planul Contabil General (PCG – the General Accounting Plan). Romania would adopt a continental type of accounting with specific inspiration drawn from the French example. Romania was not the only country to take this route to accounting reform: the Czech Republic also was inspired by the example of the French PCG.

More recently, however, doubts have grown in Romania as to whether this was a wise choice – particularly given the growing importance of IAS on the world scene and the recognition that capital markets were increasingly dominated by companies which prepare their financial statements according to an Anglo-Saxon model of accounting. These doubts culminated in the arrival of a team from the Institute of Chartered Accountants of Scotland (ICAS), financed by the British Know How Fund, to advise the Romanian government on further accounting reform. This advice, in turn, led to the publication of an Order from the Romanian Ministry of Finance in June 1999 (430/1999) which makes substantial changes to accounting regulation and sets out a timetable for further changes to the Romanian accounting system.

This chapter is divided into five further sections. The first considers the background to the initial selection of the French model and relies upon previous commentary by Richard (1995, 1998), Duţia (1995) and arguments advanced by Feleagă and Ionaşcu (1993). The second section reviews the nature, structure and content of Order 430/1999. This is followed by a review of the influences, both international and national, on the Order. Conclusions follow. The chapter suggests that, in many respects, the Order represents an uncomfortable compromise between the Anglo-Saxon and continental models of accounting and exhibits a degree of cultural intrusion upon an existing accounting system which is, at the least, unnecessary.

The French background

The idea that Romania should base its accounting reforms upon the French example was one which fitted well with the close cultural, political and economic ties between the two countries. Romanian independence from the Ottoman empire was forged by political exiles in Paris; the civic, political and educational institutions of the Romanian state of the late nineteenth century and early twentieth century were modelled on those of France; and close linguistic ties were maintained between the two countries (Romanian is a Latin language), with the political and intellectual élite in Romania being well educated in French and with the Romanian language importing large numbers of French words. Even in the communist period, the foreign policy attitudes of the Ceauşescu regime which struck a pose of independence from the Soviet bloc echoed the independence of Gaullist defence policy from that of NATO. Not least in these connections were the economic ties, for example, in the licence from Renault to produce cars (under the 'oltcit' brand) in the communist era. Richard reports that in 1993 French investments 'were ahead of those of all other foreign investments' (Richard, 1995, p. 319) in the country.

These features may all help to explain a predisposition on the part of the post-1989 Romanian authorities towards a French model of accounting but they do not seem to be either necessary or sufficient as explanations for adoption of that model. As mentioned earlier, the Czech Republic, with far fewer connections to France, was also heavily influenced in its initial accounting reforms by France. In that country Sucher and Zelenka (1995) suggest that a personal view of the then Czech

Minister of Finance was important in the adoption of a general accounting plan modelled on the French PCG.

What is notable about the Romanian case, however, is the almost complete use of the French model in the 1991 Law and 1993 implementation decree. Richard (1998, p. 321) concludes that 'the whole of [Romania's] legislation is based on French financial accounting (with all its characteristics of static accounting with fiscal and macroeconomic objectives)'. This wholesale borrowing can be seen in a number of dimensions within the Romanian legislation. Examples are the formalities for enterprise accounting organization set out in Articles 6–26 of the Romanian law; the strong tax/accounting links demonstrated by the use of *provizioanele reglementate* (regulatory provisions) which are defined in exactly the same terms as the French *provisions réglementées*; the organization of the Romanian PCG which Richard suggests is 'virtually a replica of France's 1982 chart' (1995, p. 317); and the formats of the balance sheet and profit and loss account which duplicate French formats even down to the specification of 'intermediate management balances' (*solduri intermediare de gestiune*; French: *soldes intermédiares de gestion*).

How was it that Romania adopted the French model in such a wholesale fashion? Feleagă and Ionaşcu (1993) adduce a number of arguments, arguments which have attracted criticism from Richard (1995). For Duţia (1995) the choice appears to be unproblematic: it arose, in part, from the specialized advice to the Romanian government from a variety of French (and Belgian) accounting and financial institutions which 'made a very important contribution to . . . accounting reform in Romania' (1995, p. 747). It is as well to point up the crucial role of advisers in shaping accounting reform in countries in transition: Feleagă and Ionaşcu (1993, pp. 8 and 26) also cite the critical role played by the French authors, Delesalle and Gélard, of the Enterprise Accounting System (*Système Comptable d'Entreprise (SCE)*) in influencing accounting thinking in Romania at the turn of the 1990s. Indeed, the SCE was conceived as a tool for inspiring accounting change in countries in transition (Delesalle and Gelard, 1991). The role of the ICAS team in recent years in advising on the future direction of Romanian accounting has also been of similar importance: as will be discussed later, parts of Order 430/1999 are straight translations of paragraphs from Schedule 4 of the UK Companies Act 1985.

But even if the role of advisers was critical in developing the substance of the initial accounting reforms in Romania, it does not explain fully the selection of France as the 'culturally dominant' model (Nobes,

1998). It does seem clear that the Romanian authorities made the strategic decision that accounting reform should be effected with the aim of creating a system which complied with the company law harmonization directives of the EU. The long-term political aim of joining the EU was consciously established in Romania, as indeed in other European countries in transition, in the early 1990s. Adopting wholesale a French model would, of course, ensure compliance. (Hungary, to a large extent, took a similar route in its inspiration from the German model; Kazakhstan, with no aspirations to join the EU, decided on wholesale adoption of another country's model: the basis of accounting there is essentially that of US GAAP (Generally Accepted Accounting Principles).) Within the EU the Anglo-Saxon model of accounting has been in the minority, used essentially in the UK, Ireland, the Netherlands and Denmark. It would therefore make sense to look to a continental model for inspiration and, given the close historical ties with France, it is not surprising that the specific French model of accounting would present attractions to Romania.

Feleagă and Ionaşcu go further than this. They present a number of arguments relevant to the Romanian choice – arguments which read more like *ex post* justifications, it should be said. They suggest, *inter alia*, that the Romanian situation at the turn of the 1990s was one which required an accounting system where financial data for macroeconomic purposes were as important as for stakeholder reporting; where the Romanian economy was characterized by a large number of small and medium-sized enterprises and the absence of developed financial markets so that bank and government financing of companies was critical; and where a strong tax/accounting link was not disadvantageous (it should be added with hindsight that, given the difficulties in revenue-raising in Romania, such a link might present positive advantages). All of these features could be said to be found in France, at least historically at the time when the foundations of that country's accounting system were established.

Richard criticizes these 'technical' arguments of Feleagă and Ionaşcu although his dismissal of most of them is in terms of a discussion of the Romanian accounting chart (PCG) rather than of the Romanian accounting system as a whole. He suggests that the explanation for Romania's choice lies in the conjunction of power interests. On the one hand, the interest of France, its industry and accounting profession, gave rise to a desire to promote and develop that country's economic base in Romania by 'pushing through French accounting ideology' (1995, p. 318). On the other hand, pressure existed in Romania from a pro-French camp of accounting specialists and academics (amongst whom Feleagă and Ionaşcu could be counted) who wished to strengthen their power with respect to the other parts of the Romanian accounting élite (1995, p. 316) and particularly those who supported the prior Soviet model of accounting.

Whatever the nature of the explanation for Romania's choice of the French model and the justifications for that choice, three important issues stand out. The first is that there was a mix of predisposition and strategic interest on the part of the Romanian authorities in making that choice. Equally, the role of specialist advisers was a major factor in the establishment of the French model. Finally, there were solid grounds, in terms of the Romanian economic situation, for choosing a continental model of accounting. It was never suggested that the French model was inappropriate for Romania. For these reasons it is doubtful whether one could characterize the adoption of that model as 'culturally intrusive'.

Order 430/1999 of the Romanian Ministry of Finance

It is difficult to pin down how and why doubts arose as to the wisdom of Romania's choice of accounting model. A number of factors may have been at work. Perhaps most obvious among these was the growing recognition that the French model was not well adapted to the delivery of financial information to financial markets. The Romanian government had over the 1990s been keen to develop the country's stock exchange both as a symbol of a market-based economy and as some kind of attractor for foreign investment. The recognition, also, of the importance of US investment in the country may have directed attention towards the Anglo-Saxon model of accounting, particularly in the light of actual and planned privatization of state enterprises. Also important may have been an increased awareness in the Romanian accounting community of other accounting systems. The major international accountancy firms had established offices in the country and courses on international accounting are now offered in some of Romania's leading universities (notably the ASE, Bucharest). Books have been written on international accounting matters, for example Feleagă (1995, 1996). Even this author, identified as being 'pro-French' by Richard (1995), suggested, in the context of a discussion about conceptual frameworks, that there is, perhaps, a need for change in Romania (Feleagă, 1996, p. 282). A further factor was, of course, the growing significance of the work of the IASC in the 1990s. This body, with its

Anglo-Saxon emphasis on 'due process' and standards, has, in European terms, overtaken the EU directives as a force for accounting change (exemplified, most obviously, in the EU Commission's decision in 1995 to give its support to the work of the IASC) and taken on immense influence as a result of its agreement with IOSCO.

Whatever the exact reasons for a change in attitude towards accounting reform in Romania, the agreement between the Romanian Ministry of Foreign Affairs and the UK government in 1996 to have a team from the UK, financed by the British Know How Fund, to advise on further reform marked a major change in accounting outlook. After discussions with a number of bodies in the UK, the ICAS was chosen to provide the specialist advice. It is worth noting that it was an agreement with the Romanian Ministry of Foreign Affairs, not the Ministry of Finance – which is the Ministry responsible for accounting matters.

The outcome of the advice and deliberations of the Romanian authorities appeared in April 1999 in the form of an Order from the Ministry of Finance (403/1999); an English translation of this Order was published by the British Know How Fund in June 1999.

The Order itself is entitled 'Accounting Regulations harmonised with the 4th Directive of the European Economic Community (EEC) [*sic*] and with International Accounting Standards, Volume 1'. The international orientation is thus clear. The reference to Volume 1 is significant since there are a total of four volumes planned. Volume 1 sets out the basic accounting principles and rules for individual enterprises (there was, in 1999, no current legal requirement for consolidated accounts in Romania) governing the form and content of general-purpose financial statements. Volume 2 is a translation of the IASC's Conceptual Framework; Volume 3 will contain both IAS and National Accounting Standards (the latter will comprise both mandatory and optional standards and be established in cases where no relevant IAS exists). Volume 4 will contain professional guidance notes. The sequence of accounting authority, both now and in the future, of these volumes is prescribed in the Order (Art. 3.8). Volume 1 must be in conformity with the EU Fourth Directive and with extant IAS, to the extent that these do not contradict the directive. Volume 3 must always respect the provisions of Volumes 1 and 2.

Volume 1 of the Regulations contains two chapters: the first sets out the principles, rules, formats and contents of individual entity financial statements; Chapter 2 contains definitions of 41 accounting terms and concepts. Chapter 1 itself is divided into ten sections: Table 1 sets out the subject matter of each section. The Preamble of Chapter 1 lays out a number of complex transitional arrangements for Romanian enterprises. The main features of these require listed companies to apply the regulations for the 2000 year-end and by 2006 year-end only 'small' enterprises (defined in terms of the Fourth Directive's conditions) will not be required to follow them. Starting with the 2000 financial year, enterprises may be permitted, with ministry approval, to apply the regulations in advance of the timetable, depending on the progress of a national training programme.

Volume 1 also contains a Foreword whose phrasing provides some interesting insights into the thinking behind the creation of the Order. It is clear that the Ministry of Finance views the Regulations in terms of a continuity of development of accounting since 1990. The Regulations themselves exist within the framework set up by the 1991 Accounting Law and it is made clear that this Law does not require modification, at least in the near future (Foreword, s.4). The Foreword also makes explicit the notion that the Order is only part of further accounting developments and provides a list of these. The EU and IASC dimension is paramount but reference is made also to the development of capital markets and the privatization process. An indication of the Anglo-Saxon orientation is given in the aim of:

> Instituting the possibility of adopting rules dealing with the alternative treatment of certain events and transactions which use professional judgement to meet the criterion of a 'true and fair view'. (Regulations, p. 11)[1]

Mention has been made of an English translation of the Ministerial Order, published by the British Know How Fund. Each page of this translation is footnoted by the statement 'The British Know How Fund accepts no responsibility for the contents of this document. Reference always should be made to the original Romanian text.' It is just as well that this statement is included: the document illustrates the dangers and difficulties of the translation process. Translation is always difficult in accounting but, in many places, this document is unfortunate in its use of English. There are straight mistranslations and obscure English (for example in Art. 5.12(c) where *deprecierea* is translated as 'amortisation/depreciation' instead of 'diminution in value' – a translation which makes the whole section meaningless), additions (for example the document suggests that a Statement of Total Recognized Gains and Losses forms part of the annual financial statements in Art. 3.4 – the Romanian text makes no mention of this Statement although Art. 5.58 does require a traditional equity reconciliation to be disclosed in the notes), omissions (for example a translation of the last sentence of Art. 4.22 is missing), inconsistencies (for example *întreprindere* is variously translated as 'ownership unit' or 'individual entity'). In the discussion which follows the advice of the document is taken.

International influences

It is in the shape, content and linguistic style of the Order itself that we can see the various foreign and international influences upon Romanian accounting at work. These influences can be divided into four main elements. The first two are international and explicit: the IASC and the EU Fourth Directive; the second two are foreign national influences, those of France and the UK.

The EU influence is most obviously seen in the structure of the Order which, mainly parallels, in the sequencing of its sections (Table 5.1), the Fourth Directive. The nature of the annual financial statements (Section 3) is followed by sections on form and content of those statements (5.4), accounting principles and rules (5.5), notes (5.5) and matters concerned with the approval, audit and publication of the annual report (5.6–5.10); this ordering is broadly that of the Directive. The explicit aim of harmonization with the Directive is, of course, the central influence: the content of the Order is consistent with the Directive, at some points slavishly so. Thus, for example, the balance sheet format (Art. 4.10) shows the relevant captions for formation expenses and development costs complete with the parenthesis '(insofar as legislation permits them being shown as an asset)'[2] duplicating the Fourth Directive (Art. 9) and this despite the fact that the Order does permit such capitalization (Arts 5.20 and 5.21).

Perhaps the most significant amendment to the Directive's contents lies in the nature of the requirement for a true and fair view (*o imagine fidelă*) to be given. Article 2 of the Directive specifies the nature of annual accounts, requires those accounts to be prepared in accordance with the Directive's provisions and to give a true and fair view (TFV). If applying the provisions is not sufficient to give a TFV, additional information must be given. Finally, in exceptional cases, a provision of the Directive must be departed from if applying that provision would not result in a TFV. The Romanian Order extends these requirements considerably. First, the annual accounts to which the TFV requirement applies include a cash flow statement (*situaţia fluxurilor de trezorerie*)

Table 5.1   Contents of Chapter 1, Volume 1 of Romanian Accounting
Regulations (403/1999)

Section	Articles	Subject-matter
1	1.1–1.4	Accounting procedures for individual enterprises
2	–	The accounting year
3	3.1	The annual financial statements of enterprises
4	4.1–4.30	Form and content of enterprise financial statements
5		Accounting principles and rules
	5.1–5.11	Accounting principles
	5.12–5.31	Accounting treatments
	5.32–5.45	Alternative accounting treatments
	5.46–5.86	Notes to the accounts
6	6.1–6.3	The approval and signing of enterprise financial statements; the approval of profit distributions
7	7.1–7.2	The administrators' report
8	8.1–8.2	Audit
9	9.1–9.5	The laying and delivering of enterprise financial statements and annual report
10	10.1–10.3	The publication of the enterprise's annual report (and financial statements)

although details and the format of this Statement are not contained in
the Order (Article 4.30 makes it clear that the format will be prescribed
in Volume 3). The fact that a cash flow statement is required is, perhaps,
just one example of IASC influence (IAS 1 (revised), s. 7). The second
difference relates to the fact that Romanian enterprises are required not
just to prepare their annual accounts in accordance with the 1991 Law
and the Order but also in accordance with the Conceptual Framework of
Volume 2 and the mandatory Standards of Volume 3 (Art. 4.3). This
raises the interesting issue of potential conflicts between the 1991 Law
and the 1999 Regulations on the one hand (based on the Directive) and
Volumes 2 and 3. Although the EU Directive is held to be consistent
with IAS with the exception of certain valuation issues such as marking
to market, it is by no means clear that the IASC Conceptual Framework,
particularly in its definitions of the elements of financial statements, is
so consistent. Equally, the terminology used by the IASC is not always
compatible with that used in the Directive. The mandatory Accounting

Standards of Volume 3 are not available although it is clear that these must be consistent with the Regulations of the Order (Art. 3.8). These Accounting Standards will therefore not have the role assigned to them as in the UK.

The Directive's requirement for additional information to be given is provided for in the Order (Art. 3.6) and the 'exceptional cases' clause for departure is also included – but with a wider remit. Art. 3.10 makes it clear that if 'special circumstances' (*împrejurări speciale* – the use of this term perhaps betrays a UK influence since 'special circumstances' is the phrase used in the UK Companies Act 1985 whilst 'exceptional cases' is the phrase of the English-language version of the Fourth Directive) prevail in an enterprise, departure is only possible if compliance with all three volumes (that is, including the Conceptual Framework, IAS and mandatory NAS) is inconsistent with the requirement to give a TFV. This would appear to make departures extremely unlikely.

The IASC influence is also self-evident in the Order; it is, of course, an explicit aim of the Order to harmonize Romanian accounting with IAS, in so far as this does not contradict the Fourth Directive (Foreword, s. 2; Art. 3.8). Volumes 2 and 3 emphasize that influence and the above discussion of the requirements for a Romanian TFV illustrates the integration of IAS and the Conceptual Framework into Romanian laws. The influence can also be seen in some of the detail of the Order. For example, Article 5.21 deals with valuation rules for development costs. This suggests that such costs will be included in the balance sheet only in the named situations described in Volume 3.[3] This is a reference to IAS 9, withdrawn in 1998. A similar influence can be seen at work in the maximum period for the amortization of (non-)consolidation goodwill (*fondul comercial*) of 20 years (Art. 5.22(b)) which is, of course, the maximum period specified under IAS 22 (revised 1993). IAS 22 of 1998 removed this maximum.

Perhaps more significantly, the Order prescribes the use of some accounting principles (*principiile contabile*) in the preparation of financial statements which clearly owe their origin to IAS 1 rather than the Directive. Articles 5.2–5.9 of the Order prescribe nine principles, six of which duplicate those set out in Art. 31 of the Directive with three being drawn from IAS. Article 5.8 lays down the offsetting principle (*principul necompensarii*) which forbids the offsetting of assets against liabilities and income against expenses – a notion expounded in IAS 1 paras 31–7. Article 5.10 sets out the principle of materiality (*principul pragului de semnificaţie*), a new idea for Romania where, because of the strong tax/accounting link, the annual accounts of enterprises have been used for tax assessment, requiring detailed figures to be provided. This principle relates to paras 29–32 of IAS 1. Finally, the Order incorporates the critical notion of 'Substance over Form' (SOF) in Article 5.9 (*principul prevalenţei economicului asupra juridicului*). In the 1997 revisions to IAS 1 SOF was made into a key notion in establishing the reliability of financial statements where no specific IAS exists (IAS para. 20(b)). The identification of SOF as a separate accounting principle in the Romanian Order appears to be more in the spirit of the original IAS 1 in putting it alongside other principles. As will be suggested below, the incorporation of this principle in Romanian accounting regulations introduces a potential contradiction with other components of those regulations.

Foreign national influences upon Order 430/1999

France

It is probably not surprising that, given the history of post-1990 Romanian accounting reforms, there should still be a strong French influence upon the Order. The Order, of course, operates within the framework of the French-inspired 1991 Accounting Law and until that Law is amended, the Order had to be consistent with it.

These French influences are pervasive and powerful and can be illustrated in a number of dimensions. Perhaps the most obvious lies in the existence of Volume 2 of the Order: the definitions of accounting terms. The 1982 French PCG contained a list of key accounting terminology with brief descriptions of each term; such an approach has no real parallel in the Anglo-Saxon world although the various conceptual frameworks do provide definitions of the elements of financial statements. The definition of accounting concepts is also of current concern in Romania in the deliberations of a national working party about the translation of key terms of IAS into Romanian.

A second dimension of influence lies in Section 1 of the Order: accounting procedures for individual enterprises. Two points are worthy of note here. The first is the simple point that the Order, as the 1991 Law, is, throughout, applicable to individual enterprises (*întreprinderii*), not just limited liability companies of the form outlined in Article 1 of the EU Fourth Directive or of the UK Companies Act. In this, Romania is following the French example: in implementing the Directive, France decided to amend its *Code de Commerce* (which governs virtually all enterprises) in line with the Directive. With some exceptions (notably on the publication of annual accounts) the Directive applies to all enterprises governed by the Code. Romania appears to have followed the same path (this is, of course, consistent with IAS 1 in the sense that this standard does not specify particular legal forms of enterprise).

The second dimension resides in the detail of Section 1 which essentially deals with the formalities of accounting records in enterprises and is based on Articles 6–25 of the 1991 Law. This concern for the legal form of accounting records is part of a French accounting tradition going back to the Colbertian *Édict* of 1673 and Section 1 simply replicates, for the most part, French regulations. Of particular interest is the reference to 'evidential documents' (*documentele justificative*; French: *pièces justificatives*). Such documents play a key role in French law as a means of proof (Esnault and Hoarau, 1994) for the regulation of business both by the state (including the tax authorities) and for the resolution of business disputes. In the concern for the legal form of accounting records Romania has taken on a cultural tradition which, if not inconsistent with the notion of SOF for the presentation of financial statements, points up a set of attitudes towards accounting and financial reporting far removed from the pragmatism and informality of most Anglo-Saxon accounting systems. These attitudes towards accounting records find their fullest expression in the form of an accounting plan and use of an accounting chart.

Another dimension of French influence in the Order is in the retention of the concept of 'patrimony' (*patrimoniul*; French: *le patrimoine*) to which frequent reference is made, including reference to 'patrimonial operations' (*operaţiile patrimoniale*). The concept of patrimony is well established in a number of continental accounting systems (including Spain and Italy) although its significance is not always appreciated in Anglo-Saxon countries. This significance is, perhaps, most obviously underlined in the phrasing of Article 2 (3) of the EU Fourth Directive. The English-language version of this reads:

> The annual accounts shall give a true and fair view of the company's *assets, liabilities*, financial position and profit and loss.

In the French-language version the italicized words are substituted for by the single word *patrimoine*.

'Patrimony' in a number of continental countries is a legal concept which refers to the net assets which *belong* to a business. The implication is that it refers to the *legal* rights and obligations of that business at a point of time (Roberts, 1993). The balance sheet, then, would contain only items that are legally owned and owed by the business. The emphasis is on legal form rather than economic substance. The concern for recording patrimonial operations, for constructing a patrimonial balance sheet in the Romanian Order thus sits uncomfortably with the SOF principle enunciated in Art. 5.9. It seems clear that there is a philosophical contradiction here. On the one hand, Volume 1 uses the patrimonial concept; on the other, Volumes 2 and 3 would reject it. The acid test for this concept is the accounting treatment of finance leases. In countries like France and Italy such leases cannot be capitalized in individual enterprise accounts because[4] the fixed asset which is the subject of the lease does not form part of the enterprise's patrimony (Spain has found a way around this by requiring finance leases to be capitalized as an *intangible* fixed asset: the right to use the fixed asset is a legal right). In Romania's case finance leases are now required to be capitalised (Order 686, June 1999). The Order implicitly recognizes this treatment by requiring disclosure in the Notes (Art. 5.68) of operating lease (*leasing operational*) charges to the profit and loss account.

Another French legacy to the Order lies in the procedures for the annual inventory (*inventarierie patrimoniului*) which, as the Romanian term indicates, is linked to the notion of patrimony. Following French rules (*Code de Commerce*, Art. 12), the Order prescribes that items entering the patrimony of the enterprise shall be recorded at their 'entry value' in the accounting records, this being for assets, in most cases, the purchase price or production cost (Art. 5.12). At the end of the accounting year, following the annual inventory of all assets and liabilities, an 'inventory value' (*valoarea de inventar*) for all these items shall be taken and this value compared to the entry value or, in the case of fixed assets, the carrying value (*valoarea contabila*). The nature of the inventory value depends on the type of asset or liability. Art. 5.12 sets out a series of actions to take depending on the nature of the item and whether the inventory value is higher or lower than the book value (entry or carrying, as the case may be). Crucially, if the inventory value of fixed assets is lower than the carrying value, either extra depreciation must be provided for if the difference is considered permanent, or a provision for diminution in value must be created if the difference is considered to be temporary (Art. 5.12 (c)).

All of this is taken from French law (D83–1020, Art. 7) and represents a very particular way of dealing with asset valuation. The procedures for annual inventory, the concept of patrimony, the establishment of inventory value, and the construction of provisions for diminution of value, although linked to the recent IAS 36 on the Impairment of Fixed Assets, are not at all the same. It is not clear how the requirements of Art.

5.12 will mesh with this IAS which, of course, forms an element of Volume 3. This problem is underlined by a consideration of the general nature of provisions for liabilities and charges in the Romanian legislation. Although these provisions are not defined in the accounting terminology of Chapter 2, Volume 1, their nature is described in Art. 4.24. This specification appears to have been taken from the EU Fourth Directive, Art. 20:

> Provisions for risks and charges are constituted with the aim of covering losses or debts which are clearly defined as to their nature and which, at the balance sheet date, are probable or certain to be incurred but undetermined as to value or date of when they will occur.[5]

It is perhaps unfortunate that this definition does not fit well with the recent IAS 37 on provisions, which has a more restrictive view of their constitution, based on the notion that provisions are a liability.

There are many other French influences upon the Order, for example, in the conception of the accruals principle (Art. 5.5) (*principiul independenţei exerciţiului*) which is based on the French *principle d'indépendance des exercises* and which is wrongly translated as the matching principle in the British Know How Document. But perhaps the most surprising retention of French influence in the Order is in the format for the profit and loss account (*contul de profit şi pierdere*). The 1982 French PCG prescribed only one of the four formats for this financial statement permitted under the EU Fourth Directive – the horizontal, by nature format[6] Article 4.27 of the Order provides for a vertical, by nature format.

This form of presentation is, of course, consistent with the EU Fourth Directive and IAS 1 – but it is, none the less, a surprising choice. If one central purpose of the Order is to encourage foreign investment, capital market development and a general orientation towards international accounting practice, then one would have expected to see a vertical, by function (revealing cost of sales and gross profit figures) format being, at least, permitted. The fact that such a presentation is not allowed may have something to do with the construction of the Romanian PCG and the demand by the state for financial information relevant to macro-economic policy (notably in the extraction of value-added data) and tax assessment. On the other hand, a by function analysis is required to be disclosed in the notes (Note 5, set out in the Romanian Official Journal, Nr. 480/4 October 1999).

The UK

The above discussion has indicated that French accounting thinking permeates a lot of the content and style of the Order – a fact perhaps not surprising given that this Order is within the framework of French-inspired 1991 Accounting Law. It is also clear, not just because of Volumes 2 and 3, that IAS have also brought an Anglo-Saxon flavour to the legislation. But what specific British influences have been incorporated into this accounting reform? There are a number which are immediately apparent.

Perhaps the most obvious lies in the nature of the financial statements themselves. As mentioned earlier, the annual financial statements comprise four elements: the balance sheet, profit and loss account, cash flow statement; and notes. The level of detail in the balance sheet and profit and loss account is far more British than French. French formats rely on a larger number of captions than their British equivalents – the latter reveal the minimum required by the EU Fourth Directive. Another British influence can be seen in the notes. These are described in the Order as *notele la conturile annuale*. (This Romanian phrasing is perhaps significant: in the 1991 Law the notes are referred to by a single word: *anexa*. This latter word is used in French legislation: *l'annexe*). The French approach has been to conventionalize and schematize this 'annexe', to place it on an equal footing (Matt and Mikol, 1988) with the balance sheet and profit and loss account – an approach adopted in the Romanian 1991 Law. The change of terminology in Romanian marks, it could be said, a change in approach: the notes will be just that – a set of miscellaneous pieces of information in an Anglo-Saxon style which detail, expand and comment upon the other elements of the financial statements.

The particular feature of the financial statements which is British in origin is, however, the format for the balance sheet. Article 4.10 sets out this format which is vertical; that is, captions for net current assets and total assets less current liabilities are shown. The prescription of this format is odd: this presentation of the balance sheet, although permitted by the EU Fourth Directive, is definitely minority practice in the EU; indeed, it is not known in the US. It is even more curious that the positioning of the caption 'Accruals and Deferred Income' (*Venituri în avans şi cheltuieli angajate*) is such that it is not visually part of 'Creditors due in less than one year' and 'net current assets' as it is in Schedule 4 of the UK Companies Act. In format terms, therefore, the Order has chosen a French-style profit and loss account format and a

British style balance sheet format. It is hard to see the reasons for, and benefits of, this arrangement.

British influences can also be seen in the use of language in the Romanian text. Despite a prevailing French approach to asset valuation, the shape of the rules governing this area is British. Articles 5.12–5.31 group the rules for valuation according to the historical cost accounting rules of Sch. 4 of the 1985 Companies Act; Articles 5.32–5.45 provide analogues of the alternative accounting rules (*tratamente contabile alternative*) contained in that UK legislation although there are many points of difference.

These stem from the experience of inflation in Romania and the Order makes reference to an NAS on Inflation Accounting in Volume 3 and government revaluations. However the rules for the treatment of any revaluation reserve (Arts 5.4–5.45) broadly follow similar rules in para. 34, Sch. 4 of the UK Companies Act.

There are other UK influences on the language and content of the order but it is often difficult to disentangle what is specifically British and what is inspired directly by IAS. Mention should, however, be made of the implicit relationship between tax and accounting within the Order.

It does seem clear that in the Order there has been a deliberate attempt to alter the strong tax/accounting relationship which exists in the 1991 Accounting Law. This Law was modelled on French regulation and practice in which the tax-deductibility of expenses depended upon them being registered within accounting records and where the annual accounts of enterprises form part of the annual tax return. Specific intrusions of tax existed in the existence of 'regulated provisions' and the tax-deductibility of provisions for diminutions in value. In the 1999 Order one can see some modifications of this strong linkage. Regulatory provisions (*provisioanele reglementate*) are nowhere mentioned in the Order; nor does a caption appear for them in the balance sheet. Curiously, however, an account code (14) for these provisions is still listed in the chart of accounts published in the Romanian Official Journal (Nr. 480/4 October 1999). Indeed, very little reference is made to tax matters, as one would expect, although there is a critical note required (Arts 5.69 and 5.70). These two articles require disclosures of the difference between tax charged and tax payable in the financial year, provided that this difference is material, and a reconciliation of the accounting profit for the year 'and the taxable profit as shown in the tax return'.[7] This is in accordance with the EU Fourth Directive, Art. 43, 1(10) and (11).

These words are significant in the sense that they suggest that deferred tax can arise and that accounting profit cannot be assumed to be the same as taxable profit. The disclosure of the reconciliation mirrors a requirement in Spanish legislation when that country moved from an accounting system based on fiscal imperatives to one where there was a clearer separation of accounting and tax matters. Whether, in practice, this separation will be achieved in Romania will depend heavily upon the behaviour of the Romanian tax authorities with respect to accounting records and statements and also the behaviour of enterprises.

One acid test for the influence of tax upon accounting is in the calculation and treatment of depreciation of fixed assets. In the UK accounting depreciation is based on an estimate of the 'useful economic life' of fixed assets (para. 18, Sch. 4, 1985 Companies Act); depreciation for tax purposes is based upon a system of 'capital allowances' determined by the UK tax authorities.

The relevant article for depreciation in Romania (Art. 5.16) is almost a word-for-word translation of para. 18 of Sch. 4 – except in one crucial respect. In place of 'limited useful economic life' is substituted the phrase 'normal life of limited functioning'.[8] This phrase, which is difficult to translate elegantly, omits a reference to the word 'economic'. This may be significant in that it allows depreciation to be established without regard to the circumstances of enterprises and in line with nationally (and tax) set asset lives.

Conclusion

How should this accounting reform be assessed? Perhaps the first approach should be to view it in the context of its stated objectives: to develop Romania's accounting system in continuity from the 1991 Accounting Law in line with the European and IASC frameworks. It is clear that, broadly, this aim has been achieved. The Order is consistent with the EU Fourth Directive and Volumes 2 and 3 in particular will enshrine in Romanian legislation both the IASC conceptual framework and the body of IAS.

It is when we look at the detail of the reform that doubts arise. The prevailing accounting philosophy in the Order is French-inspired and the range of actual and potential conflicts and confusions between a system based on legal formalities and tax domination of accounting and the broader IAS spirit is quite wide. How will Romanian enterprises deal, for example, with the construction of provisions, asset impairments, asset recognition and so on given that Volume 1 adopts an approach which is not necessarily consistent with Volumes 2 and 3? Will there really be an accounting for economic substance given the continuing notion of patrimony? Will the Romanian tax authorities continue to exert an undue influence upon the way that enterprise accounting is done?

It is clear also that the Romanian government has been encouraged to look towards a more Anglo-Saxon orientation for its accounting system with the aim of encouraging more foreign investment and making the financial statements of listed companies and privatized state enterprises more transparent to international investors. How far will the reform assist this aim?

Again, a claim can be made for the reform to have done this by requiring such enterprises to use IAS in their financial statements. But the retention of a by-nature profit and loss format and the prescription of a British-style balance sheet may just indicate a certain confusion about the nature of Romanian rules to the outside world. Equally, the credibility of the financial statements for outside investors is related to the quality of the account preparers, the enforcement of the accounting rules and the quality of audit. It is unclear how easy it will be for Romanian accountants trained first in the pre-1990 period and then retrained in the French-inspired accounting framework of the 1991 Accounting Law to adapt to a system of accounting where professional judgement is called for. Much will depend on the development of the National Training Programme. Audit plays a critical role in establishing credibility and one cynical view of the substance of the 1999 reform is that it substitutes an Anglo-Saxon 'accounting ideology' for a French one and, in so doing, provides market opportunities for the 'big five' accounting firms in terms of audit.

Other questions remain to be answered. How will the Romanian PCG fit into the requirements of the 1999 Order? If Romanian enterprises are required to operate the PCG, how far will the detailed formalities of accounting procedures implicit in the use of such charts militate against the need to show more flexibility? Much will depend on the attitude of the Romanian tax authorities. In this context it is noteworthy that the new accounting regulations apply to individual enterprises. Other continental European countries have introduced IAS into their accounting systems for listed companies which produce consolidated accounts. Such financial statements do not, in the main, have fiscal consequences since the group is not a taxable entity; they can, therefore, operate a 'dual-track' financial reporting system and preserve, to a large extent, a close tax/accounting link for accounting in individual enterprises.

This is not the case for Romania. Volumes 2 and 3 of the Order will apply to all 'non-small' individual enterprises and it is unclear whether fiscal imperatives will allow the exercise of professional judgement necessary for the operation of IAS.

This last point raises a more general question about the nature of foreign intervention in the development of accounting systems in countries in transition. The IASC has recognized that it is not self-evident that the body of its standards and its conceptual framework are suitable for such countries (and developing countries) by establishing a Working Party to examine this subject. Equally, China, which has broadly taken an IASC route to its 1991 accounting reforms has moved relatively slowly in taking this path and has preserved the right to impose fiscal (and other) national rules over and above IAS.

Romania, it seems, has taken on a more directed Anglo-Saxon approach in this recent accounting reform and superimposed it on a largely incompatible French accounting tradition. The problems of reconciling legal form and economic substance, capital market and bank/creditor orientation, tax exigencies and investor information requirements, accounting training based on procedure and training for professional judgement all loom large for the future. In a real sense these problems are ones which apply in all countries in transition; the pity is that in Romania these issues have been complicated by an attempt, aided by a set of foreign advisers, to apply both 'Anglo-Saxon' and 'continental' accounting traditions to the preparation and publication of financial statements for all 'non-small' enterprises in the country. It is perhaps in this mix of accounting traditions and the additional problems that it will undoubtedly throw up that there is a true cultural intrusion.

Notes

1   Instituirea posibilității și regulilor privind tratamentul alternativ al unor evenimente și tranzacții prin prisma judecății profesionale, astfel încât să fie respectată cerința de 'imagine fidelă'.
2   (când legislația permite capitalizarea acestora).
3   'Cheltuielile de dezvoltare vor fi înscrise în bilanț numai în anumite situații descrise în Volumul 3'.
4   The practical objection to capitalization is, however, a tax matter.
5   'Provizioanele pentru riscuri și cheltuieli se constituie în scopul acoperirii pierderilor san datoriilor clar precizate în ceea ce privește natura lor, dar care, la data închiderii bilanțului, sunt probabile sau certe, dar nedeterminate ca valoare sau ca data de producere'.

6   Reference is made in the French PCG to a vertical format (*en liste*) but this format is essentially a rearrangement of the horizontal one with no netting off of captions permitted – an illustration of the strong French accounting principle of non-compensation (*non-compensation*). This principle is also reproduced in the Order (Art. 5.8).
7   'şi rezultatul fiscal, aşa cum este prezentat in declaraţia de impozit'.
8   'durată normală de funcţionare limitată'.

References

E. Delesalle and G. Gelard, 'Exporter la Comptabilité – Le Système Comptable d'Entreprise', *Revue Française de Comptabilité*, May (1991), 75–85.

T. Duţia, 'The Restructuring of the System of Accounting in Romania during the Period of Transition to the Market Economy', *The European Accounting Review*, 4 (1995) 4, 739–48.

B. Esnault and C. Hoarau (1994). *Compatibilité Financière* Paris: Presses Universitaires de France.

N. Feleagă, *Sisteme Contabile Comparate* (Bucharest: Editura Economică, 1995).

N. Feleagă, *Îmblânzirea Junglei Contabilităţii* (Bucharest: Editura Economică, 1996).

N. Feleagă and I. Ionaşcu, *Contabilitate Financiară: Volumul 1* (Bucharest: Editura Economică, 1993).

N. Garrod and S. McLeay (eds), *Accounting in Transition: The Implications of Political and Economic Reform in Central Europe* (London: Routledge, 1996).

D. Krzywda, D. Bailey and M. Schroeder, 'A Theory of European Accounting Development applied to Accounting Change in Contemporary Poland', *The European Accounting Review*, 4 (1995), 4, 625–57.

J. M. Matt and A. Mikol (1988) in *Principles Comptables at Information Financière* (Paris: Editiens Comptables Malesherbes).

Ministerul Finanţelor, *Reglementări Contabile Armonizate cu Directiva a IV-A a Comunităţilor Economice Europene (CEE) şi Standardele de Contabilitate Internaţionale* Vol. 1 (Bucharest: Editura Economică, 1999).

G. G. Mueller, *International Accounting* (New York: Macmillan, 1967).

C. W. Nobes, 'Towards a General Model of the Reasons for International Differences in Financial Reporting', *Abacus*, 34 (1998), 2.

J. Richard, 'The Evolution of the Romanian and Russian Accounting Charts after the Collapse of the Communist System', *The European Accounting Review*, 4 (1995), 2, 305–22.

J. Richard, *Les Comptabilités et leurs Pratiques* (Paris: Dalloz, 1996).

J. Richard, 'Accounting in Eastern Europe: From Communism to Capitalism', in P. Walton, A. Haller and B. Raffournier (eds), *International Accounting* (London: Thomson Business Press, 1998).

A. Roberts, 'Reflections of a True and Fair View in France', *University of Reading Discussion Papers in Accounting, Finance and Banking*, No. 36 (1993).

A. Roberts, 'The Very Idea of Classification in International Accounting', *Accounting, Organizations and Society*, 20 (7/8) (1995), 638–44.

P. Sucher and I. Zelenka, 'The Influence of French Accounting on Recent Developments of Czech Accounting', Unpublished Working Paper, Thames Valley University (1995).

6
Reforming Pension Systems in Transitional Economies: Case study of Kazakhstan[1]

Yelena Kalyuzhnova

Introduction

Reform of pension systems in the transitional economies has been driven by a number of macroeconomic imperatives: first, to achieve the fiscal retrenchment that has become necessary given the relatively small tax base of many transitional states. The small size of their tax base has made it difficult for them to continue to meet the large contingent liabilities, stretching well into the future, created by the existence of unfunded pension schemes. 'Many governments have failed to accept or understand that, in a market economy, a tax system should be based on laws that establish tax rates and rules for objectively defining the tax bases and should have one paramount objective – to raise revenue as efficiently and equitably as possible' (Tanzi, 1999, p. 23). Second, reform of the pension system has also been necessary because, under central planning, responsibility for providing many social services rested at the level of the firm. Large state monopolies were, effectively, mini-welfare states for their employees. Third, it is widely recognized that funded pension schemes increase the savings rate and hence provide a deeper pool of investment capital for economic development. Obviously, the question of pension reform is intimately related to the more general issue of transfer payments and income distribution policy in transitional economies, among which are interest payments on the public debt.

However, beyond these macroeconomic factors, the relationship between the development of funded pension schemes and that of financial markets is a crucial one: funded pensions cannot exist without the ready availability of financial instruments that match the investment horizons of future pensioners. In the Western countries that have moved from unfunded to funded pensions, for example the UK, these financial markets and instruments had been in existence long before pension reform was attempted. The same was true of the institutional investors and fund managers needed to establish and operate such schemes. However, in the transition economies, as in the developing economies more generally, these types of financial markets are rarely well developed. Indeed, in the transitional economies the problem exists in a particularly acute form since the financial systems were almost entirely bank-dominated, as other chapters in this volume have already discussed. This has necessitated the development of financial markets in parallel with the move from unfunded to funded pension schemes. The enormous practical difficulties that this dual reform presents is the subject of this chapter, which explores the issues through a detailed case study of Kazakhstan.

Pension systems as part of the macroeconomic changes

This section explains the reasons for the breakdown of the pensions systems developed under central planning as the transitional economies began their reforms in the early 1990s. The breakdown of unfunded pension schemes is a phenomenon that has occurred in the developed world as well as in the transitional economies. As de Castello Branco remarks:

> Pension funds world-wide are showing signs of financial stress, making the future size of public pension benefits and/or contribution rates uncertain. As the systems mature and contributions start to fall short of what is needed to pay off the implicit pension debt, the budgetary costs of excessively generous benefits render unreformed systems financially unsustainable and this builds uncertainty into the systems. (de Castello Branco, 1998, p. 8)

However, in the transitional economies these problems have existed in a particularly acute form. All the pension systems of the transitional countries were inherited from the centrally planned system and were based on the pay-as-you-go principle (PAYG) (James, 1997; Kopits, 1992) under which all citizens were eligible for a wide range of benefits (including disability, welfare benefits and so on) as well as old-age pensions. The funding (25.5 per cent of wages) was provided solely by employers.

Employees made no contribution to the plan, and benefits received under the plan were unrelated to the amounts contributed. Payments to retirees were adjusted for inflation once every five years, but since inflation was suppressed in the centrally planned economies the actual adjustments were relatively modest. The retirement age was generally 55 for women and 60 for men with the exception of Poland, where the retirement ages were 60 and 65 respectively. The whole social provision system was the responsibility of the government and of the company where the worker was an employee. The notion of personal or family responsibility to provide for future needs or retirement did not exist.

This system was designed to work under the conditions of the centrally planned economy but was by no means appropriate for transitional conditions, due to the high inflation, drastic increase in earnings, and the decline in national income and employment that was experienced in all transitional countries. By the beginning of the 1990s contributions started to decline due to the fall in industrial output, as well as a rising dependency ratio. Therefore the relations between the government budget and the old-age, disability and survivors' pensions, as well as other social assistance schemes and cash benefits, were unclear. All these schemes are financed from the same source and administered by the same authorities.

The increase in unemployment and the switching of some part of population to the informal sector of the economy caused a rapid decline in the number of contributors (Table 6.1).

The increase in the number of pensioners could be explained by demographic factors as well as by the fact that for some transitional countries the increase in unemployment caused the introduction of new

Table 6.1   Number of pensioners and contributors in some countries of transition (average annual growth rate), 1990–96

Country	Number of pensioners	Number of contributors*
Kazakhstan	3.6	−8.5
Latvia	3.0	−17.7
Russia	1.9	−2.2
Ukraine	1.6	−2.9

* Employment figures for Russia and Ukraine.
Source: IMF, WP/98/151.

legislation which lowered the retirement age. In some transitional countries the liberalized laws granted disability pensions; this again exaggerated the situation. Therefore the system dependency ratio increased, and as a logical consequence of this, the financial pressure became an additional burden to the transitional governments. This burden pushed them to consider new mechanisms and schemes that would make pension finance more flexible and take away from the state responsibility for the ageing society. Most of the transitional countries experienced high inflation, especially at the beginning of transition. Retaining the indexing mechanisms developed under central planning thus placed pension systems under considerable strain. Consequently, some transitional governments took the route of incomplete indexation, thus reducing the pension expenditure / GDP ratio by keeping the growth rate of average pensions well below the growth rate of nominal GDP. However, not all the transitional countries followed this path. In countries like Kazakhstan or Russia, for instance, the government response took the form of an accumulation of pension arrears, which in most cases were never paid in full (especially in the Russian case after the 1998 August financial crisis). Therefore, in the 1990s in some CIS countries, where expenditure growth was contained by the accumulation of pension arrears, pension expenditure did not rise in relation to GDP.

The decline in the living standards was an immediate consequence of such growth. The annual growth of the Gini coefficient,[2] for example, for Russia and Ukraine was three to four times higher than in the UK or US. Between 1989 and 1996 salaries dropped 48 per cent in Russia, which made it even more difficult for the transitional governments to find ways of supporting existing pension systems (UNDP, 1999).

However, it is important to stress that rapidly worsening inequality is not a general phenomenon for transitional economies. At the present time two patterns of inequality have emerged: the Central European pattern (where economies experienced a relatively modest increase in income inequality) and the Southeastern and FSU pattern (where a rapid increase in income inequality took place). 'Social transfers in the form of pensions, unemployment benefits and child allowances increased (relative to GDP) or remained constant in Central Europe, whereas they fell or stagnated at lower levels in Southestern Europe and Former Soviet Union' (UNDP, 1998, p. 20).

Thus during the 1990s the PAYG pension systems in transitional economies can be summarized as exhibiting the following five main features:

1 In the majority of cases the number of contributors decreased (a reflection of the increase in unemployment); at the same time a rapid growth in the number of pensioners took place. This made the system's dependency ratio rise rapidly (IMF WP/98/151, p. 7).
2 Before 1990 the retirement age was low; however, the financial difficulties of the transitional period initiated an increase in the retirement age in some cases.
3 The replacement rates are low for most CIS countries.
4 Weak links between contributions and pension benefits. This is a common feature of the PAYG systems. In the transitional period this was exaggerated by the dependency of the pension size on wage history (contributions) for a limited number of years.
5 Inequalities in the PAYG systems. There are a number of examples of such inequalities which have risen without the conscious direction of policy: for example, some sectors of the economy (in some countries) were exempt from contributions; there are cases of favourable early retirement; as a rule the retirement age for women was lower than for men; however, female life expectancy was higher than male life expectancy, but the net present value of the female worker's pension would substantially exceed that of the male worker.

Due to the declining real sector of the economies as well as continuing fiscal difficulties, the transitional governments have been unable to fulfil their obligations regarding state pension payments and have tried to find different ways to approach this problem.

Therefore, taking into consideration all the failures of the existing PAYG systems, the transitional governments found themselves having to make essential changes in the current pension systems. All the programmes which were produced by the governments included reform within existing PAYG systems as well as the introduction of a completely new system, for transitional countries – the mandatory fully funded pillar (FF system).

Alternatives to PAYG systems

Strictly speaking, before the government decides on the approach for any pension reform, the authorities should evaluate the economic costs of one or another pension programme by looking at its costs and benefits which relate to the total payments and the size of economic activity. Siebert (1997) selected some criteria for evaluating social policy regarding pension development and among them the satisfaction of an intertemporal budget restriction is the main requirement for a new pension system. In other words, there is a strong link between contributions today and future benefits. Another of his points is related to the main goal of a pension system, which is the provision of income after retirement. This goal should be separated from redistributional functions. In this context preference should be given to a system that provides a level of retirement benefits with fewer contributions. Therefore capital accumulation, growth and employment should be taken into account. The final criterion – the actuarial fairness principle – is mainly concerned with the realization of a maximum of equivalence between the present value and benefits for the individual.

One option in a pension reform programme is to attempt to improve and shore up the existing PAYG systems. Practically all the CIS countries made changes in their PAYG systems in the light of the existing schemes' financial weaknesses. Despite their initial enthusiasm for reform, they none the less often took a piecemeal route. The financial collapse of a traditional unfunded social security system could be prevented by some changes in its basic parameters and restrict its cost rate within a reasonable level of payroll taxes. In order to achieve this it might be necessary to increase the retirement age as well as enhancing the administrative efficiency of the system. The pursuit of these objectives could be done through keeping the targeted benefits low, as well as the level of payroll tax. However, if payroll taxes become high, use of notional defined contribution plans may protect against labour market distortions and high evasion of taxes that are likely to ensue.

Summarizing, the whole set of changes could be introduced in the following list of measures (IMF WP98/151):

1   Improving contribution collection.
2   Modifying the indexation formula.
3   Increasing the eligibility age for retirement.
4   Tightening benefits.

However, while these efforts at strengthening the PAYG system were necessary, they did not confront the underlying structural problems created by the governments' commitment to pay future unfunded pensions. One of the key problems here is the elimination of the informal labour market. By reducing the size of the informal market, productivity will grow, which will lead to economic growth. Moreover, none of these methods would be able to provide an environment for long-term savings or would encourage the development of a financial market.

To deal with these structural problems a more radical approach seemed necessary, and the most popular area for debate concerned the introduction of new privately funded savings schemes. In other words, the current system of PAYG would be replaced by a defined contribution retirement income system. The main arguments in favour of such a change are: more adequate pension incomes; lower costs; and a more healthy economic system as a whole. In any case, the result of the pension reform should be targeted not at the macro system as a whole, but should first of all provide a retirement income to the aged population; only secondly should it concern the impact of the pension system on the economy. However, the shift from the traditional defined benefit PAYG system to a defined contribution fully funded system has obvious implications for both the adequacy of pension benefits (which is mainly related to the predictability of pension benefits upon retirement as well as an assurance from the government that retirees will have a decent standard of living) and pension financing. The ensuing debate often found the Ministry of Finance and the Ministry of Social (or Labour) Policy on opposite sides: the Finance Ministry favoured reform and privatization of the pension system, while the Social Policy Ministry attempted to defend the existing unfunded system, even though the latter was becoming increasingly unsustainable.

In view of these considerations, transitional governments have had to consider an alternative to the PAYG system – a mandatory fully funded pillar (FF). The general common feature of this new system is the creation of individual retirement accounts, where mandatory saving is accumulated and invested in financial assets. The main logic of this approach is the establishment of proper economic incentives, which will reduce distortions in capital accumulation and labour supply. The main principle here would be the enhancement of contributory compliance and the development of the financial market.

The macroeconomic situation also plays a role, where there is space for savings, investment and growth. These aspects of reform would be particularly relevant to the transitional economies given their financial needs. In this respect the FF system would be capable of providing an explicit link between benefits and contributions and therefore reduce labour supply distortions. In addition, the FF system would be able to prevent further distortions in the long run by the requirement of a lower contribution rate in order to cover a given replacement ratio, as in theory (and from past practice) the average yield of pension funds is higher than the growth rate of the wage bill. Practical evidence also suggested that the FF system helped to improve the link between economic growth and the financial market (for example the Chilean experience in Holzmann, 1997). However, it would be unrealistic to assume that the effect of these reforms would not touch other areas of the economy, and the Chilean contemporary development is a good example in this respect.

The major differences between PAYG and FF systems are: administrative costs (an FF system will require additional costs compared with a PAYG system, namely spending money on marketing and sales workforces, as well as costs for administering a large number of small accounts); disability risks (private markets can provide better social insurance than the PAYG system); effects on savings; financial market development and growth (all these aspects would be better off in the FF system due to the reduction in labour supply distortions; lower contribution rate, higher possibility to increase savings as well as at least partial investment of the private pension funds' resources to the private financial market); distributive and transparency concerns (the FF system eliminates distributive problems which the PAYG system has due to the weak link between contributors and benefits); as well as political-economy aspects. The political-economy aspects can be explained as follows: in theory the FF systems are considered to be more insulated from the political risk in that the given government will run a fiscal deficit or the public will be forced to bear high tax rates in order to support the repayment of the debt to the social security system. In the FF system, where the contributors are recorded in individual accounts, this risk is substantially reduced. However, it might not be true in some practical transitional cases where the transparency of the reforms, as well as the legal institutions, are weak, and the law cannot prevent the interference of the government in the private sphere. The argument regarding the PAYG system as a high political risk, due to the legacy of the communist past and costly post-communist transition, where the population maintains mistrust of the public sector, is quite simplistic and does not reflect the present situation in the majority of the transitional countries. Of course the population has little respect for corrupted and incompetent governments; however, there is even less faith in the newly established unknown private pension funds, which are reminiscent of previous financial pyramids (see below the example of Kazakhstan). All these issues were explicitly discussed in the literature (WP/98/151).

There are three basic models of fully funded pension schemes already in existence (Table 6.2): Australian–Chilean, German and Swiss models.

Table 6.2 Pension models

Australian–Chilean	German	Swiss
Mandatory occupational pension scheme (Australia) Mandatory private savings scheme (Chile) These schemes are supplemented by small public first pillar systems in order to provide poverty relief.	Large mandatory publicly managed PAYG pension scheme (first pillar) Retirement income provision through private (occupational) pension schemes (second pillar) has minor role.	Sizeable mandatory publicly managed PAYG pension scheme (first pillar) This scheme is supplemented by equally large mandatory private pension scheme (second pillar).

The specific feature of the Chilean pension system is that it is heavily regulated and practically managed by the private sector. At the same time Chile has a public pillar in the form of a minimum pension which is guaranteed by the government. The size of the minimum guaranteed pension is around 25 per cent of the average salary of a worker who has spent a minimum of 20 years of contributions in the country. In the case of a worker who has 40 years of contributions and 20 years of retirement life, he will achieve 60 per cent of a replacement rate if the real return is 5 per cent and real wage growth is 2 per cent. The total costs will depend on the number of pensioners who will rely upon the minimum pension (approximately 1 per cent of Chilean GDP). The treatment of past service is expected to be a recognition bond for the people who switched to the private system of employment. The private tier used to set aside around 10 per cent for long-term capital accumulation. Therefore the role of the private pension funds in the capital market is significant. The Chilean pension system strictly restricts the right of pension funds to invest outside Chile.

The German model may also encourage the development of the capital market for index-linked assets and could also prevent shortfalls as hedging strategies (Davis, 1998, p. 18). This model is dominated by the PAYG system. In 1990 the total assets of private pension funds, as a proportion of GDP, was only 3 per cent. The company-led provision has been slow to develop outside the public sector and among workers in financial institutions. The current German pension system provides 70 per cent of the average net wage earned as a pension benefit for the person who has a 45–year contribution record.

The Swiss pension system is a multi-pillar compulsory system. The public pillar consists of two major parts: nearly 20 per cent of the average covered wages and the payments based on the number of years of contributions; another part is based on the average lifetime indexed earnings. Altogether, the public pension cannot exceed more than 40 per cent of average wages. The compulsory second pillar includes a mandate from the employer (compare with Chile, where the mandate is imposed on the worker). Unlike in Chile, the Swiss workers have the choice of purchasing nominal or real annuities, or have scheduled withdrawals without longevity insurance (Vittas, 1997, p. 39).

Problems in applying fully funded models to the transition economies

A number of problems arise with an attempt to apply any of these models to a transition country. In the first place, there will be an increase in the fiscal deficit, since during this 'transitional' period the government is still obliged to keep to payment commitments for the workers assigned under the PAYG system. Second, the transitional pension systems suffer from a number of common weaknesses: the significant discrepancy between the pension system and demographic old-age dependency ratios as well as low retirement ages; disability provisions, widespread and growing evasion; and on going suffering from the adverse effect of pension indexation. One of the major lessons (which was quite explicit in the Chilean experience) is that radical pension reform is technically and financially feasible, but it will require quite a high transitional cost and the absence of a developed financial market could be a barrier. The adoption of any pension programme will contain policy issues, which would include the future cost of public pensions, reconsideration of the indexation policy, streamlining and activation of the legislative framework, and integration of the newly created private pension funds to the financial system.

Another problem is related to the question of the capability of the countries' financial and regulatory infrastructure to absorb the changes. Pension reform and the establishment of private pension funds require a number of preconditions in terms of financial sector development, for instance a relatively well-developed securities market. The question which arises is how well-developed should the securities market be in order to conduct pension reform? More generally, to what extent is the institutional infrastructure of financial markets in the transition economies capable of supporting widespread use of fully funded pension schemes?

An important difficulty that any transitional government faces in the reform of its pension scheme is the lack of properly developed financial markets. The difficulties with the establishment of the financial market in the new transitional economies have been exacerbated by the recent South Asian and Russian financial crises. Before these crises the international community, as well as national governments, were quite enthusiastic about the establishment of new financial markets with a number of significant privatizations on the way. A further problem is that in a number of the transition economies there is still widespread popular distrust of the financial sector, given previous examples of financial pyramids scandals (in Albania, Russia and Kazakhstan). By the same token, these pyramid schemes are a consequence of the lack of a properly functioning financial sector: where people lack reliable savings vehicles and regulation is weak they may be tempted by the often extravagant promises made by the operators of these schemes. 'One of the most important causes of the growth of the pyramid scheme phenomenon was the inadequacy of the formal financial system' (IMF Working Paper WP/99/98, p. 5). Most significantly, perhaps, is the lack of any institutional infrastructure of financial institutions, markets and instruments necessary to operate privately funded schemes.

The Chilean experience of pension funds suggests that they could play an important role in generating financial resources for the long term as well as serving the growth of capital markets. Therefore this section examines the interaction between pension funds and capital markets.

A macroeconomic policy would be just one of the many conditions which would be required for successful economic development. Another important issue for facilitating relations between pension reforms and the capital market is institutional infrastructure, which should be based on effective regulatory reform. As Norton and Arner point out in the previous chapter, there are some institutional and technical conditions which need to be fulfilled in order to develop the capital market, namely: macroeconomic stability which will provide appropriate fiscal and monetary conditions; and a legal and institutional framework which will provide reassurance of transparency and permanence, employing widely the rule of law in transitional systems as well as practical implementation of the newly created legal infrastructure and wider understanding of the above principle.

These conditions should be implemented, together with considerable attention to financial instruments with a long investment horizon, for example bonds and equities. Previous experience suggests that pension funds could become a source of long-term savings in order to support the development of the bond and equity markets. A credible and well-managed pension system can accumulate long-term resources. For instance the Chilean pension system was expanded from 1 per cent of GDP in 1981 to 43 per cent in 1994. In this respect the accumulation of financial resources has particular economic significance due to the fact that contractual savings are not affected by inflation through interbank borrowing and lending.

The problem of allocating pension fund assets into equity or bonds markets is mainly a question of the country's perception regarding risk and investment limits (regulation). 'Regarding the pension funds, The Commission has proposed on 11 October 2000, a directive on the co-ordination of laws, regulations and administrative provisions relating to institutions for occupational retirement provision. Investment rules will be based on the "prudent-man" principle and ensure that pension funds can invest in risk capital markets'. (Commission on the European Communities, 'Communication from the Commission to the Council and the European Parlament.' Progress Report on the risk capital action plan. Brussels, 18.10. 2000 COM (2000) 658 final. p. 27). Different countries hold different views on this issue: Malaysia and Singapore place pension assets in debt instruments, including governmental bonds; a small share of assets go to equities; continental Europe has quite tight investment limits; Chile does not allow investment in equities and this is still the subject of strict rules.

A quite complicated issue, especially for the transitional economies, is the question of investing in foreign assets. The local financial markets in transitional economies are still in a rudimentary state and diversification between local and foreign assets may increase portfolio return. Moreover, such an approach will help in reducing investment risk. However, unlimited investment in foreign markets could isolate domestic markets from the benefits of the creation of pension funds in the country with long-term financial resources. Therefore it is up to the government to decide what kind of policy the country will employ regarding the above issues. In any case, a transitional government should realize that a country that does not yet have an established and transparent capital market as well as a pension system is weak. In these circumstances the economic system will require tight and precise investment rules – a prudent policy. Step by step these rules could be modified (relaxed) once the domestic capital market starts to mature.

Here the question which will arise relates to the capability of pension fund managers and institutional investors to manage risky investment projects. It will require expertise in structuring collective investment schemes as well as a regulatory infrastructure to ensure that fund managers do not take excessive risks and that customers are protected.

A particular problem with some investment schemes that are not properly regulated is that investment managers may be tempted to follow a high-risk/high-return investment strategy. If they can achieve high returns in the first few years of the fund's existence they may tempt many potential investors to invest with the fund. However, such a high-risk strategy, aimed at short-term maximization of returns to attract market share, may not be consistent with the long-term investment horizons necessary if pensioners are to be guaranteed a reasonable retirement income. This is likely to be a particular problem in the transition economies where investors are inexperienced and mostly unsophisticated – witness the attractiveness of pyramid schemes.

Behind every pension fund there is a manager, whose performance is frequently evaluated. Managers are interested in keeping their jobs; therefore the short-term results are crucial in this sense, and obviously this personal factor is shortening their investment horizons, pushing them away from allocating too much into stocks. There is also some evidence of a negative impact on the economy when they invest in stocks due to the tendency to favour layoffs. The basic problem is the one outlined above – the different incentives faced by fund managers, who may aim to maximize market share by showing high-yielding short-term results, and pensioners, who want to maximize retirement income, not immediate returns. There is a clear risk of fraud in this context: managed funds are particularly vulnerable to this type of behaviour, because it involves the exchange of money now for an often vague promise of money in the future.

The logical question is how far the security market is developed to meet the demand for pension funds. For the transitional countries this is not a simple question. Private pension funds can also appear as a powerful source for privatization: they could help to accumulate resources. Furthermore, pension funds could contribute significantly to improving corporate governance and controlling corporate performance. Institutional investors could contribute to the expression of opinions in corporate affairs once the pension funds started to grow. In this way they could help to create more robust structures of corporate governance, lower monitoring costs and so on. For instance, in Latin American countries, particularly in Chile, pension fund managers are required to vote for independent directors.

Pension funds could play a crucial role in financial innovation as well as in the modernization of the capital market. In return, capital markets could provide pension funds with a good opportunity for risk management and portfolio return. Therefore this mutually reinforcing link will definitely require the appropriate macroeconomic conditions, including low inflation, relatively small budget deficits and positive long-term real interest rates. Once private pension funds are established, long-term financial resources should accumulate rapidly. They can then play a major role in modernizing securities markets, stimulating innovation, fostering better accounting and auditing standards, and promoting more disclosure of information.

The creation of the financial market cannot be accomplished overnight. It requires a long time as well as efforts from all parties (government, participants in the market and so on). Therefore the transitional governments cannot simply abolish the PAYG system and rely only upon newly established pension funds. The creation of the latter is difficult enough; operating them could be impossible for some of the countries.

Pension reform in Kazakhstan

The specific problems of pension reform in the circumstances of a transition economy will now be considered from the perspective of the case study of Kazakhstan. This case study illustrates the genuine difficulties that arise when the government tries to shore up the existing PAYG system, as well as the problems involved in putting a more viable funded system in its place.

The Pension system in Kazakhstan in the 1990s

In 1991 the Kazakhstani government introduced changes in the pension law which were supposed to provide indexation of the pension levels three or four times during the year based on equivalent changes in the minimum wage. The implication of this law became apparent in 1996 when average pension payments were substantially increased compared with the inflation rate. At the same time the item 'pensions' was removed from the national (republican) budget and therefore only the residue of contributions was left as the source of pension finance.

The situation deteriorated due to the effects of demographic factors, increased size of pensions, liberal rules for eligibility to receive benefits as well as decreasing economic activity. This led to a substantial increase in the actual number of people who wished to retire through special privilege rules. The total proportion of pensioners in the population increased from 14 per cent in 1990 to 16.8 per cent in 1994. For example, the World Bank estimates that over one-half of pensioners were on early retirement pensions. However, in the light of the emigration from Kazakhstan, in 1993–96 the number of pensioners declined (IMF, WP/98/151).

At the same time the contribution level dropped significantly. The contribution rate has constantly declined since 1993. The contributions were negatively influencing the profits of the newly privatized enterprises, which of course was not the case in the socialist system, where the notion of 'profit' did not exist. Another problem was in the non-determination of the contributions of the employee. Therefore non-payment could have no possible influence on the future pension of a particular employee. Pension revenue over GDP was declining. At the same time pension expenditure over GDP was constant at around 4.5 per cent, but at the expense of accumulating large arrears. Accumulation of the pension arrears is in a sense a route to resolving the operational imbalances in pension funds due to the delay by enterprises in making their contribution payments.

By 1999 the share of pensions in total public expenditure in Kazakhstan was over 24.2 per cent (Table 6.3). In industrial countries this figure is 14 per cent; at the same time the figure for income per capita is several times higher.

There were also operational administrative problems, which were linked with the organization of the pension policy from above (governmental level), and also practical implementation from below (oblast or regional level, country level). In reality, pension funds were sometimes diverted at the operational level to cover other social expenditures, to the detriment of pensioners. The funds which were targeted to finance other

Table 6.3   Kazakhstan: public pension expenditure, 1993–99 (in per cent of total expenditures of the government, including credits)

1993	1994	1995	1996	1997	1998	1999
17.2	16.3	17.7	25.3	38.2	25.1	24.2

Source: Statistical Agency of the Republic of Kazakhstan.

social obligations were 'borrowed' sources from the pension fund, but were seldom paid back.

At the oblast level there was also a difference in contributions due to the fact that some oblasts were collecting a surplus of contributions, while others were facing a deficit. The absence of a monitoring system, which would have allowed the control of reallocation of funds from one oblast to another, made it difficult to balance the pension system.

The demand in social need increased, while social expenditure dropped sharply. At the beginning of 1996 the pension non-payments were 36 billion tenge (US$500 million), which was 45 per cent of the total pension payments. At the end of 1996, the pension non-payment figure reached 58.2 billion tenge (US$808 million). A total of 75 per cent of the non-payments were considered as non-collectible debts. The Kazakhstani PAYG pension system would become impossible to finance if the system remained unchanged.

Development of a new system

The initial reforms of the first pillar of the PAYG pensions system were started by the creation of a Working Group in 1996 (piecemeal reform). The main components of this included:

1 Increase in retirement age: beginning from 1997, increase by six months per year until the age of 63 (men) from 60 and 58 (women) from 55 by 2002. The remarkable fact here is that the average life expectancy in Kazakhstan is 63.
2 The benefit formula included 60 per cent of the highest recent wage, increased by 1 per cent of base salary above the minimum eligibility criteria (25 contribution years for men and 20 for women). As in other countries, for example Bulgaria, Romania, Russia, Slovenia and Ukraine, the pension contributions are tax-exempt.

'However, since these measures were accompanied by a 50 per cent increase in the pension ceiling, they did not alleviate the financial pressures on the pension fund' (IMF, WP/98/11). In March 1997, the Working Group published and distributed a Concept Paper introducing reforms to the pension system. Later in the spring of 1997 this document was revised and campaigners were travelling throughout the country trying to explain the main changes for pensioners and workers.

When other transitional governments introduced a mandatory FF component of the pension system, the Kazakhstani government took a quite drastic step, adapting completely to the FF system.

The Concept Paper was a basis for a new pension law, which would establish a new pension system. There would be three sources of pension payments: during a period of 30 years, payments would be financed by a tax of 15 per cent of payroll to be paid by employers; a private, mandatory defined contribution scheme (accumulation scheme) would be financed by a deduction of 10 per cent of a worker's wages; and the third scheme would be a private, voluntary defined contribution funded by additional contributions from employers, employees, or both. Contributions for the last scheme would be deductible from taxes up to a certain limit tied to average wages.

Most of the preferential categories were removed, but several exceptions remained, (for example the military, women with five or more children, and the people who lived in the Semipalatinsk nuclear testing area during 1949–63).

In a sense, the newly designed Kazakhstani pension system is a replication of the pure Chilean pension model. The introduction of the new system is supposed to generate a deficit equivalent to nearly 2 per cent of GDP in the first year of the reform. There are two crucial points here which will influence the evolution of the fiscal burden, namely the elimination of the old pension entitlements and speed of introduction of the payroll contribution so that the financing of the old system can be phased out.

The reduction of evasion will be achieved through the looser benefit–contribution link. This will also be the way to ensure that the revenue side will be the source for the bulk of the adjustment. 'The aggregate cost of the transition, in present value terms, has been estimated at about 40 of GDP' (IMF, WP/98/11, p. 34). The natural hope of the Kazakhstani government is revenue from privatization, which could partially cover these costs; however, the rest of these costs will be covered by debt issuance.

A new law was passed on 20 June 1997 with an effective date of 1 January 1998. Therefore the new pension system includes a mandatory private saving pillar (fully funded defined contribution scheme) and a minimum pension, which is guaranteed by the state, which augments the contributions-related pension. Supplementation by voluntary savings is also expected.

Regarding investment-related issues, it is envisaged that the new private pension funds will be active investors in Kazakhstani government securities, bank deposits, private bonds, equities and perhaps abroad. For the first step of the pension reform's implementation it is expected that pension funds will be invested mostly in government securities. In

Table 6.4   Pension indicators, Kazakhstan 1994–99

Indicator	1994	1995	1996	1997	1998	1999
Number of pensioners, M (000s)	2 999	2 980	2 917	2 940	2 853	2 037
Number of employed people, N, (000s)	5 415	4 994	4 380	3 629	3 071	2 314
System dependency ratio (M/N), %	53.5	60	66.6	80.3	92.9	88

Source: Kratkii Statisticheskii Yezhegodnik Kazakhstana, 1998, p. 15, 28.

As Table 6.4 shows, the number of people employed in Kazakhstan has dropped significantly in recent years. At the same time the dependency ratio has increased since 1994 and reached 88 per cent in 1999.

Table 6.5   Pensions and wages, Kazakhstan, 1995–99

Indicator	1995	1996	1997	1998	1999***
Average monthly pension (tenge),* P	997.8	1 876	3 283	3 554	3 964
Average monthly wage (tenge),** W	4 786	6 841	8 583	9 683	11 043
Pension to wages ratio (P/W), %	20.8	27.4	38.4	36.7	35.9

*   Data according to the Ministry of Social Security of the Republic of Kazakhstan, stated at the beginning of year.
**   Without small enterprises and peasant farms.
***   Data for January–September 1999.
Source: Kratkii Statisticheskii Yezhegodnik Kazakhstana, 1997, 1999.

this connection the Kazakhstani authorities were planning to extend the maturities of government securities. A comparison of recent data on pensions and wages has demonstrated (Table 6.5) that during the last three years the pension/wage ratio has stabilized at the level of 36–8 per cent.

Implementation of the pension reform

'At the beginning of 1998, Kazakhstan put into effect a pension reform program to transform the public pension system into a fully funded system...Under the new system, all workers are required to save 10 percent of their earnings in accumulation funds' (Gurgen et al., 1999,

p. 69). At the end of that year the number of such accumulation funds reached 13, of which one was state-owned.

Currently in Kazakhstan the National Pension Agency supervises pension funds. There is one state accumulation fund (which was established by the government and is only authorized to invest in securities issued by the government, deposits of the state banks and international financial institutions), 14 private funds and 6 asset management companies. According to the National Securities Commission the net pension assets exceeded 64.5 bn tenge (US$460.7) on 1 January 2000. A sum of 30.6 bn tenge of the total amount belongs to private pension funds and 33.9 bn tenge is located in the state pension fund. There is a growth in pension assets. However, most people prefer to keep their money in the state accumulation fund – 2.9 million persons, which is 75 per cent of the total fund savings. The pension fund of Naronduii Bank consisted of 395 000 people; fund 'Kazakhmys' – 60 000 people; 'Umit' – 35 000 people; and 'Ular' – 34 000 people. 'Pension funds had invested around Tenge 53 bn in different financial instruments with government debt securities and sovereign Kazakhstani eurobonds dominating – 60.13% and 29.58%, respectively' (*Kazakhstan Weekly News*, 20 September 1999).

This fact demonstrates that the attitude of the population is slowly changing. But the government still needs to do more to restore public confidence in the pension system and financial institutions in general so that the population wants to participate in the scheme with additional voluntary contributions and employers are forced to comply with the law and make the required payroll tax payments.

'The share of expenditure on entitlements to the old pension system made up roughly 60% of expenditures for social security in 1998' (*Kazakstan: Economic Trends*, 1999, p. 35). This is approximately 97476.6 mn tenge. There is a constant decline from year to year in the social security item of the Kazakhstani budget. In 1999 the government cut social spending drastically (for example in the first six months the decline was nearly 31 per cent of spending in 1998).

Assessing the plans to change the pension system in Kazakhstan, one can say that the creation of the new scheme imposes a double burden on the working population: on the one hand they have continually to support the older population; on the other hand they have to save for their own pensionable age. Therefore the transformation of the pension system should be done gradually, over a long period of time.

The financial mechanism of the new system is as follows: a part of the same contribution revenue is reallocated from the PAYG pension fund to the private funds (and, it is hoped, to the financial market). Part of the reallocated money should find its way back to the state budget via government bonds. This is in a sense a costly process due to the fact that financial intermediates will take their share and interest at market rates will have to be paid by the taxpayer. The remaining part of the budget deficit will have to be financed by rearranging the state budget, namely reducing public investment as well as pension benefits (which has already been done).

However, pension reform has not yet boosted the capital market in Kazakhstan, as was originally planned. It would be difficult to predict the exact date of a significant investment in corporate securities by the pension funds, although it is clear that it will not happen earlier than the end of 2001.

In evaluating this irrevocable shift to the FF system which Kazakhstan made, it is important to assess the net present value of pledged state pension benefits. In theory the new system is supposed to produce cheaper and better pensions and take the burden of pension provision from the state. However, it is clear even now that the operating costs of the new FF system are high, which is partially related to the transfers of members' accounts between the different fund management companies.

At the present time Central Asia is faced with two major obstacles in the investment sphere. The first lies in the undeveloped character of the securities markets in the region. The second relates to the changes in consumer behaviour after the collapse of the centrally planned economy system, where the changing pattern of consumer spending took place, leaving the habit of saving in the past.

The non-liquidity of the Central Asian securities market and the associated limited scope for portfolio diversification, as well as a lack of suitable domestic investment assets, will push Kazakhstani pension funds to look for a 'foreign-asset preference'. However, the pension funds could help to promote the future development of the capital market in Kazakhstan.

At the present time there are many worries among participants of the pension reform and the population in Kazakhstan. This is indicated by the fact that the current Minister of Labour and Social Protection, N. Radostovets, expressed his doubts about the overall efficient functioning of existing Kazakhstani pension funds as well as the safety of their assets. However, the Kazakhstani government is trying to convince the population that it is not in a position to change the way in which the pension system is being reformed, and characterizes the speeches of the Minister of Labour and Social Protection as jeopardizing the government's position.

In reality, as was already mentioned in the previous section, the population cannot forget recent financial pyramid scandals (for example Smagulov's pyramid) and quite a substantial part of the population considers the FF pillar in Kazakhstan as a new pension pyramid, with government as the main player. The rule of this game is simple – obligatory contributions, legalized by governmental law, for every employed citizen in Kazakhstan. Practically all collected assets are invested in the securities of the Ministry of Finance. This means that all pension assets will facilitate the deficit of the state budget, which amounts to a virtual tax since the probability of return on payments is not high. The lack of significant changes in the economy prevents the provision of returns any higher than was the case for pension funds.

There are still contradictions and disagreements between the National Securities Commission and the Ministry of Labour and Social Protection. According to the Minister, N. Radostovets, 10 per cent of all pension assets are supposed to be used to finance the real sector of the economy. Particular emphasis was laid on the oil pipeline project Atyrau-Samara. However, G. Shalgimbayeva, the Executive Director of the National Securities Commission, stated that pension assets will not be invested in the real sector of the Kazakhstani economy. The explanation for such reluctance was given in the light of the sacred character of the pension assets; therefore their use should be directed to risk-free financial instruments (*Kazakhstan Weekly News*, 17 January 2000). Such arguments are not satisfactory, especially in respect of the profitable nature of the oil pipeline project Atyrau-Samara. This again demonstrates the unwillingness of some governmental bureaucrats to appropriately direct pension assets. Perhaps it is simplest to direct such investment to easing the state budget deficit, which at the present time requires additional capital injections.

Kazakhstan is only at the beginning of its pension reforms and development of a capital market. But one thing is obvious now – none of the financial or pension reforms will be successful without the proper functioning of the real sector of the economy. It would be an important step in the state governance to ensure that the development of pension reform is accompanied by restructuring of the enterprises. Perhaps the safer way to pension reform for Kazakhstan (as well as in other transitional countries) would be a mixed system, rather than a single privately funded pillar. Realistically, it is premature to expect that the Chilean model of pension reform will be successfully implemented in transitional countries. The gradual approach, in which it would be possible to combine elements from both PAYG and FF systems, would minimize the financial risks facing funded systems. For the new pension in Kazakhstan to work it will be necessary to fulfil two essential conditions: the state must provide, with clear and immutable rules, for the next 30 to 40 years of investing for future pensions; a change of government must not affect such a policy. Industrial growth should be higher than inflation growth; in other words: pension investment will show a return over time.

Conclusion

All PAYG systems in transitional countries were affected by macroeconomic changes: a large output loss, rising unemployment and high inflation. At the present time quite a few CIS countries have already started to address the shortcomings of their PAYG systems via piecemeal reforms.

Kazakhstan decided to move a step closer to long-run fiscal sustainability and has embraced systemic pension reform. It appears that the Kazakhstani reform path will lead eventually to the adoption of the main features of the Australian–Chilean pension model – dominated by a mandatory, privately managed pension scheme.

Therefore the switch is mandatory for all participants, including participants in the old PAYG system. The government will honour all pension rights accumulated under the old system (Palacious and Rocha, 1997). Initially only 40 per cent of contributions will go to the FF system.

Despite the high contribution rates, the financial situation of pension funds in Kazakhstan has deteriorated from the moment of its inception in 1991–92. It was also aggravated by the fact that pension funds carry the burden of providing non-contributory benefits – special privileges out of contributions.

Kazakhstan is undertaking far-reaching reforms, which could both ease the pressure on the budget in the long term and transform the Kazakh fledgling capital market by creating for the first time a pool of long-term savings. 'Most experts agree that the Kazakh reform plan is very ambitious' (IMF/98/11, p. 34). It would be a great mistake to overestimate the stability and viability of pension reforms implemented in transitional economies. In some countries it has not solved anything; others have solved a few old problems, but created new ones. There are worldwide challenges for the twenty-first century: erosion of the traditional contribution base and the world trend of changing labour market arrangements. The newly established pension systems in the transitional countries will have to face these problems.

'The success in implementing pension reform in Kazakhstan will be crucial not only to establishing a sustainable pension system in the country in the long run, but also in view of its role as a model for pension reform in the region' (IMF/98/11, p. 34). In any case it will take a long time for transitional economies to build credible pension systems.

Notes

1 I am grateful to my friend Michael Taylor for his encouragement and for his idea that I should write such a chapter. My thanks go to Pietro Vagliasindi and George Tridimas for their helpful comments. I also appreciate the help of Sylvia Smelt in shaping this chapter. Lastly, my gratitude to my husband Andrei for his unconditional love and support.
2 The Gini coefficient provides a summary measure of inequality. The value of the Gini coefficient ranges from zero (perfect equality) to one (perfect inequality).

References

M. de Castello Branco, 'Pension Reform in the Baltics, Russia and Other Countries of the Former Soviet Union (BRO)', (International Monetary Fund Working Paper WP/98/11, Washington, 1998).

J.F. Charles, 'The Swiss Social Security', *Basic Principles and Structure* (Federal Social Insurance Office, Bern, 1993).

Commission on the European Communities, "Communication from the Commission to the Council and the European Parliament." Progress Report on the risk capital action plan. Brussels, 18.10.2000 COM (2000) 658 final.

P. Davis, 'Policy and Implementation Issues in Reforming Pension Systems' (EBRD Working Paper No. 31, London, August 1998).

Economic Survey of Europe (1990), *Demographic Ageing and the Reform of Pension Systems in the ECE Region*. N3:48.

E. Gurgen, H. Snoek, J. Craig, J. McHugh, I. Izvorski and R. von Rooden, 'Economic Reforms in Kazakhstan, Kyrgyz Republic, Tajikistan, Turkmenistan, and Uzbekistan' (IMF, Occasional Paper No. 183, Washington, DC 1999).

R. Holzmann, 'Pension Reforms, Financial Market Development and Economic Growth: Preliminary Evidence from Chile' (Staff Papers, IMF, Vol. 44, No. 2, June 1997).

E. James, *The World Bank's Three-Pillar System: Will it Provide Income Security to the World's Aging Population?* (American Institute for Contemporary German Studies, No. 26, March 1997, Washington: The Johns Hopkins University).

Kazakhstan Weekly News, 20 September 1999 and 17 January 2000.

Kazakhstani National Statistical Office 'Kratkii Statisticheskii Yezhegodnik Kazakhstana 1997' (Almaty, 1998).

Kazakstan: Economic Trends, July–September quarterly issue (1999), Brussels.

G. Kopits, 'Social Security' in Vito Tanzi (ed.), *Fiscal Policies in Economies in Transition* (International Monetary Fund, Washington, 1992).

R. Palacious and R. Rocha, *The Hungarian Pension System in Transition* (World Bank, mimeo, November 1997).

H. Siebert, 'Pay-As-You-Go Versus Capital Funded Pension Systems: the Issues' (Kiel Working Paper No. 816, The Kiel Institute of World Economics, 1997).

V. Tanzi, 'Transition and the Changing Role of Government' in *Finance and Development* (IMF, Vol. 36, No. 2, June 1999).

UNDP *Poverty in Transition?* (Regional Bureau for Europe and the CIS, New York, July 1998).

UNDP *Human Development Report* (New York: UNDP, 1999).

D. Vittas, 'The Argentine pension Reform and its Relevance for Eastern Europe' (World Bank Policy Research Working Paper No. 1819, Washington, June 1997).

Part III

Supervision and Regulation of Financial Markets

7
International Standards and the Transitional Economies

*Douglas W. Arner**

Law and financial development

The importance of law and law reform to the process of transition and development has been underlined by the recent financial crises in Mexico in 1994, in East Asia in 1997–98, and in Russia in August 1998.[1] One generally agreed conclusion of the many analyses that have followed on these events is that an underlying cause of these crises, or at least an exacerbating factor, was weaknesses in domestic financial sectors and improper sequencing of the liberalization of international capital flows.[2] This is especially significant in the context of transition economies, where development of a functioning financial sector has been (and continues to be) one of the greatest challenges. In this respect, attention to legal reform is essential to financial stability in transitional economies in that it not only underlies efforts to develop financial systems but moreover can strengthen such systems in order to reduce potential vulnerabilities to financial crises. Legal reform can also help countries resist possible international economic contagion (pressure stemming from adverse investor 'herd' behaviour) from financial crises elsewhere which can be extremely dangerous to the development of fledgling financial systems, including those in transition economies.

The financial stability and viability, and hence development, of an economy depend on two fundamental factors.[3] The first factor is the macroeconomic and structural conditions in the real economy which affect financial decisions and form the environment within which the financial system operates. The second factor is the robustness of the financial system itself, comprising the financial markets, institutions and arrangements through which financial transactions are carried out. By their nature, the component elements that comprise a robust financial system depend on legal structures and institutions. Unfortunately, at the beginning of the transition process in 1989, this was was little understood and therefore received very little early emphasis.

Legal structures and institutions serve as the underlying framework for the operation of modern financial markets and are important elements underpinning their development. Transition economies, however, by definition did not need such structures and institutions, but rather functioned (although not well) through central planning and administrative fiat. It was only in the 1990s that attention began to be focused on the need to develop structures to support functioning financial markets as one very significant aspect of the transition process. Today, legal structures and institutions are seen as necessary both to establish and maintain the rules by which participants in the market must play and to build confidence in the financial environment and thereby encourage finance and investment.[4] Further, an effective legal system enables financial commitments to be created and honoured and also governs the conduct of the market in which the underlying transactions occur. Vibrant financial markets require not only that appropriate legal rules exist, but that they operate in an environment where they are effective. While the phrase 'rule of law' has been repeated since the beginning of the transition process, until recently the meaning of the idea and its effective implementation received very little practical attention; for that reason, transition and financial sector development were seen as the field of economists and the role of law was viewed as largely irrelevant.[5] Difficulties and set-backs in the transition process during the 1990s have caused the focus to shift somewhat to the 'rule of law' and related institution-building.[6]

The development of appropriate regulation of financial markets and the creation of effective financial legislation promote financial development and stability in two fashions. First, prudential regulation protects depositors and strengthens their confidence in the financial system as a whole, thereby encouraging savings, investment and the development of effective financial intermediaries.[7] In transition economies, developing a functioning financial sector has become a key goal, necessary to transition and the development of an effectively functioning market economy.[8] Second, a clear and effective legal infrastructure promotes reliance on and respect for contracts that underpin financial dealing.[9] While the 'rule of law' was thought of during the early transition process as an amorphous goal, the development of a functioning legal system is now strongly emphasized, as understanding has developed of the role of law in encouraging business activity generally and in reducing the dangers of corruption and other governance problems. Law therefore must be seen to play a central role in creating and promoting the development of a decentralized, non-corrupt financial system. Additionally, weaknesses in the banking system or in the capital markets of a country can threaten financial stability and development, both in individual countries and internationally, through contagious failures in market confidence, such as those that occurred following the Mexican peso crisis in 1994 and in East Asia beginning in 1997.[10] Thus there has been growing international attention to methods to strengthen financial systems, with various international bodies increasingly acting to develop principles to underlie such efforts at reform.[11] In order to be meaningful, such international principles must be implemented through legal reform, encompassing broad legislative, institutional and cultural changes. Legal reform in transition economies raises special challenges because the transition countries have begun from a starting-point of essentially non-functioning legal systems and general lack of understanding and regard for the role of law in a market economy.

What, then, are the most significant principles underlying financial market stability and development and how is a robust supporting legal system to be developed? This chapter attempts to answer these questions, arguing that the minimum content of the requisite financial laws and the necessary elements of the legal system that makes those laws effective can be discerned through analysis of the demands of the 'rule of law' in the context of financial markets and through recognizing that internationally acceptable minimum financial standards can be distilled from a developing consensus on underlying principles necessary to support the requisite elements of financial systems. Of particular importance are the pronouncements of those international bodies concerned with promoting effective regulation and supervision of financial markets. This chapter will also argue that these principles and their implementation have special importance for transition economies and that it is a project long overdue in its development and implementation.

International financial standards

While financial laws and regulations and their enforcement are fundamental to the development and functioning of sound financial markets, the post-communist countries launched their transition to a market economy with no such institutions. While there was simply no need for them under central planning, the question remains as to what are the legal and regulatory arrangements towards which the transition economies should be moving. Just as there is no archetype for a market economy, there has historically been no unique set of laws and regulations and mechanisms for their enforcement that underpin sound finance: indeed, there is wide variation in these institutional arrangements and practices in market economies worldwide.[12] From this diversity, though, has come a range of experiences and many valuable lessons. Through several international forums government officials and regulators have begun to draw on these experiences to develop 'core principles' for effective financial law and regulation, with these efforts today coordinated through the Financial Stability Forum, established at the instigation of the Group of Seven Indutrialized Nations (G-7). These forums also serve as a mechanism for harmonization of legal and regulatory systems in increasingly globalized and integrated financial markets that expand the potential for jurisdictions with weaker systems to attract financial activity away from those with stronger arrangements. The most important of these underlying principles is that of the 'rule of law'.

While the importance of the rule of law is increasingly emphasized in discussions of the requirements for transition and development, it is little understood or defined in practice.[13] This is especially the case in relation to the role of the rule of law in financial development and transition. The rule of law as applied in the context of financial activities involves issues such as the enforcement of financial contracts, the creation of efficient insolvency and collateral laws and the existence of clear standards of corporate governance. Another key aspect of the development of the rule of law is the effort to combat corruption and money laundering and enhance integrity, which is of great significance in the financial sector, both in initial investments and in on-lending operations.

In the context of transition economies, as noted above, functioning legal systems and the rule of law were unnecessary and non-existent. However, when questions of transition were first being analysed in the late 1980s, law was not seen as significant to financial development; rather, emphasis was placed on various models of mass privatization and 'big-bang' transformation, the theory being that appropriate structures would develop naturally as part of the transition process. In the event, this has not been the case; rather, drastic transitions undertaken without attention to the institutional fabric, including law, have not generally proceeded as successfully as more gradual transition processes integrating development of supporting institutions.[14] As a result, increasing attention is devoted to supporting institutions and the development of the rule of law in transition economies. Unfortunately, until recently, there has been no general consensus on what factors are significant, especially with respect to financial sector development.

Following the Mexican financial crisis of 1994–95 and the US and international rescue operation that it required, leaders of industrial nations recognized the need to develop mechanisms to deal with the potentially systemic dangers of such financial crises.[15] In response to an initiative at the Lyon summit of the G-7 in June 1996, representatives of the countries in the G-10 and of emerging market and transition economies jointly sought to develop a strategy for fostering financial stability through the analysis of key experiences in previous crises and for elucidating basic standards and principles to guide individual nations in the development of stronger financial systems.[16] The primary conclusion to emerge from this study was that a financial system that is robust is less susceptible to the risk of a crisis in the wake of real economic disturbances and is more resilient in the face of crises that do occur.

Experience and study have shown that three key elements are necessary for the development of a strong financial system: (i) the creation of an institutional setting and financial infrastructure necessary for a sound credit culture and effective market functioning; (ii) the promotion of the functioning of markets so that actual and potential stakeholders exercise discipline over financial institutions (typically referred to as effective corporate governance); and (iii) creation of regulatory and supervisory arrangements that complement and support the operation of market discipline.[17] At the beginning of the transition process, none of these elements existed; throughout the 1990s, failures in each of these key elements have led to significant difficulties in various nations. For instance, lack of all three elements can be seen to underlie Russia's crisis in 1998, and corporate governance issues are viewed as central to problems over the past several years in the financial system of the Czech Republic. Countries that have effectively addressed these issues (for example Poland) have been more successful in both financial sector development and overall transition.

Once the key elements are identified, the question arises as to how to develop them effectively in respect of any given financial system. As a result, within this framework for sound financial systems, a number of international organizations have sought to expound agreed minimum principles and standards to be implemented to encourage and improve confidence in and viability of domestic financial systems. The aim of such standards is to promote sound financial institutions, to minimize systemic risk and to encourage savings and investment activity through increased confidence in financial markets, both domestically and internationally. The efforts of these various organizations and the respective principles and supporting documents are now coordinated by and through the Financial Stability Forum, established by the G-7 and administratively headquartered at the Bank for International Settlements (BIS), in Basel, Switzerland.[18] Relevant areas of concern include: the public sector (including policy transparency and data dissemination); banking; securities; insurance; corporate (including governance, accounting and auditing, and bankruptcy); and payment and settlement.[19]

It must be noted at the outset, however, that these international principles and standards are just that: minimum internationally agreed guidelines that leave great latitude in their implementation and effectiveness. Despite their increasing importance, the mere adoption of such standards by any given country will not ensure the viability and development of its financial system. Rather, the question arises as to how to implement these general principles in the legal and institutional framework of a given country. None the less, these principles do for the first time give guidance concerning the minimum requirements to develop in a country's financial system to prepare it for participation in international financial markets.[20] As has been most clearly demonstrated by the volatility of recent international capital flows to and from emerging market economies worldwide, especially in Russia and East Asia, such participation is not without its dangers. Individual countries are therefore increasingly interested in developing effective regulatory and other legal mechanisms that can provide their own financial systems with some measure of protection from such outward capital movements, while at the same time encouraging investment flows to their economies. Such efforts must be seen to be especially significant in the context of the recent development of the financial services liberalization provisions of the General Agreement on Trade in Services (GATS) of the World Trade Organization (WTO).[21]

More importantly for transition economies, the development of an international consensus on the requisite elements of a stable and robust financial system is extremely significant. Obviously, the process of transition and how to achieve it was a new question and one for which answers have not easily been developed. Different countries have pursued different models, based on the theories of different academics, consultants, and international and domestic bureaucracies. A constant, however, is the need to develop functioning market-based financial systems. Before the development of this emerging consensus on principles underlying stable and robust financial markets, financial sector transition and development had to be viewed as at best a haphazard process. While today there is still certainly no single road-map to successful financial sector development, at least there is now, for the first time, general agreement as to the goals to be achieved. This can only be viewed as a very significant step forward and one that is long overdue.

Sound financial and institutional infrastructure

Prudential regulation and market transparency are central to a viable financial system. However, supervision and regulation are only impor-tant if investors actually engage in financial transactions. Accordingly, laws promoting prudential regulation and market transparency must be supported by the development of an effective legal and institutional infrastructure that fosters, in practical terms, financial transactions, including payment, settlement and custody arrangements. These prac-ticalities extend to effective corporate governance, leading to improved corporate performance and increased investor confidence.[22] Finally, both regulation and supervision and the underlying legal infrastructure rely necessarily upon effective accounting and auditing standards and practices.

These sorts of issues have not been addressed in any coherent fashion until very recently. The result has been that they were generally ignored in the transition economies until the mid-1990s. In practical terms, however, the underlying legal and institutional infrastructure should have been addressed at an early stage; the reality, however, has been a general emphasis on larger macroeconomic issues rather than institu-tional and supporting (microstructural) issues in the initial stages, with supporting infrastructures such as accounting, auditing and payments systems not receiving attention initially.

In addition to a sound public law regulatory framework, private law must provide individual investors with a means for participating in financial transactions and for enforcing their rights with respect to their investments. The basic functions of the legal/judicial framework in supporting the financial system are: first, to establish clearly the rights, responsibilities and liabilities of the parties to financial transac-tions; second, to establish codes to support market forces in maintaining appropriate incentives and adequate information; and third, to provide means to enforce legal obligations and claims efficiently. These features may be referred to as the institutional infrastructure for the provision of finance.

In relation to transition economies, these three functions clearly underlie the entire process of transition from centrally planned to market economies. First, property rights, responsibilities and liabilities largely existed in a completely different form and context under the previous system. Establishing meaningful individual property rights is clearly a *sine qua non* of transition, and logically would have proceeded first with the creation of such rights in the various civil codes and constitutions of the transition economies. Second, with property rights arises the need for legal definition of rights of governance and contract, along with systems of information (namely accounting and the press) that are necessary to make property rights meaningful. Interestingly, such ideas were not addressed until after efforts of mass privatization. Third, systems of dispute resolution and enforcement are necessary to make property rights effective. While it seems clear today that a functioning judicial system is necessary to implement and protect property rights, this is still a massive challenge in many countries (and certainly not limited to transition countries).

Necessary legal infrastructure for financial transactions

Based on the experiences of law reform teams within international financial institutions, lessons gained from recent international financial crises and the extensive literature on the topic,[23] core areas of the legal infrastructure that are necessary for the development of functioning decentralized financial markets and the creation of a sound business environment can be identified. While it is also a priority for transitional economies to develop stable macroeconomic frameworks and policies, these policies must be strengthened and supported by the development of an environment of effective laws and institutions. Indeed, experiences in Central Asia have shown that in the context of potentially very lucrative investments (for example in the energy sector), the legal and institutional environment can in fact be as, if not more, important than the existence of a stable macroeconomic framework.

While the following list is by no means exhaustive, these core areas are of great importance and, when combined with an appropriate 'second level' of financial regulation and supervision discussed below, create the necessary environment for the development of viable financial markets.

First, clear and defined property rights must be established as a fundamental precondition for financial transition and development. The creation of property rights is of course a cornerstone of the transition process. In many ways, without the creation of property rights, transition is not possible.

Second, a regime supporting binding and enforceable contracts is necessary in order for financial activity to develop beyond close networks. Investment is predicated on binding and enforceable contracts, without which parties cannot effectively structure their transactions.

Third, adequate company law incorporating principles of good corporate governance is essential for corporatization, privatization and the development of a decentralized financial system.[24] Prospective investors need to be assured that the legislative and contractual frameworks within which corporate entities operate provide adequate protection of their legitimate interests and expectations. The importance of effective corporate governance has been underlined by the G-7, the OECD and recent international financial crises. In addition, its impact can be seen directly in the context of investors' decisions not to invest in companies (and sometimes even countries, of which the clearest recent example is Russia) which are viewed as problematic in this respect.

Fourth, adequate lending infrastructure, including secured transactions law, is necessary to the development of banks and banking.[25] The role of an adequate lending infrastructure is at the heart of recent problems in East Asia and Mexico. A proper legal framework for lending encourages extended loan duration and improved currency matches, and enhances the development of domestic financial markets.

Fifth, clear rules governing foreign investment and public–private partnerships (concession law) must be established to enable foreign investment and participation in economic transition.[26] Without clear rules on foreign investment, foreign capital and expertise will not enter a market. Clear rules discourage corruption and enhance respect for the rule of law as well as aiding in the transfer of funds and technology necessary to transition and development. Public–private partnership arrangements require a legal infrastructure that recognizes the legitimate needs and expectations of the parties.

Sixth, effective insolvency provisions, including those for financial institutions, are required to enable the redirection of capital and the closure of inefficient enterprises, hence improving governance and performance.[27] Once again, East Asia has underlined the significance of functioning insolvency procedures, not only for economic renewal, but also for adequate protection of investor rights in the context of a business failure.

Seventh, fair and reasonably predictable tax laws are essential to supplement other legal infrastructure and to clarify the role of the government in a transition economy.[28] Fair and reasonably predictable tax laws are an absolute necessity both for the adequate functioning of domestic governments and for the encouragement of investment and growth. The negative impact of Russia's unclear and ineffective tax system on financial development is generally recognized.

No overall international consensus has evolved in respect of underlying legal infrastructure; however, consensus has developed in a number of areas, including corporate governance and accounting standards (see below). Further, consensus is currently being sought in respect of secured transactions and insolvency.

Effective corporate governance

Corporate governance has been a key ongoing issue in many transition economies and can be considered as perhaps the most significant issue to be faced following the initial challenges of monetization and stabilization.[29] The foundation of good institutional governance – the oversight and control by directors, managers and staff – is a sound business strategy and a competent and responsible senior management. Obviously, management ability and business acumen have developed and will continue to develop in transition economies only with time, experience and education.

In addition, good governance requires comprehensive internal control procedures and policies, including means to ensure that staff act in the interest of the institution and do not engage in insider dealing, disclose proprietary information, or provide credit on grounds other than objective assessments of potential returns and risks. Maintenance of good institutional governance also requires that owners, directors and senior management have adequate incentives and are subject to appropriate legal sanctions in the event that they behave improperly. These sorts of requirements, unlike development of quality management, can be influenced by the legal framework, most clearly through property, contract and company law and accounting standards.

In relation to financial institutions, which naturally were all state-owned and controlled before 1989, special problems arise. Around the world, government ownership of financial institutions has frequently been the basis of management failures because political pressure may place prudential and commercial considerations second to other objectives.[30] With many financial institutions still in state hands in the transition economies, these problems are likely to continue. Another major cause of management failure, often at the root of banking problems, is insider lending or lending to related enterprises, when lending decisions are not based solely on the borrower's creditworthiness. This is an issue that has plagued financial institutions in transition economies since the beginning of the transition process and is one of the most difficult to address. Good institutional governance is more likely to be sustained if there are outside shareholders (that is, depositors, creditors, investors and other actors with a sufficient direct stake in an institution) to bear some of the cost and effort of exercising diligent corporate oversight. These sorts of relationships, however, clearly require a developed legal and judicial framework in order to be effective. How can this be achieved? One of the most direct methods is liability for management and owners of financial institutions in certain clear cases on insolvency. Of course, this means also that there must be an effective system of insolvency.

Efficient markets for subordinated debt encourage large holders to exercise oversight in much the same way as private shareholders. Good interbank markets in which bank creditors have effective systems for counterparty appraisal and exposure control, and the ability to reduce credit lines or increase risk charges to poorly managed banks also help to promote oversight. Finally, a key feature of effective corporate governance is that institutions, including financial institutions, must be allowed from time to time to fail. An effective insolvency regime requires adequate legislation and effective judicial and administrative mechanisms as a necessary functional framework.[31]

The Organization of Economic Cooperation and Development (OECD) has been active in the area of corporate governance for a number of years, beginning in 1996 with the commissioning of a study of corporate governance. In addition, the G-7 has recently mandated the OECD to develop a comprehensive set of corporate governance principles to serve as the primary guidance in this area – a project which in currently ongoing.[32] As a result of the G-7 mandate, he OECD Council, meeting at Ministerial level on 27–8 April 1998, called upon the OECD to develop, in conjunction with national governments, other relevant international organizations and the private sector, a set of corporate governance standards and guidelines.

The OECD Principles[33] seek to strike a balance between the various, sometimes conflicting, concepts of corporate governance, and to promulgate standards of good corporate behaviour. The core values underlying the Principles are fairness, transparency, accountability and responsibility.

In addition, the EBRD published *Sound Business Standards and Corporate Practices* on 15 October 1997 to help companies in the region understand some of the broader concerns that lenders and investors have when considering a potential loan or investment opportunity in the region.[34] These Standards delineate guidelines for businesses to consider in their dealings with customers, shareholders, lenders, employees, suppliers, communities in which they operate, and government and local authorities. Such relationships build upon the basic requirements for success of a company having a sound strategy, competent management, valuable assets and a promising market.

Respecting relationships with shareholders (that is, corporate governance), as the core aspect, investors and lenders must understand clearly and be satisfied with the manner in which shareholders can oversee the performance of the management and participate in key decisions. More specifically, this includes as a basic matter setting out in legal form in the company charter the roles and responsibilities of the various management structures and shareholders and the creation and continued existence of transparent shareholding structures, including disclosure of voting rules and beneficial ownership of large blocks of shares. This serves to prevent and allay fears of self-dealing. A well-functioning board of directors legally required to act in a fiduciary manner on behalf of the entire company, combined with disclosure requirements to prevent interested transactions, further strengthens corporate governance. In addition, rights of minority shareholders must be legally protected against dilution or other loss of value through inappropriate dealings. This includes the necessity for procedures to protect the integrity of the shareholders' registry. Protection of shareholders' rights also requires the provision of properly audited accounts and other relevant corporate information in an annual report.

Effective payment, settlement and custody mechanisms

Ineffective payment, settlement and custody arrangements undermine the proper functioning of financial markets. In the area of payments and settlements, two organizations have been active. The first, the Committee on Payment and Settlement Systems (CPSS), which operates under the aegis of the G-10 central bank governors at the BIS, addresses issues related to the development of practices fostering efficient and viable payment and settlement systems and has recently published a set of Core Principles in this regard.[35] The second, IOSCO's Emerging Markets Committee, in which regulators from 64 emerging market countries participate, has released a report proposing the basis for the development of a legal framework for clearance and settlement in emerging markets.[36] The report highlights the main legal concerns which must be addressed in order to achieve an efficient clearance and settlement system for securities in emerging markets.

Internationally acceptable accounting and auditing standards

Effective financial regulation and supervision and the legal infrastructure supporting financial transactions depend on the timely provision of financial information that is understandable and reliable. The development of both financial institutions and financial transactions is impossible without financial information based on reliable accounting and auditing standards. Such systems did not exist in any meaningful fashion under central planning, and the development of adequate systems of valuation and accounting was one of the key difficulties initially faced by Western advisers in the transition economies.[37] Over ten years later, systems have had a chance to develop, although problems still remain.

Credible accounting systems are central to the provision of information needed by investors and others with an actual or potential stake in an enterprise to evaluate the past performance of an enterprise, to help predict its future performance and to determine its financial strength. Effective accounting standards should serve four basic needs: accuracy; relevance and transparency; comprehensiveness; and provision in a timely and regular manner. The best assurance that financial statements contain *understandable* information is if they are prepared and presented in accordance with accounting standards and principles that are generally acceptable internationally. The work of the International Accounting Standards Committee in publishing *International Accounting Standards* has been instrumental both in forming the content of optimal national standards and in providing standards with which individual financial institutions and other enterprises may prepare their accounts.[38] The best assurance that such financial statements are *reliable* is if they have been audited to standards that are broadly acceptable internationally. Auditing mechanisms are essential to ensure that accounting norms are effectively applied and maintained and to monitor the quality of internal control procedures, with both internal and external audits being necessary.

As described above, effective systems for providing information are essential to stakeholder monitoring, with accounting standards based on principles and rules that command wide international acceptance being crucial in this regard as they facilitate the comparison of performance across countries.

Oversight, however, cannot be effective without remedies and sanctions in the event of unacceptable performance. Markets, therefore, along with legal and regulatory structures, need to exercise an appropriate level of control over institutions and stakeholders need to be able expeditiously to exercise contractual sanctions allowed for in their claims on institutions, for example by being able to take possession of collateral in a timely fashion. As has been noted, these underlying legal institutional issues are crucial to successful transition, but require effective legislation and time.

Rigorous accounting and auditing standards also help prevent money laundering and other financial crime, an important function given the potentially disastrous impact such problems can have on both individual financial institutions and confidence in the financial system as a whole. In this area, the Financial Action Task Force (FATF) on Money Laundering has made recommendations and established principles and guidelines that serve as the basis for the development of laws to combat the practice.[39]

Effective regulation and supervision of financial markets

Effective prudential regulation and supervision of financial markets and institutions (including banks, insurance companies, securities intermediaries and pension funds) are essential to the financial stability and efficient functioning of any economy because of the central role of the financial system in collecting and distributing savings and investment. In transition economies the financial system was principally an administrative process based on central plans, with finance serving as simply a method of record-keeping. Financial institutions only existed as administrative entities within the state; regulation and supervision were therefore meaningless, except from the standpoint of monitoring the implementation of the plan system. As economies were monetized and transformed from state control, financial institutions began to take on completely new roles and at the same time to begin to give rise to dangers completely new (or long forgotten) to transition economies – roles and risks very familiar indeed to any market economy (for example financial intermediation and consequent systemic risk). Regulation and supervision became necessary; however, while the risks were well known to Western economists and central bankers, this did not translate into emphasis in the transition economies.[40] This changed with the advent of significant financial crises in a number of countries, especially the Baltics and Bulgaria in the early and mid-1990s, and highlighted by Mexico's experiences in 1994–95.[41]

Official oversight of the financial system encompasses financial regulation, including the formulation and enforcement of rules and standards governing financial behaviour as well as the ongoing supervision of individual institutions. Regulation and supervision play an essential role in fostering stable and robust financial systems, and should seek to support and enhance market functioning rather than to displace it by establishing basic 'rules of the game' and seeing that they are observed.[42] As individual transition countries experienced significant financial crises, attention began to focus not just on macroeconomic factors, but also on the need for regulation and development of the rule of law.

At the most basic level, prudential regulation and supervision serve to promote the public confidence on which decentralized financial systems are based. Further, supervision and regulation are essential complements to effective management and market discipline. The requirements of different financial market segments, however, have different motivations and requirements. The task of such regulation and supervision is to ensure that financial institutions operate in a prudent manner and that they hold capital and reserves sufficient to support the risks that arise in their business. In addition, regulations can be themselves a source of vulnerability to the extent that they are too lax, too intrusive, poorly designed, outdated or inadequately implemented. Strong and effective financial regulation and supervision therefore provide a necessary public good. However, in transition economies, the needs were greater even than those in market economies: financial regulation and supervision were needed to support the development of functioning financial institutions and systems. Unfortunately, this was only seen clearly through the negative effects of financial crises, of which that in Albania probably opened the most eyes to the very real dangers of lack of financial regulation and supervision, not only to economic transition and development, but to political stability and public order.

A fundamental guiding principle in the design of all regulatory/supervisory arrangements is that they should seek to support and enhance market functioning, rather than to displace markets. Obviously, this highlights the immense change from the role of the financial system in a centrally planned economy to that in a market economy. As a result, bureaucracies in transition economies have not always found it easy to understand their new role and that of the institutions and markets that they are dealing with. Luckily, this is much less so today than in the early 1990s, but must be the focus of continued training and educational initiatives, which are now being increasingly institutionalized through the Financial Stability Institute, based at the BIS in Basel.[43]

In the broadest sense, regulatory/supervisory authorities collectively need to pursue three broad objectives: define clearly the types of institutions subject to regulation and oversight along with the jurisdiction of each regulatory/supervisory agency for those institutions; promote the reliability, effectiveness and integrity of market infrastructure, in particular payments and transactions systems; and foster efficient operation and competition in the financial system. In a broad sense, these objectives can serve as a road-map for reform: the first stage must be to establish the regulator and what it has authority for, typically through a central bank law or law establishing an individual regulatory authority. The second step must be for those regulators to have an understanding of what a financial market is and what it does; otherwise, they will not be able to support its needs and protect it from risks. Third, in order to foster the operation of and competition in the financial system, rules need to be in place for participants in that system and their relationships with one another, with the regulator, and with the general public (that is, a banking law, a securities law, an insurance law and so on).

In the context of this broad framework, core aspects of regulation and supervision should be highlighted. First, supervisory and regulatory authorities must be independent and accountable. This applies also to central banks, whether they have supervisory responsibilities or not. Ideally, this should be set down in the law establishing the regulator and/or central bank and its relationship to the government. Second, authorities need to have powers of licensing, prudential regulation, consolidated supervision, and access to accurate and timely information as well as the ability to engage in remedial action. As a general matter, this should be set down in the law establishing the regulator or in the legislation governing specific financial markets (for example the banking law); while regulations will be important in this regard, the general principles should be clearly placed in the legislation. Finally, authorities must have adequate powers and resources to cooperate and exchange information, both with other authorities in their own jurisdiction and with those from outside, concerning the status of financial institutions or financial intermediaries. This is a factor that is often underemphasized. Ideally, financial sector legislation should be viewed as an opportunity to design the overall plan of the financial system; for example, what sort of institutions will be allowed, what they will be allowed to do, who will monitor them, and how those responsible authorities will relate to one another and the government. Unfortunately, despite the clear opportunity at the beginning of the transition process to do just this, it has rarely been done, although Poland has taken a more coherent approach than most and has been quite successful in doing so. It is worth mentioning that China is also seeking to take a coherent (and planned) approach to development of its financial sector, in order to solve its significant problems before opening.[44]

Banking supervision and regulation

Approaches to effective regulation and supervision differ significantly between banking and securities activities, reflecting fundamental differences between the nature of these activities. For that reason, transition economies must carefully consider their approach to banks and banking. Banking basically transforms the liquid deposits of many small and dispersed savers into illiquid loans to borrowers. These loans are extended on the basis of bank–client relationships and private information. This combination of liquid deposits and illiquid loans, however, is potentially unstable because of the risk that depositors begin a run on a bank if its liquidity becomes doubtful, a risk that is increased further because of the limited information depositors have about banks. Prudential oversight in banking provides a measured alternative to the disruptive discipline of bank runs and is often accompanied by government provision of deposit guarantees.

In market economies, banking crises have tended to occur when financial markets were recently liberalized but when supervision and regulation were not upgraded to cope with expanded activity.[45] In transition economies, the challenge has been to build institutions for sound finance in step with the expansion of financial activity. Such synchronization is undoubtedly difficult to achieve, and not surprisingly there have been many banking crises in transition economies. Not only did the severe economic upheavals early in the transition render many enterprises and banks insolvent, but also banking crises have persisted even as the transition advances and the economies stabilize. Behind the Baltic banking crises (Latvia and Lithuania in 1995–96) lay pervasive connected lending by new private banks that had rapidly expanded their activities. In the recent Russian crisis, a number of banks had built up large open foreign exchange positions by writing forward contracts that were inadequately hedged. In each episode, there were serious gaps in the prudential regulation and supervision of banks that allowed imprudent exposures or fraud to go unchecked.

In transition economies, banks, more so than stock markets, are the major suppliers of funds to new and old enterprises. Banks have a major role to play as the predominant savings outlet in such countries. Therefore it is important to create a legal and regulatory framework that allows banks to channel savings to enterprises in an efficient manner while also minimizing the system's exposure to corruption and instability.

In the area of banking regulation and supervision, the Basel Committee on Banking Supervision, composed of the G-10 central bank governors, has been most active, especially with its recent publication of *Core Principles for Effective Banking Supervision and Regulation*.[46] In the Core Principles, summarized briefly below, the Basel Committee, in conjunction with regulators from 16 other jurisdictions including transitioning and emerging economies, has produced 25 basic principles that should underlie banking supervisory policies and structures, outline the basic framework for effective banking supervision and serve as a basic reference for supervisory and other public authorities in all countries and internationally. In addition, a methodology for implementation has been produced.[47] Detailed guidance in the implementation of the Core Principles is in turn provided through the Basel Committee's compilation of its ongoing pronouncements over the years.[48]

As a precondition, an effective system of banking supervision requires the delineation of clear objectives and responsibilities for those involved, along with operational independence and adequate resources. This should be established as part of the legal framework for banking supervision, which should also provide for authorization and ongoing supervision of banking organizations; adequate regulatory powers; and legal arrangements for confidentiality and information-sharing between supervisors. The legal framework must clearly define permissible activities of banks and restrict the use of the term to regulated entities, with clear requirements for licensing and changes in ownership, whether through merger or transfer.

Powers and responsibilities for prudential regulation must include appropriate minimum capital requirements; and appropriate evaluation of banks' lending, investment, asset quality evaluation and loan provisioning policies. In addition, supervisors must ensure the existence of adequate management information systems and compliance with limits on exposures to single or groups of related borrowers. Such supervision must extend to requirements to prevent connected lending and other non-arm's-length transactions. Beyond credit risk monitoring, supervisors must monitor banks' market risk systems as one aspect of banks' overall risk management systems – an especially difficult task in volatile markets with thin banking experience such as those in transitional economies. Adequate internal controls also must be ensured, including appropriate 'know-your-customer' mechanisms and ethical standards to prevent money-laundering and financial crime.

Beyond initial systems, ongoing supervision requires both on-site and off-site monitoring, including regular contact with bank management to provide a thorough understanding of each institution's operations. This must include both solo and consolidated information collection and analysis, along with independent validation of information supplied by supervised institutions. Consolidated supervision of banking groups is essential. In order for such ongoing supervision to be effective, each bank must maintain adequate records drawn up in accordance with consistent accounting standards and practices, preferably of an international standard.

In order to be effective in their supervisory efforts, supervisors must have adequate powers to bring about timely corrective action in circumstances where banks fail to meet the prudential requirements outlined above. This should include the ability to revoke banking licences in extreme cases.

Finally, because of the increasingly cross-border nature of banking activities and the greater risks that such activities lead to in the international financial system, banking supervisors must practise global consolidated supervision over their authorized internationally active banking organizations. A key component of this is contact and information-sharing with other supervisors, especially host country supervisors. Host country supervisors in turn must require local operations of foreign banks to be conducted to the same high standards as required for domestic institutions.

Before the development of its Core Principles, the Basel Committee had historically been most active in establishing internationally agreed minimum standards for adequate capitalization for financial institutions.[49] These standards should constitute a minimum floor in this respect: capitalization standards applied in practice need to be higher if the risks are higher because of vulnerabilities to external disturbances, a history of weak macroeconomic performance, or undeveloped financial markets.

Another area of necessary focus for banking regulation is the provision of appropriate safety net arrangements. While no international consensus has yet emerged in this area, given its impact in the recent East Asian crises, greater attention is likely to be forthcoming. The high cost to society of a collapse of the banking system is a principal reason why authorities in virtually all countries provide some sort of a safety net for depositors, usually in the form of deposit insurance. This involves the potential outlay of public funds in the event that the stability of the banking system is threatened. Such arrangements (or the general belief in *de facto* government guarantees) inevitably create moral hazards because they hold open the prospect that stakeholders will be at least partially indemnified from losses from failing institutions. These problems were most clearly illustrated during the US savings and loan (S&L) crisis of the 1980s and have been (and in many cases continue to be) a feature of recent banking weaknesses in East Asia.

Securities regulation

Securities activities, in contrast to banking activities, are market-based and require transparency and public disclosure of information for the markets to function well. This information is necessary not only for the accurate valuation of equities and bonds in securities markets, but also for the holders of these securities to protect their rights and to perform a corporate governance role. However, as clearly demonstrated by the social disruption caused by failures in securities regulation in, *inter alia*, Albania, there are also considerable risks in regulatory failures. Standards and institutions that promote market transparency generate investor confidence in capital markets. In many countries in transition, individual investors lack confidence in their securities markets and in equity investments. Further, the failure in several countries of large investment funds that were mostly unregulated has caused investors in some cases to lose confidence in the marketplace. Many jurisdictions have not established adequate requirements for information to be provided to investors in connection with public offerings and investment funds. Investors, in turn, are unable to assess the accuracy of the information on which they need to make investment decisions.

Failures in the regulatory framework for securities regulation have opened the possibility of significant financial fraud and market manipulation in the transition economies, clear examples of which have been seen in, *inter alia*, Albania, Bulgaria, Romania and Russia.

In the area of securities market oversight, the International Organization of Securities Commissions (IOSCO) has taken the lead with its recent publication and adoption of *Objectives and Principles of Securities Regulation*.[50] In addition, it has developed a framework for minimum content of public offer prospectuses.[51] This latter document is intended to set a basic framework for international offering documents acceptable to regulators and stock exchanges around the world. Such a framework could serve as an internationally acceptable basis for the further development of stock exchange listing requirements and prospectus regulations throughout the region.

The IOSCO *Objectives* sets out three main objectives of securities regulation: (i) the protection of investors; (ii) ensuring that markets are fair, efficient and transparent; and (iii) the reduction of systemic risk. To achieve these objectives, IOSCO has developed principles to be implemented as part of a legal framework for securities and capital markets.

As a starting-point, the responsibilities of the securities regulator should be clear and objectively stated, with the regulator operationally independent and accountable in the exercise of its functions and powers. The regulator must have adequate powers, proper resources and the capacity to perform its functions, and must have staff who are required to observe the highest professional standards, including appropriate confidentiality and disclosure of personal interests. In addition, in the exercise of its functions, the regulator must adopt clear and consistent regulatory processes. In order to support proper enforcement, the regulator must have comprehensive inspection, investigation and surveillance powers as support to comprehensive enforcement powers.

As part of the regulatory regime, appropriate use should be made, to the extent appropriate to the size and complexity of the relevant market, of self-regulatory organizations (SROs), which might include such institutions as stock exchanges, that would exercise direct oversight responsibility for their respective areas of competence. Any SRO should, however, be subject to the oversight of the regulator in respect of observing standards of fairness and confidentiality when exercising any powers and delegated responsibilities.

Regardless of the division of responsibilities between the regulator and any SROs, the regulatory system should, overall, ensure an effective and credible use of inspection, investigation, surveillance and enforcement powers and implementation of an effective compliance programme. As one aspect, clear and appropriate authority and mechanisms need to be established for information-sharing and co-operation with domestic and foreign counterparts.

In regard to market intermediaries, regulation must provide for minimum entry standards, initial and ongoing capital requirements and other prudential requirements (such as those dealing with market risk and off-balance-sheet activities). Market intermediaries must also be required to comply with standards for internal organization and operational conduct that aim to protect the interests of clients and under which management of the intermediary accepts primary responsibility for these matters. Appropriate areas include risk management and controls and custody arrangements.[52] In addition, procedures for dealing with the failure of a market intermediary need to be created to minimize damage and loss to investors and to contain confidence shocks that might pose a systemic risk to the financial system through contagious panic. More specific requirements address the special risks posed by collective investment schemes (for example, unit trusts or mutual funds), including the establishment of licensing and regulation of those who wish to market such schemes. Legal rules must be drawn up governing the legal form and structure of such schemes, including the segregation and protection of client assets. Disclosure of risks and asset valuation, pricing and redemption of units must also be delineated.[53]

In order to provide adequate market information, issuers of securities must meet requirements for full, timely and accurate disclosure of financial results and other information material to investor decisions. Legal safeguards should exist to ensure that holders of securities in a company are treated in a fair and equitable manner. In addition, accounting and auditing standards must be of a high and internationally acceptable quality (see below). Beyond the primary market, the secondary market also requires attention. Trading systems including securities exchanges must be subject to regulatory authorization and oversight, including ongoing supervision to ensure maintenance of trading integrity and transparency through detection and deterrence of manipulation and unfair trading practices. In addition, proper management of large exposures, default risk and market disruption is essential, as is regulatory oversight of the clearing and settlement system.

The objectives as set out in the IOSCO publication thus extend beyond the traditional arena of financial regulation and supervision (that is, protection of investors and reduction of systemic risk) to cover fairness, efficiency and equity of markets. Historically, securities regulation has not been accorded similar prominence to that accorded to banking. However, experience has shown (both in the US and increasingly in Europe) that requirements for adequate disclosure and transparency in securities markets increase investor confidence in such markets, thereby encouraging development and expansion.[54] In the transition economies, this has been demonstrated most successfully in the continued successful development of Poland's highly regulated capital markets.

Insurance regulation

Like securities regulation, insurance supervision has historically not received the attention given to that of banking. With the growth of financial conglomerates and the consequent spread of potential systemic risks throughout the financial system, and the development of significant insurance company assets available for investment, insurance regulation is an area of increased concern for regulators.

The International Association of Insurance Supervisors has published *Insurance Supervisory Principles* to serve as guidelines for the regulation and supervision of insurance markets and is in the process of developing guidelines or standards in the areas of licensing, use of derivatives, on-site inspections, solvency, reinsurance, market conduct and investment policies.[55] The IAIS has enunciated general principles that identify subject areas that should be addressed in the laws of each jurisdiction, with further guidance specifically tailored to the needs of emerging markets.[56]

Under the IAIS *Principles*, an insurance supervisor is expected to protect policyholders by ensuring that companies comply with the laws governing the business of insurance, intervening as necessary using the powers available under the legislation. Specific responsibilities (presented in more detailed general principles) include licensing and changes of control. Standards of corporate governance and internal controls should be established. Prudential rules should cover assets, liabilities, capital adequacy and solvency, derivatives and 'off-balance-sheet' items, and reinsurance. Supervisors should have monitoring and inspection powers, including financial reporting, and on-site inspection and access to information. Supervisors should also be given appropriate sanctions powers. Finally, they must be able to coordinate their activities, not only with other financial supervisors in their own jurisdiction and in other jurisdictions, but also in the context of appropriate confidentiality.

Financial conglomerates

Financial conglomerates, common throughout the transition economies (exceptions are Poland and China, where such entities are currently prohibited), present special concerns due to their conjunction of banking, securities and insurance activities and the differing regulatory rationales for each. The Joint Forum on Financial Conglomerates, in which the Basel Committee, IOSCO and IAIS participate, is presently developing a framework for the supervision of financial conglomerates and for the exchange of supervisory information.

Currently, the Joint Forum has developed the following principles, which form a Compendium:[57] Capital Adequacy Principles; Fit and Proper Principles; Framework for Supervisory Information Sharing; Principles for Supervisory Information Sharing; Coordinator guidance; Risk Concentrations Principles; and Intra-group Transactions and Exposures (ITEs) Principles.

These requirements will be relevant to many countries in the region, given the general trend towards legislation permitting universal banking and the provision of a range of financial services across the region, a development connected to common legal attributes of many EU Member States and aspirants (addressed below).

EU financial services directives and accession

While the work of international financial forums forges globally accepted core principles, EU requirements relating to financial services are more directly relevant for those post-communist countries aspiring to accede to the European Union. Given the composition of many of the international bodies concerned with promoting effective regulation and supervision of financial markets, it is not surprising that European Union requirements relating to financial services have influenced the content of the emerging international standards and reflect their content. None the less, EU standards have been more immediately relevant for countries in the region with EU membership aspirations.[58]

The EU framework for financial services provides minimum standards for banks and other financial institutions, securities regulation, stock exchange regulation, company law and regulation of institutional investors, all based on the premise of universal banking and an open internal market. However, this framework is not complete, given that it builds progressively on existing national systems of financial and commercial laws rather than trying to replace them with a complete new system.

Ten transition economies are signatories to Europe Agreements with the EU[59] which oblige them to take on board the *acquis communautaire*. A primary obligation of the accession states is the approximation of existing and future state legislation in the financial services sector to that of the EU. Moreover, under the existing Europe Agreements, EU financial companies will have the right to operate on the territory of the respective accession candidate country by the end of a transition period at the latest. Accordingly, the accession states will need to have in place a fully EU-compatible system of banking and financial services regulation by the date of accession.

As an aid to this process of incorporation of the *acquis*, in April 1995 the European Commission issued a White Paper identifying the key measures required to undertaken in each sector of the internal market. The White Paper proposed a sequence under which the accession candidates should seek to approximate their domestic legislation to that of the EU. It proposed that the Community legislation in the financial services area should be adopted in two stages: the first involves the introduction of the basic principles for the establishment of financial institutions; the second (although some elements are important for the first stage) aims to strengthen prudential supervision of investment firms in order to bring them up to international standards. This second stage of the Commission framework for the accession candidates focuses on the various EU provisions for free movement of capital and services in the financial sphere.

The experience of the EU shows that regional integration can play a role in promoting the adoption of sound principles and practices in economies and in supporting their implementation. The fundamental principle of mutual recognition and a system of a single licence ensure that these directives provide a set of minimum norms while at the same time avoiding the creation of obstacles to competition among financial institutions. Moreover, since most of the potential new members are countries in transition, the EU is well placed to help address the special challenges that they face.

Conclusion

Most transition economies have made substantial progress (albeit at different rates) in establishing the basic legal framework for the operation of a market economy.[60] The next level of development to be attained has a dual focus. The first goal is the increased integration of transitional economies into the international financial system. This process entails necessary changes in the legal framework and culture. Further, EU accession countries face the immediate domestic challenge of harmonizing their laws and institutions with the requirements of the *acquis communautaire*. However, integration into the international financial system is not without its dangers and must be based on coherent sequencing of liberalization preceded by the development of an effectively functioning financial system in each country.

In achieving such a goal, the following framework is suggested. First, a transition country needs to establish a centre for coordination of the overall work programme (typically the central bank, Ministry of Finance or specialized financial services arm of the government). This will take responsibility for coordination of the work programme, use of any consultants, mobilization of funding and review of implementation. Second, a plan must be developed that looks at the financial sector as a whole. Questions to be addressed include: what is the current status of the financial sector? What are its strengths and weaknesses? Are there any significant failures? What are the needs for the coming years? The idea is that the financial sector should not be looked at piecemeal, but rather as part of a coordinated plan to establish coherent and meaningful rules for participants and regulators in order to secure its future development. It should be noted, however, that this is not a plan for how the sector should function; its aim is, rather, to formalize the rules of the game so that development in the context of stability can take place toward the overall goal of an open, effectively functioning financial system. Third, the legislation and regulations governing the market and its participants must be analysed *vis-à-vis* international standards and best practices and any gaps addressed in a coherent and effective manner. It is especially important to secure coordination of authorities and establishment of independence and clear objectives, while at the same time to be forward looking (for example, how the system interacts with a given's country's WTO, EU or other commitments) and non-interventionist. This must be seen as no small task and one that may require time, but one that will pay dividends in financial and overall economic development in the future.

As a second goal, the transition countries must continue to strengthen the role of the rule of law in their respective systems. An emphasis on the rule of law will strengthen investor confidence and assist the overall transition process within each country. As discussed above, without the development of financial markets and a culture incorporating the rule of law, transition will not be successful and will always remain vulnerable.

Notes

*The opinions expressed here do not necessarily represent those of the EBRD. This chapter was originally prepared as background research for the European Bank for Reconstruction and Development's *Transition Report 1998* and presented at a conference at the University of Reading entitled 'Entering the World Financial Market: East and Central Europe and the CIS Countries' in September 1998 from which this volume is drawn. The author would like to thank Gerard Sanders, David Bernstein, Anita Ramasastry, Michael Taylor and Steven Fries for their assistance and comments.

1 For an analysis of recent financial crises and the importance of law reform, see D. Arner, M. Yokoi and Z. Zhou (eds), *Financial Crises in the 1990s* (2001).

2 See, e. g. , Rudi Bonte, 'Supervisory Lessons to be Drawn from the Asian Crisis, Basel Committee on Banking Supervision', Basel Committee on Banking Supervision Working Paper No. 2 (June 1999).

3 See EBRD, *Transition Report 1998: Financial Sector in Transition* (1999).

4 See generally EBRD, *Law in transition* (spring 1999) (focusing on the role of law in financial markets in transition economies).

5 See K. Pistor and P. Wellons et al. , *The Role of Law and Legal Institutions in Asian Economic Development, 1960–1995* (1998).

6 For an overview of progress, difficulties and transition generally since 1989, see EBRD, *Transition Report 1999: Ten Years of Transition* (1999).

7 See R. Lastra, *Central Banking and Banking Regulation* (1996), ch. 2.

8 For an in-depth treatment of this issue, see EBRD, *Transition Report 1998*, esp. pp. 93–145.

9 See R. La Porta, F. Lopez-de-Silanes, A. Shleifer and R. Vishny, 'Legal Determinants of External Finance', *Journal of Finance*, 52 (July 1997) 1131–50; idem. , 'Law and Finance', *Journal of Political Economy*, 106 (1998) 1113.

10 See Group of Ten (G-10), 'A Strategy for the Formulation, Adoption and Implementation of Sound Principles and Practices to Strengthen Financial Systems', *Report of the Group of Ten (G-10) Working Party on Financial Stability in Emerging Markets, Financial Stability in Emerging Market Economies* (April 1997); Group of Twenty-two Systemically Significant Countries, *Reports on the International Financial Architecture* (Oct. 1998).

11 For details, see D. Folkerts-Landau and C-J. Lindgren, *Toward a Framework for Financial Stability* (Jan. 1998). See also the website of the Financial Stability Forum at http://www. fsforum. org (summarizing the various organizations and principles). Additional information on reform of the 'international financial architecture' is available at the International Monetary Fund (IMF) website at http://www. imf. org

12 See E. Wymeersch, 'Corporate Governance in Western Europe: Structures and Comparisons', *Law in transition* (Autumn 1999) 46; and K. Haupt (ed.), *Comparative Corporate Governance* (1998).

13 For discussion of the role of the rule of law in economic development, see T. Carothers, 'The Rule of Law Revival', *Foreign Affairs* (1998) 95; C. Clague, P. Keefer, S. Knack and M. Olson, 'Property and Contract Rights in Autocracies and Democracies', *Journal of Economic Growth*, 1 (1996) 243 p.243; D. North, 'Economic Performance Through Time', *American Economic Review*, 84 (1994) 359; M. Olson, 'Dictatorship, Democracy, and Development', *American Political Science Review*, 87 (1993) 567; and idem. , 'Big Bills Left on the Sidewalk: Why Some Nations are Rich, and Others Poor, *Journal of Economic Perspective*, 10 (1996) 3.

14 The best examples here are those of Hungary and China; the contra example has been Poland.

15 See D. Arner, 'The Mexican Peso Crisis: Implications for the Regulation of Financial Markets', *NAFTA: Law and Business Review of the Americas*, 2 (1996).

16 G-10, 'A Strategy for the Formulation, Adoption and Implementation of Sound Principles and Practices to Strengthen Financial Systems'. G-10 docu-

ments are available at the Bank for International Settlements (BIS) website at http://www. bis. org

17 See ibid. ; see also Reports on the International Financial Architecture; and R. White, 'What Have We Learned from Recent Financial Crises and Policy Responses?' BIS Working paper No. 84 (Jan. 2000).

18 For more information and links to the various standard-developing organizations and their efforts, see the Financial Stability Forum's website at http://www. fsforum. org

19 The Financial Stability Forum maintains a Compendium of standards and standard-setting bodies at its website.

20 See M. Taylor, 'International Financial Standards and the Transition Economies', *Yearbook of International Financial and Economic Law 1998*, 3 (1999) 345.

21 See J. Norton, 'International Financial Law and International Economic Law: Implications for Emerging and Transition Economies', *Law in transition*, (Spring 1999), 2.

22 In addition to a sound public law regulatory framework, private law must provide individual investors with a means for participating in financial transactions and for enforcing their rights with respect to their investments.

23 See sources cited in note 9.

24 See OECD, *General Principles of Company Law in Transition Economies* (1997).

25 See EBRD, *Model Law on Secured Transactions* (1994); see also J. Norton and M. Andenas (eds), *Emerging Financial Markets and Secured Transactions* (1997).

26 See J. Taylor and F. April, 'Fostering Investment Law in Transitional Economies: A Case for Refocusing Institutional Reform', *Parker School Journal of East European Law*, 4 (1997) 1.

27 See Asian Development Bank (ADB), *Law and Development at the Asian Development Bank* (Apr. 1999), pp. 7–36.

28 See IMF, *Code of Good Practices on Fiscal Transparency* (IMF, Apr. 1998).

29 See generally EBRD, *Law in transition* (Autumn 1999) (focusing on corporate governance).

30 See P. Honohan, 'Banking system failures in developing and transition countries: Diagnosis and predictions', BIS Working Paper No. 39 (Jan. 1997).

31 For this reason, legal reform in the area of insolvency is an important focus of the EBRD, and the EBRD Office of the General Council analyses insolvency within the context of its survey of commercial law extensiveness and effectiveness, presented in the annual *Transition Report* since 1996. See EBRD, *Transition Report 1999*, Annex 2. 2. For explanation of EBRD survey practice, see Taylor and April, 'Fostering Investment Law'.

32 For details, see the OECD website at http://www. oecd. org

33 OECD, Directorate for Financial, Fiscal and Enterprise Affairs, Ad Hoc Task Force on Corporate Governance, *OECD Principles of Corporate Governance*, SG/CG(99)5 (April 1999) (available at http://www. oecd. org).

34 EBRD, *Sound Business Standards and Corporate Practices: A Set of Guidelines* (Oct. 1997).

35 See Committee on Payment and Settlement Systems, *Core Principles for Systemically Important Payment Systems* (Dec. 1999).

36 IOSCO, *Report of the Emerging Markets Committee, Towards a Legal Framework for Clearing and Settlement in Emerging Markets* (Nov. 1997).

37   See D. Cairns, 'Improving Financial Reporting in Transition Economies', *Law in transition* 8 (Spring 1999).

38   For details, see the International Accounting Standards Committee website at http://www. iasc. org. See also M. Steinberg, D. Arner and C. Olive, 'The Development of Internationally Acceptable Accounting Standards: A Universal Language for Finance in the 21st Century?', *Yearbook of International Financial & Economic Law 1998*, 3 (1999) 87.

39   Financial Action Task Force on Money Laundering, *The Forty Recommendations* (1996 rev'd). Additional information is available at the FATF website at www. oecd. org/fatf

40   The classic treatments are by Thornton and Bagehot in the nineteenth century: H. Thornton, *An Enquiry into the Nature and Effects of the Paper Credit of Great Britain* (1802) and W. Bagehot, *Lombard Street: A Description of the Money Market* (1873).

41   See M. Goldstein and P. Turner, 'Banking Crises In Emerging Economies: Origins And Policy Options', BIS Economic Paper No. 46 (Oct. 1996).

42   See C. Goodhart, P. Hartmann, D. Llewellyn, L. Rojas-Suarez and S. Weisbrod, *Financial Regulation: Why, How and Where Now?* (1998).

43   Additional information is available at the BIS website.

44   For discussion, see J. Norton and Y. Huang (eds), *Financial Regulation in Greater China* (2000).

45   See Goldstein and Turner, 'Banking Crises'.

46   Basel Committee on Banking Supervision, *Core Principles of Effective Banking Supervision* (Sept. 1997). Basel Committee documents are available at the BIS website at http://www. bis. org

47   Basel Committee on Banking Supervision, *Core Principles Methodology* (Oct. 1999).

48   Basel Committee on Banking Supervision, *Compendium of Documents Produced by the Basel Committee on Banking Supervision* (1997 updated).

49   See J. Norton, *Developing International Bank Supervisory Standards* (1995).

50   IOSCO, *Objectives and Principles of Securities Regulation* (Sept. 1998). IOSCO documents are available at the IOSCO website at http://www. iosco. org

51   IOSCO, *International Disclosure Standards for Cross-border Offerings and Initial Listings by Foreign Issuers* (May 1998).

52   IOSCO, *Risk Management and Control Guidance for Securities Firms and their Supervisors* (May 1998).

53   Further requirements are discussed in IOSCO, *Principles for the Supervision of Operators of Collective Investment Schemes* (1997).

54   See B. Steil, *The European Equity Markets* (1996) and J. Seligman, *The Transformation of Wall Street: A History of the Securities and Exchange Commission and Modern Corporate Finance* (1995, 2nd edn).

55   IAIS, *Insurance Supervisory Principles* (Sept. 1997).

56   IAIS, *Guidance on Insurance Regulation and Supervision for Emerging Market Economies* (Sept. 1997).

57   Joint Forum on Financial Conglomerates, *Supervision of Financial Conglomerates* (Feb. 1999 as updated).

58   For details, see C. Hadjiemmanuil, 'Central Bankers' "Club" Law and Transitional Economies: Banking Reform and the Reception of the Basel Standards

of Prudential Supervision in Eastern Europe and the Former Soviet Union', in Norton and Andenas, *Emerging Financial Markets*.

59   Poland, Hungary, the Czech Republic, Slovakia, Bulgaria, Romania, Estonia, Latvia, Lithuania and Slovenia.

60   For the results of the EBRD's empirical survey of the status of the commercial legal and regulatory systems of its countries of operations, see EBRD, *Transition Report 1998* (1998) ch. 2, Annex 2. 1 and ch. 6. See also A. Ramasastry and S. Slavova, 'Market Perceptions of Financial Law in the Region – EBRD Survey Results', *Law in transition* (Spring 1999) 24 and A. Ramasastry, S. Slavova and D. Bernstein, 'Market Perceptions of Corporate Governance – EBRD Survey Results', *Law in transition* (Autumn 1999) 32.

8
Building Supervisory and Regulatory Capacity in the Transition Economies

Michael Taylor[1]

Introduction

As several chapters in this volume have already indicated, the costs of regulatory failure in a number of the transition economies have been substantial. These costs range from the immediately apparent, for example the increased burden that resolving banking crises places on already strained government budgets, to the less obvious and indirect, including those that arise from the inefficiencies resulting from ineffective or unnecessarily burdensome regulation. The absence of effective regulation may impede the development of a modern financial sector in other ways, particularly since markets that appear to favour well-connected insiders will not be attractive to foreign investors and firms. Hence building effective supervisory capacity is central to building a market-based financial system and to the successful integration of the transition economies with world financial markets. This chapter reviews some of the main policy-related problems that can arise in a transition economy context as they attempt to construct this capacity.

The development of effective regulatory institutions belongs to what has come to be termed the 'second generation' of institutional reforms. The first generation of reforms were intended to create functioning markets through the abandonment of central planning combined with economic liberalization and market opening, including withdrawal of the state from ownership and from intervention in market entry, market exit and pricing. By contrast, second-generation reforms instead attempt to build institutional capacity with a view to cementing and enhancing the welfare gains achieved through the first-generation reforms. This process of institution-building is necessary because the network of institutions and social interactions between markets, the state and civil society establishes the capacities of a society to use its resources optimally. When institutions lag the development of markets, this produces, in the words of the head of the OECD's Programme on Regulatory Reform, a 'gap' between actual and potential welfare (Jacobs, 1999). In other words, society could be making better use of its resources than is possible given the constraints of a particular set of institutions. Thus second-generation reforms are, according to Jacobs,

> those that align relationships between the state, the market, and civil society to reduce the gap in potential welfare. These kinds of reforms are needed to sustain and consolidate the move to market-led growth, which is evolving so rapidly that it is straining the capacities of lagging or obsolete institutions to perform important functions such as providing security, repairing market failures, and maintaining democratic legitimacy within the policy structure.

For the transition economies to achieve the full benefits of the market-led reforms in which they engaged in the early 1990s they have needed to move to the second stage of reform in which state institutions are adapted to meet the new demands of a market-based economy. The failure to adapt institutions quickly enough has been illustrated at a number of points in this volume, most notably in the instances of the banking crises of the Baltic republics. Applied to the specific example of the regulation of the financial services sector, the second generation of reforms means building the capacity effectively to supervise and regulate financial markets and institutions.

The main building blocks of supervisory capacity can be considered under several different headings. The first is the clarity of regulatory objectives. This is necessary in the first place to demonstrate that complete government non-intervention in the financial markets is not a viable policy option, despite the aspiration of an early generation of reformers who reacted strongly against any role for the state. At the other end of the spectrum, the construction of regulatory institutions in economies where heavy state involvement has been the past norm runs the risk that regulatory institutions will be perceived, both by market participants and those charged with operating them, as a return to the former traditions of state intervention. Thus it is necessary to draw a clear distinction between state intervention, which aims to replace the market mechanisms with administrative decisions, and regulation, which aims to improve market efficiency through correcting market failures. Furthermore, clarity of regulatory objectives also helps ensure that regulation is proportionate to the ends it is intended to fulfil. The vaguer are regulatory objectives, the greater will be the temptation for regulatory agencies to engage in regulatory 'creep' – that is, to extend the regulation beyond that which is necessary to correct the market failure it has been established to address. By contrast, clear and precise regulatory objectives both minimize the scope for a constant 'ratcheting up' of regulation and make it easier to hold regulators to account for their actions.

A second issue, closely connected with the clarity of regulatory objectives, is the need to construct *effective* regulatory institutions. 'Effective' regulation is responsive to market developments and flexible enough to accommodate them while at the same time discharging its primary objectives (Jacobs, 1999). It is also independent of political interference – in the terminology of this chapter the government needs to develop a 'credible commitment' not to interfere with the regulatory process. To do otherwise would be to return to the type of state interventionism which seeks to replace market-determined outcomes with those based on other criteria. Effective regulation also requires that the moral hazard arising from the governmental involvement in the financial system be contained. The fact that financial institutions are subject to regulation or that depositors enjoy some form of special deposit protection should not been regarded as equivalent to a governmental blanket guarantee that all creditors of a financial institution will receive support from the government should it fail. Owners and managers in particular need to be convinced that the state will not rectify the losses resulting from their mistakes or excessive risk-taking. This is also requires a form of credible commitment by the government.

The structure of the rest of this chapter is as follows: the next section explores the issue of the role and functions of the regulatory state, and especially the problem of establishing effective and proportionate regulation in the early years of transition. The third section then discusses the need for the state to create institutions that give expression to a credible commitment not to interfere in the regulatory process. The various components of regulatory independence are discussed, as is the issue of the location of the regulatory agency in the government machine. The role of the central bank in regulation is also examined. The fourth section then considers the issue of credible commitment from the perspective of reducing moral hazard. This requires consideration of the structure of deposit insurance schemes, the need for prompt corrective action, and the role of the state as the shareholder of banks. The focus throughout most of the chapter will be on the regulation of the banking system since this forms the largest component of transition economy financial sectors. The regulation of the non-bank financial sector, including securities markets and insurance companies, raises similar issues but the prominence that will be given to banking regulation in this chapter reflects its importance for the transition economies.

The role and functions of the regulatory state

Under the pre-transition economic model the state dominated economic life. In particular, the entire banking system was state-owned. Although on the surface it appeared to comprise a number of different institutions (a central bank, an investment bank, a foreign trade bank, and a savings bank for the general public) in practice all these different institutions were regulated by instructions from the central bank (Kornai, 1992). Hence many observers have referred to this as a 'monobank' system. Pricing and allocation decisions were determined entirely by the state, the entire short-term and most of the long-term (with the exception of limited foreign currency borrowings) supply of credit to the real economy was handled through this system, and the investing public had only one potential repository for their savings – deposits with the savings bank arm of the monobank system.

The transition process involves dismantling the monobank system and encouraging competition in the provision of finance to the real sector. At the same time, non-bank financial institutions and markets also need to be developed. The assumption underlying many of the early efforts at reform in the transition economies was that the development of the financial system could be entrusted almost exclusively to competitive forces. This was simply a special case of the more general assumption that the competitive market was a largely 'natural' product, and that the free play of individual self-interest could be entrusted to produce outcomes which maximized social utility. This assumption gives rise to a conception of the role of the state that is usually referred to as the '*laissez faire*' or 'invisible hand' model. According to this view the government might legitimately perform some basic functions necessary to support a market economy, including the provision of law and order and national defence. However, other than providing this limited range of public goods the role of the state is illegitimate.

Proponents of this view are among the leading critics of most forms of governmental regulation of business. According to one strand of this opinion regulation is unnecessary since self-correcting forces can be relied upon to correct market imperfections which are therefore deemed to be merely temporary phenomena. A alternative view, associated with the Chicago school of political economy of which Geroge Stigler is the leading representative (Stigler, 1988), argues that although market imperfections may be more than merely temporary phenomena, the costs of regulation will always outweigh any potential benefits that it can deliver. The work of the public-choice school has aimed to show, in particular, how departures from the normative model of *laissez-faire* are due to the interaction of group interests and the self-seeking behaviour of politicians and bureaucrats. It has resulted in a powerful body of theory which purports to establish that many (if not most) instances of regulation serve a narrow sectional interest rather than the public interest. Thus behind most regulations are the interests of a cartel or the aggrandizement of bureaucrats. In terms of practical policy prescriptions this school of thought inclines towards unregulated (that is 'free') banking; and it also criticizes the attempt to regulate securities markets by requiring the disclosure of information and prohibiting insider dealing. Indeed, on some formulations, insider dealing is merely the hidden hand's way of introducing information into the market which disclosure regulation singularly fails to deliver.

Traditionally the primary alternative to the *laissez-faire* model of the state has been the public-interest model. This argues that there are certain examples of market failure that are sufficiently serious and pervasive as to require governmental intervention. According to this view unregulated free markets in the provision of financial services may lead to monopoly pricing, to externalities like bank runs, to defective credit supply to firms, and to widespread fraud on the investing public. Most of the economic concepts and analysis underpinning this approach to the role of the state was developed by the Cambridge school of economics in the late nineteenth and early twentieth centuries, most notably in the work of Henry Sidgwick, Alfred Marshall and A. C. Pigou (Pigou, 1946). The application of the concepts developed by these economists to the regulation of business, and to financial services regulation more specifically, only took place several generations later. More recently, the justification for a regulatory role of the state in financial services has been given further impetus by the emergence of the economics of information since the early 1970s. This has stressed the pervasiveness of the information imbalances which exist between consumers and producers of financial services which, it is argued, occur in a more acute form in these markets than in many others (Stiglitz, 1994). Thus there is now what may be termed a 'standard textbook' account of financial regulation that grounds the need for it in the pervasiveness of negative externalities and of information asymmetries.

The theoretical recognition of the existence of market failures in the financial sector has been reflected in the practical realities of the transition economies. Governments in these countries have learned, sometimes on the basis of hard experience, that deregulation and market liberalization are insufficient concepts to guide the reforms needed to establish sustainable market-led growth, much less to maximize social welfare. Benefits have often been less than expected, while costs have been higher than necessary. The impetus to deregulation provided by the model of the *laissez-faire* state has in fact provided a dangerous one for a number of transition economies; its main result has been the failure to develop regulatory institutions and the creation of regulatory gaps that have misled or crippled markets and harmed consumers. This is evidenced, for example, in the early experience of a number of transition economies where, to encourage the development of a competitive banking system, the authorities permitted relatively unrestricted access to banking markets, as occurred for example in the Baltic republics, discussed elsewhere in this volume. The result was a series of examples of 'wildcat' banking, with poorly managed and poorly regulated institutions often incurring substantial losses that the government ultimately had to underwrite. Similarly, the contrasting experiences of Poland and the Czech Republic in developing their securities markets provides illustration of the importance of strong regulation. Whereas Poland's securities markets have flourished under the regulation of a powerful securities and exchange commission, the Czech Republic relied initially on a self-regulating system. This resulted in a securities market that was widely believed to be dominated by insiders, with the result that foreign interest in the market waned. Only belatedly did the Czech Republic accept that its securities market would not develop sufficiently without some element of governmental regulation.

Thus the experience of the early years of transition suggests the need to move beyond the ideologies of the 'small state' that were often invoked by the first generation of reformers and the advocates of 'shock therapy' to a more positive and proactive view of the state in cooperation with civil society. This is not the same debate that occurred in the early 1990s about 'governing markets', which was triggered by active state interventions in the fast-growing East Asian tiger economies (though it may learn from those experiences), but a different debate about essential complementarities between the state, the market and civil society. In the current debate, the quantity of the state becomes less important than its quality.

However, the quality of the state – in the sense of the public infrastructure needed to support policy objectives – is something that the theorists of public-interest regulation have often taken for granted. The textbook public-interest theory of governmental regulation concentrates on the existence of market failures; the concept of government failure is, if not altogether alien to it, at least something that it relatively neglects. The problem with the traditional public-interest theory of regulation is that it presupposes that the state possesses the institutional infrastructure to deliver its regulatory objectives. It assumes, for example, that the government possesses a bureaucracy that has the skills and honesty to perform the functions required of it; that once the government has taken its decision to regulate it can impose its decision on the regulated industry without its designs being subverted by political or improper pressure; and that the government is capable of distinguishing between those market failures that it is economically efficient for it to correct through regulation and those which it is not. Governments of all kinds may fail to meet these standards and it is, perhaps, significant that the intellectual groundwork for the public-interest view of regulation was laid in Britain at the end of the nineteenth and the beginning of the twentieth century. The fact that Britain at that time enjoyed a civil service that was widely respected both for the intellectual quality of its members and for their personal probity and integrity was surely a factor in building public acceptance of the case for government intervention in a wide range of economic activities.

By contrast, the problem in many transition economies is that the bureaucracy was developed for the purpose of administering the central plan; in Kornai's (1992) terminology it was responsible for 'vertical' coordination of economic decisions. The idea of government agencies responding flexibly to market developments, and accommodating market-determined outcomes, which is the essence of high-quality regulation, is alien to the inherited culture of many transition country bureaucracies. Thus building regulatory capacity requires that the government bureaucracy acquires both the skills and the culture necessary to perform the new range of tasks required of it. This takes time to accomplish, and perhaps requires generational change within the government agencies themselves before it is fully established. However, since the questions that this issue raises are mainly related to problems of the recruitment and retention of professional staff and the internal organization of regulatory agencies, they will not be persued further in this chapter.

Instead, the main thesis of this chapter is that in designing regulatory institutions the incentives to which they are subject, and to which they in turn give rise, are of the upmost importance. The insights of the public-choice school show that in at least some cases governmental regulation can depart from a publicly interested ideal, and that it can instead serve to promote narrow sectional interests, whether of the industry or of government. None the less, although the public-choice theorists are right to emphasize the weaknesses of government, the observation that governments as well as markets can fail does not necessarily lead to the conclusion that therefore the *laissez-faire* model of government is to be preferred. Rather the problem is to strike a balance between market failure and government failures, and this above all means designing an institutional structure that is capable of providing the right incentives to governments and regulators (Wolf, 1993).

One pervasive feature of the behaviour of governments in the transition economies has been encapsulated in Shleifer and Vishny's metaphor of the 'grabbing hand'. (Shleifer and Vishny, 1998). This analysis of the state has been inspired by the authors' experience in advising a number of transition governments, but is intended to be of more general application. Indeed, the grabbing-hand model is presented by its authors as an alternative to either the *laissez-faire* or public-interest models of the state. They argue that at the root of the grabbing hand analysis 'are models of political behavior that argue that politicians do not maximize social welfare and instead pursue their own selfish interests. . . . Because the grabbing hand model starts with politics, it can describe a 'descriptive theory of government choices and thus coherently analyze the pathologies – as well as their good uses – of the public sector.' It should be evident from this description that the grabbing-hand model has much in common with the public-choice school discussed above. While its authors may try to present it as an alternative to either the public-interest or *laissez-faire* models of the state, it is in reality neither since it aims to develop an explanatory framework whereas both the other models set out to be normative, that is, to assess the case for government intervention in specific cases.

None the less, the grabbing-hand model is of considerable explanatory power. In discussing regulation Shleifer and Vishny argue that one of the chief arguments against state intervention, from a grabbing-hand perspective, is the opportunities for corruption that it creates. Whereas a public-interest theorist concerned about corruption might focus on the selection of government officials, and their reward structures, Shleifer and Vishny argue instead that their analysis implies that 'deregulation and liberalization are far more important for fighting corruption than the improvement of incentives and personnel selection inside the bureaucracy. To the extent that some regulation is unavoidable, the grabbing hand approach suggests that individual bureaucrats must have as little discretion as possible in exercising their powers. ' Hence to the extent that regulation is necessary, one important feature of regulatory institutions is that they should, as far as possible, be rule-governed rather than permitting substantial discretion to individual regulators.

A closely related incentive problem, which is especially acute in the transition economies, but which also exists elsewhere, is how governments can credibly commit to the regulatory arrangements that they have established. This means permitting regulatory decisions to be taken according to clear procedures, based on the best technical judgement of the regulators themselves, with a view only to correcting instances of market failure where the benefits of regulation can be demonstrated to outweigh the costs. However, the creation of a regulatory apparatus presents politicians with an obvious temptation. It provides them with an opportunity to influence economic decision-making in an indirect way, which might substitute for the abandonment of the direct controls formerly exercised under the central planning system. Thus the issue may be summarized as one of ensuring that a government which has withdrawn from the attempt to replace the market with the state does not see regulation as an opportunity to reintroduce a command economy via the back door. The government needs to be able to show credibly that in creating a regulatory structure it does not intend to use that structure to subvert the first generation of market-oriented reforms.

The problem of incentives for regulators is compounded by a further incentive problem created by regulation, that of moral hazard. Efficient resource allocation requires that risks be borne by investors who operate on the basis of risk-adjusted return on capital. Government intervention, even when necessary for other reasons, often creates moral hazard problems by suggesting that governments could be made to share those risks. Moral hazard arises, for example, when depositors or other creditors of a bank believe that they will be bailed out by government, thus removing from them the incentive to monitor the activities of the institutions to which they lend money. The management and owners of these institutions also have incentives to take excessive risks if they believe that the government will bail them out; if they make mistakes the costs will be borne by the government, but if their risk-taking is successful they stand to acquire all the gains. This is an important problem, because many opportunities for such moral hazards exist from past and current practices of government intervention. Moreover, government-owned banks may be subject to a special form of the moral hazard problem, leading to excessive risk-taking by management in the belief that public funds will ultimately be available to address their mistakes. Thus in most countries, pervasive moral hazard obscures assessment of true investment risks. At its worst, moral hazard can so distort resource allocation that it contributes to macroeconomic crisis, as was seen, for example, in the moral hazard-induced banking crises in East Asia.

Thus one of the main conclusions that flows from this analysis of the problems of building regulatory capacity – designing the right incentives for government agencies, the containment of moral hazard, and the ability of governments credibly to commit to regulation that is proportionate and flexible – is that the design of institutions is of fundamental importance in structuring the incentives of governments and their agents. The rest of this chapter considers some of the aspects of institutional design that have been adopted in the transition countries in an attempt to deal with these problems.

Credible commitment: regulatory independence

As noted above, the government needs to secure a credible commitment to regulation, pursuing only the tasks that are necessary to correct unambiguous instances of market failure. One way in which it can do this is by establishing an independent regulatory agency. The reasons for setting up these bodies – to shield market interventions from political interference and to improve transparency, stability and expertise – are well known. Independent regulatory agencies are definitely a sound improvement when compared to regulatory functions embedded in government ministries without clear mandates or objectives. It is telling that the market impacts of market-opening have been greatest in precisely those sectors – financial services and telecommunications – where independent regulators are most prevalent, although the causality is still unclear (Jacobs, 1999). Moreover, the Basel Core Principles on Effective Banking Supervision explicitly requires (Core Principle 1) that the bank regulatory agency must possess 'operational independence and adequate resources'.

There are some very good reasons why independence from political pressures is important in all fields of regulation. Short-term political objectives do not always coincide with the need for regulation to operate according to a clear and stable set of rules. Politicians can notoriously be influenced by short-term factors – ranging from the latest newspaper headlines to a large donation from a wealthy supporter. For these reasons they may be tempted to interfere with the regulatory process in order to achieve an outcome which fits in with their immediate goals. But interference has its costs, especially the loss of consistency in regulatory decision-making. If the regulatory function is not perceived to be stable, and the rules by which the sector is regulated are subject to political pressures, potential investors may be deterred. Hence the development of financial markets and institutions will be hampered by a regulatory system which is unable to demonstrate the necessary degree of independence from political interference.

None the less, the question remains how regulators can be made independent of political interference. In a number of Western countries independence is greatly buttressed by the transparency of political processes, the role of the media, and the absence of a close government–business nexus. However, in many transition economies these elements of the environment in which regulatory agencies operate are either lacking or still in the course of being developed, and hence even greater attention must be given to the institutional arrangements to ensure independence. These factors are summarized in Box 8. 1.

Box 8.1   The institutional arrangements

The agency's funding

Independence is best guaranteed if the agency has a source of funds separate from the general government budget. One option is to fund the agency directly from the beneficiaries of regulation (the customers of financial services) which in practice means via a levy on the regulated industry.

Arrangements for the appointment and, more critically, dismissal of regulators

Independence is best served if there are clear rules on hiring and firing, which depend on regulators' competence and probity, not on the decisions they reach. Ideally two independent bodies – for example government and parliament – should be involved in the appointments process. Regulators should also enjoy security of tenure. They must be able to speak and take action without fear of dismissal by the government of the day.

The agency's governance structure

Multi-member commissions are less likely to be influenced by the views of any one individual, and also help ensure consistency and continuity of decision-making over time.

The openness and transparency of regulatory decision-making

Inevitably many regulatory decisions involve commercially sensitive material which it would be difficult to disclose. But the presumption should be in favour of openness in the decision-making process, making it possible for both public and the industry to scrutinize regulatory decisions.

Appeals against regulatory decisions

The existence of an appeals mechanism helps ensure that regulatory decisions are made consistently and are well reasoned. Without a formal appeals mechanism, those affected by regulatory decisions may resort to informal means, especially by seeking to influence regulators by subjecting them to political pressure.

An independent regulatory agency would be one which exhibits many if not all of these features. Of course, institutional structures are not themselves adequate to ensure independence, and on the other hand, independence should not be carried so far that it undermines the agency's accountability. If independence is poorly designed, the regulator can seem unaccountable, and outside of essential controls of the democratic system. Majone has argued that a mix of approaches is necessary: '[A] highly complex and specialized activity like regulation can be monitored and kept politically accountable only by a combination of control instruments: legislative and executive oversight, strict procedural requirements, public participation, and, most importantly, substantive judicial review' (Majone, 1993). Achieving the right institutional balance will, to a large extent, be a matter of incoporating these elements within the legal, political and historical framework of individual countries.

Perhaps the simplest way to secure an appropriate degree of independence for financial services regulation is for the function to be located in the central bank. The case for combining banking supervision with the monetary policy function has been extensively examined (Goodhart and Schoenmaker, 1992). The chief argument for combination is that banks are the instrument through which the central bank's monetary policy is transmitted to the wider economy and therefore it needs to be concerned with their soundness as a precondition for an effective monetary policy. In addition, since the central bank also acts a lender of last resort (LLR), it needs to have access to information about the financial condition of the institutions which might apply to it for emergency liquidity assistance. On the other hand, however, there are also a number of powerful arguments in favour of a separation of function, including that the failure of individual banks can attract blame to the bank supervisors and thus undermine the credibility of the central bank if it is also the bank supervisor. Thus, it is argued, it is better for the central bank's relationship with routine banking supervision to be relatively arm's-length to avoid such reputational contagion. Another reason for separating the supervision and monetary policy functions is that a central bank might be tempted to operate a lax monetary policy if it is concerned about the financial health of banks it is also responsible for supervising. By keeping monetary conditions loose, the central bank may avoid the failure of banks for which it might be blamed, but at the expense of higher inflation in the longer run.

The arguments for separation and combination of function are thus finely balanced, but two considerations would appear to tip the weight of argument in favour of combination in the transition economies. The first is that the central bank is able to provide a relatively high degree of regulatory independence. In an effort to achieve credible commitment for an anti-inflation strategy, many transition economies established independent central banks as one of their first institutional reforms. These central banks often have very strong guarantees of their independence from political pressure, in some cases (for example in Estonia and Latvia) being established as independent entities under the Constitution. In many of these countries the governor of the central bank enjoys a high degree of security of tenure and the central bank has its own dedicated funding sources (including unremunerated reserves placed with it by the rest of the banking system and seigniorage income when the latter is not transferred to the Ministry of Finance). Thus the institutional arrangements for central bank independence are also very closely aligned with our critieria for regulatory independence.

A subsidiary reason for combining banking supervision with monetary policy in the transition economies is that the central bank is usually better placed to attract and retain staff with the right level of skills and expertise than are other government agencies, owing to its relative budgetary autonomy and the prestige that many central banks in Central and Eastern Europe and the Former Soviet Union have been able to establish. This means that central banks are often much better placed to develop the human resources necessary for high-quality regulation than are government departments.

Thus in a transition economy context there are a number of important considerations, especially concerning independence of the regulatory function, that support the combination of banking supervision with monetary policy within the central bank. This is the model that most transition countries have adopted: with relatively few exceptions (Hungary being the most prominent) the central bank is also the banking supervisor. However, one question that remains is how the other financial sectors should be supervised, given that the discussion so far has concentrated only on banks. As a non-bank financial sector begins to emerge in these economies, there is also a need for these markets and institutions to be adequately supervised.

If banking supervision is located in the central bank, both for the reasons usually cited and to provide a stronger guarantee of regulatory independence, then one option might be for the central bank to assume these other regulatory functions as well. This would mean that it took responsibility for the supervision of securities firms and markets, insurance companies and also pension funds in addition to banks. The benefits of this approach are that it ensures that these regulatory functions will also be performed with the same independence as banking supervision and that regulatory capacity-building will be facilitated by the central bank's prestige and access to resources on which we have already remarked. Moreover, in countries with small financial systems, especially ones in which the non-bank financial sector remains relatively undeveloped, it may be difficult for separate specialist agencies to provide cost-effective regulation given their comparatively small size. Combining all financial regulation within the central bank thus permits significant scale economies to be realized by using its IT, data collection and human resource functions.

However, relatively few countries in the world have adopted this approach,[2] and none of the transition economies has done so (Central Banking Publications, 1999). This may reflect a number of serious drawbacks about this type of regulatory structure. In the first place, it involves the central bank taking on responsibility for a wide range of financial activities about which its staff can be expected to have no special expertise. While central bank staff will normally be sufficiently familiar with commercial bank practices to be able to perform supervisory duties effectively, they can be expected to know much less about securities markets and even less about the regulation of insurance companies and pension funds. Second, granting the central bank such extensive regulatory responsibilities may result in it being perceived to be excessively powerful, especially if it also possesses the ability to steer an independent course in the conduct of monetary policy as well. Third, and most important, the extension of the central bank's regulatory responsibilities to non-bank financial institutions may appear to be an implicit extension of its guarantee of financial assistance beyond banks. Thus creditors of securities firms or pension funds might expect the central bank to make the same efforts to ensure that they will be repaid as it will do to ensure that bank depositors can be repaid if a bank encounters financial difficulties. Not only would such an extension be unjustified, since other financial institutions do not suffer from the special insolvency risk of banks that is the main reason for the existence of a lender of last resort, but it also risks a dangerous extension of moral hazard. If all creditors of financial institutions believe that they will be protected to the same degree as depositors with a bank the result will be a level of risk-taking that is socially sub-optimal.

A possible alternative to centralizing all regulatory functions in the central bank would be to create an integrated financial regulatory authority as a separate agency responsible for banking, securities and insurance regulation. Regulatory consolidation has occurred in a number of developed world financial markets – Britain providing one of the most obvious examples – but this process has been prompted by considerations like the blurring of boundaries between categories of financial institution and contract which arguably are of little importance for the transition economies (Taylor, 1995; Briault, 1999). Whereas Britain and the United States have witnessed an erosion of the central role played by banks in the financial system, in emerging markets and transition economies most finance remains intermediated by the banking system. Hence the argument that the consolidation of regulation is necessary to reflect the increased integration of financial services hardly applies.

On the other hand, two considerations might support the integration of financial regulation in the transition economies. The first is that, although their financial systems are bank-dominated, one consequence has been that banks have become the most active participants in other financial markets, including the securities market, and have developed linkages with non-bank financial institutions like insurance companies. Thus conglomerate groups are often dominant in transition country financial systems, and an important reason for establishing a unified regulator is that it is better able to assess the risks and the adequacy of capital across such a diversified financial group. The second reason is that an integrated regulatory agency might be better able to exploit economies of scale in administrative and support services and especially in the employment of scarce human resources. When regulatory skills are in short supply, the argument that they are best centralized within a single agency gathers particular force (Taylor and Fleming, 1999).

None the less, only Estonia, Hungary and Latvia among the transition economies have moved in the direction of establishing an integrated regulatory agency. Other transition economies have considered the option, but have not so far reached a definitive conclusion. One of the main stumbling blocks to creating such an agency in a transition country context has been to ensure that it will enjoy an equivalent degree of independence to that already guaranteed to the banking supervision function while it remains within the central bank. Ensuring independence for regulatory agencies, as we have seen, requires a number of interlocking factors, and in practice it has been difficult to deliver them. Given the importance of maintaining a credible commitment to independent regulation in the transition economies, there is thus a strong case for retaining banking supervision within the central bank, or in an agency with close links to the central bank, as in Finland.[3]

Credible commitment: reducing moral hazard

As we have seen, regulation is market-distorting in the sense that it gives rise to moral hazard. Thus another important aspect of institutional design is to ensure that the government's commitment not to bail out creditors (other than depositors), owners or managers of a failing financial institution can be made credible. Without credible commitment in this area, owners and managers will have an incentive to take excessive risks while creditors will devote insufficient resources to monitoring the risks in their lending. The result will be a level of risk-taking that is greater than would be socially optimal.

There are several aspects of institutional design that can lend themselves to developing a credible commitment to contain moral hazard. Of these, prompt corrective action, which has so far been formally adopted in the United States, Japan and Korea, is intended to counteract moral hazard which may arise if owners and managers believe that their mistakes will be forborne by the authorities (the regulators and, ultimately, the finance ministry). As already noted, the incentives created by the existence of government guarantees to the banking system, whether explicit or implicit, are asymmetric. Owners and managers have incentives to take excessive risks, since they stand to reap all the gains if their gamble is successful, but the government will absorb the losses if it is unsuccessful. The problem is to counteract this distorted incentive, and prompt corrective action seeks to achieve this by applying a rule-based exit policy to banks while they still have positive net worth.

The prompt corrective action rule links the regulatory response to the level of a bank's capitalization. As a bank's capitalization falls through each of the mandated threshold levels, the regulator is required to take increasingly stringent actions; for 'undercapitalized' institutions, these include establishing a capital restoration plan and restricting deposit-taking, asset growth, dividends and management fees. There is also a statutory exit rule which calls for 'critically undercapitalized' banks (that is, those with a ratio of capital to risk-adjusted assets of 2 per cent or less) to be closed while they still have positive net worth. Conversely, well-capitalized banks receive the 'carrot' of increased banking powers and a lighter regulatory regime.[4]

Prompt corrective action provisions seem relevant to the problems of the transition economies in a number of respects. One problem that the prompt correction action is concerned to address is the risk of forbearance by the regulatory authorities as the consequence of some form of regulatory capture. This risk is especially acute in some of the transition economies, given the political–banking nexus which exists in many of them. Even if the regulatory authorities wish to take action they may be prevented from doing so by higher political authority: it is the political authorities rather than the regulators themselves who have been 'captured'. As the IMF stresses in *Toward a Framework for Financial Stability* (Folkerts-Landau and Lindgren, 1998), regulatory agencies may come under government pressure to exercise forbearance. A bank closure may be delayed because the government optimistically believes that the institution can be resurrected or because the closure might provoke popular discontent. But the price of delay may be only to increase the costs of rectifying the problem. A regulatory authority which uses its discretion to close a bank may be more open to influence or improper behind-the-scenes pressure than one which is clearly obliged to do so under the law. Even more serious is the practice in some countries of pressuring regulators into granting actual dispensations from a particular regulatory requirement in order to favour firms closely associated with the government, the governing party or the governing family. Hence the introduction of prompt corrective action provisions can help to ensure the consistency of regulatory decision-making in circumstances where the regulatory agency might otherwise be open to external pressure to exercise forbearance.

In addition, prompt corrective action provisions can improve the credibility of regulatory decisions. Where a regulatory agency is a relatively new creation, and the legitimacy of regulation is still a matter for debate, there would appear to be an advantage to having certain courses of action clearly mandated in its enabling statute. By enacting the requirement that banks be closed when they still have positive net worth, for example, regulators may find it easier to justify their actions than if the decision is based purely on regulatory discretion.

Hence there would appear to be a number of advantages in adopting prompt corrective action provisions in transition economies. While the independence of regulatory agencies may go some distance towards insulating the regulatory process from extraneous considerations, as Shleifer and Vishny discuss, other incentives may incline regulators to make socially sub-optimal decisions if they continue to enjoy a large region of discretion. Thus in addition to the independence of the regulatory agency itself, a regulatory process that relies on rules rather than discretion would appear to be desirable.

Moral hazard is greatest when the governmental offer of support to the banking system is implicit rather than explicit. To the extent that there is only a rather general, vague expectation that governments will be prepared to bail out troubled banks, a wide range of creditors may be encouraged to believe that they will be the beneficiaries of a government rescue package. Although it might be argued that this consideration points to the need for the government to give a credible commitment never to bail out a troubled bank – something that the application of a prompt closure rule would help reinforce – in practice such a commitment could never be established. The political economy of banking points towards the inevitable involvement of the government in bank rescues, at least when retail depositors form a large political constituency and the banking system is large relative to the rest of the economy (that is, if it is equivalent to more than 20 per cent or so of GDP). The lesson of history, both in the early twentieth century and more recently, is that it is politically impossible for a government to stand aside while its banking system collapses.

Given that the government can never deliver a credible commitment not to become involved in a rescue of the banking system, it should, as the least worst alternative, establish clear rules from the outset about which classes of creditors will be assisted and to what extent (Garcia, 1996). This requires the government to establish a deposit insurance system with a comparatively restricted range of application. Only 'small' depositors should be covered, and it should be clear that other classes of creditors should not expect government assistance. The creation of a deposit insurance scheme crystallizes a government's potential liability in the event of a bank failure and if it is established as a funded scheme (that is, as a pool of resources built up over time) it may be possible for at least medium-sized banks to be closed with minimal fiscal consequences. The deposit insurance agency will also need to be established as an independent agency, with guarantees of its independence akin to those already discussed in the context of a regulatory agency. It should, however, be separate from the regulatory agency to avoid the conflicts of interest which might arise, for example, in the event that the regulator was also the deposit insurer; in this eventuality the regulator might be tempted to exercise forbearance to avoid potential calls on the deposit insurance scheme.

The existence of a system of deposit insurance enables regulators to take action to close unsound banks without being unduly influenced by concern for the welfare of existing depositors with the institution. Moreover, systems of deposit insurance also help stabilize banking systems by reducing the incentives for depositors to seek to be the first in the queue to liquidate their deposits. However, the creation of a system of deposit insurance also creates a problem of 'moral hazard' in that it may increase the incentives for bank management to take excessive risks, if they believe that the public safety net will not be confined to depositors but will be extended to other creditors as well. Thus there is also a need for the regulatory institutions of a country to demonstrate a credible commitment that only depositors within the terms of the deposit insurance scheme will be compensated in the event of a failure of the bank.

Conclusion

This chapter has reviewed the main elements of effective regulatory capacity in the transition economies. It has been argued that these 'second-generation' reforms are essential if the transition economies are to reap the full benefits of their historic leap towards market-based financial systems. Regulation performs an essential function in correcting market failures, but it has to be recognized that governments, as well as markets, may fail. The objective should be to construct institutions that are capable of delivering high-quality regulation, meaning regulation that is responsive and flexible and which is clearly differentiated from the kind of state intervention which seeks to substitute administrative mechanisms for market mechanisms.

The main outlines of an institutional structure of regulation which can secure credible commitment for the government to pursue these goals have also been offered. In the first place, the regulatory agency must possess substantial independence from government. There is a case for the banking supervision function to be discharged by the central bank on the grounds that this will provide it with an adequate degree of political independence. However, if alternative regulatory structures are adopted, the issue of independence should be given a central place. Equally important is that regulation should be rule-driven rather than discretionary to reduce the scope for corruption or other abuses of the system. A rule-based bank exit policy was cited as a specific example of how this rule-based framework might be established. Finally, the importance of the government establishing a credible commitment only to compensate small depositors with a failed bank was also stressed. To extend the governmental safety net to other creditors runs the risk of encouraging excessive risk-taking.

Constructing this type of institutional framework in the transition economies would go a significant way towards cementing the first generation of reforms. As stressed in the introduction, the ultimate effectiveness of regulation depends on the 'fit' between markets, institutions and civil society. Many transition economies are well down this track, but for others there is still a serious disconnection between the institutions and the environment in which they must operate.

Notes

1 The views expressed in this chapter should not be attributed to either the Monetary and Exchange Affairs Department or the International Monetary Fund.
2 The main examples are Singapore and the Netherlands Antilles.
3 The Finnish model of financial regulation deserves study by many of the smaller transition economies. Under this system banking and securities regulation is combined in the Financial Supervisory Agency which, although legally separate from the central bank, has close administrative links with it (its staff are central bank employees, for example, and it shares the central bank's computer systems). Insurance and pensions regulation is the responsibility of a separate agency, the Insurance Supervisory Agency. For a more extensive description see Taylor and Fleming (1999).
4 It should be noted, however, that the prompt corrective action provisions are tied to the level of a bank's capitalization; hence if the calculation of a bank's capitalization cannot be accurately performed, the use of prompt corrective action will be inhibited. Establishing the true level of a bank's capital adequacy is a problem in many transition and emerging economies, and should be seen as a necessary preliminary to the adoption of a prompt corrective action technique.

References

C. Briault, *The rationale for a single national financial services regulator* (London: Financial Services Authority, Occasional Paper No. 2, 1999).

Central Banking Publications, 'How Countries Supervise their Securities Markets, Banks and Insurers', (London: Central Banking Publications, 1999).

D. Folkerts-Landau and C. Lindgren, *Toward a Framework for Financial Stability* (Washington, DC: International Monetary Fund, 1998).

G. Garcia, 'Deposit Insurance: obtaining the benefits and avoiding the pitfalls' (Washington, DC: International Monetary Fund Working Paper WP/96/83, 1996).

C. Goodhart and D. Schoenmaker, 'Institutional separation between supervisory and monetary agencies', *Giornale Degli Economisti E Annali Di Economia* (Italy), Vol. 51 (September–December 1992).

S. Jacobs, 'The Second Generation of Regulatory Reforms' (paper delivered at the IMF Conference on Second Generation Reforms, 8–9 November 1999, available at the IMF website: www. imf. org).

J. Kornai, *The Socialist System* (Oxford: Oxford University Press, 1992).

G. Majone, 'Controlling Regulatory Bureaucracies: Lessons from the American Experience', *EUI Working Papers in Political and Social Sciences* (European University Institute, Florence, Italy, 1993).

A. C. Pigou, *The Economics of Welfare* (London: Macmillan and Co. 1946 [1932]).

A. Shleifer and R. Vishny, *The Grabbing Hand* (Cambridge, MA: Harvard University Press, 1998).

G. Stigler, *Chicago studies in political economy* (Chicago: University of Chicago Press, 1988).

J. Stiglitz, *Whither Socialism?* (Cambridge, MA: MIT Press, 1994).

M. Taylor, *Twin Peaks: A regulatory structure for the new century* (London: Centre for the Study of Financial Innovation, December 1995).

M. Taylor and A. Fleming, 'Integrated Financial Supervision: Lessons from the Northern European Experience' (Washington, DC: World Bank Policy Research Working Paper No. 2223, November 1999).

C. Wolf, *Markets or governments: choosing between imperfect alternatives* (Cambridge, MA: The MIT Press, 1993).

Conclusion

Yelena Kalyuzhnova and Michael Taylor

Four essentials for success in financial sector transition

It is already more than a decade since the former centrally planned economies began a major shift towards market-based financial systems. On the way they were faced with the challenges of adapting to a series of new developments, with new rules of the game as well as with the legacy of the previous period of central planning. It has affected all spheres of the national economies, but the burden of these factors is most clearly recognizable in the financial sector.

Before transition, socialist countries had centrally planned economic systems and undeveloped or non-existent capital markets. The move to a market-based economic system required transitional governments to introduce radical changes, including the development of a financial sector that was capable of allocating capital according to market incentives rather than the requirements of the central plan. The challenges of this transformation have been – and remain – enormous, and are highly dependent upon other sectors of the economy (for example macroeconomic conditions, industrial development and so on).

Without financial sector reform further macro- and microeconomic improvements and economic growth will be inhibited. A well-managed, well-regulated and prudently run financial sector can boost the effectiveness of the allocation of capital and hence the development of the real economy.

Throughout the book the authors have highlighted four essential key elements of a sound financial system for the transitional economics, namely: an effective institutional framework; an adequately functioning banking sector as the core of the financial system; the creation of a system of non-banking institutions to supplement the banking sector; and finally, a sound financial system infrastructure. The conclusions reached by the various contributors to this volume can be summarized under these four main headings.

Institutional framework

Economic history contains a number of examples of the sharp divergence of economic theory and institutional reality. Financial transition signifies shifting from one coherent financial system to another. It is necessary to emphasize that this process is not about modification or the creation of new elements within the existing system. It is an extreme change, which affects the entire character of this system. Transition reflects a more complex combination of economic as well as institutional changes, where the latter are important, essential and creative. As has been emphasized by Shrivastava in his contribution to this volume, institutions are complementary in that the efficiency of each is enhanced by the presence of others, and hence the development of these institutions would ultimately involve other interrelated institutional changes. The revivified discipline of political economy provides a number of important insights, Shrivastava argues, into the role of institutions in economies in transition. He argues that all institutions (including financial) require a complex set of formal rules, informal sanctions and behavioural norms. He shows that a major element of policy design should be to seek to identify and encourage complementarities between different aspects of institutional reform.

Banks' soundness

As mentioned above, there are problems and issues which are directly associated with moving from a monobank system to one operated on competitive principles. From the moment when the monobank banking system shifts from the planned method of credit allocation decisions to the allocation of credit according to price, the ultimate consequence is the appearance of problems of insolvency and repayment challenges with which borrowers are faced in the transitional economies. In this respect the problem of bad loans becomes crucial. In his chapter Tridimas has modelled the bad loans problem as a tax on financial intermediation used by the government of a transition economy to assist state-owned enterprises. Employing a firm-theoretic model of bank behaviour, he examined how in a monopolistic setting bad loans affect the equilibrium volume of bank deposits and loans. The effects depend on the size of bad loans, the characteristics of the loan demand, deposit supply and expected net bank return functions, and, contrary to informal accounts found in the literature, may imply a larger volume of financial intermediation than in the absence of bad loans. Whether the larger volume of financial intermediation that may result from the existence of bad loans is sufficient to outweigh the deadweight costs that an overhang of bad loans also entails is, however, a moot point.

The Polish way of achieving modern, competitive but prudently managed banking systems from the initial conditions set by the former Polish state banking system has been described by Szymkiewicz.

Poland is widely regarded as being in the vanguard of transition. Hence the policy choices that were made to transform its banking sector are of considerable importance in understanding a successful case of transition. Szymkiewicz stresses a number of factors in Poland's banking sector restructuring, in particular the progress made in elaborating a legal framework corresponding to the international banking norms. She also highlights the recent changes in the capital structure of the Polish banking system, most notably the privatization and consolidation of the banking sector, with an increasing presence of foreign banks in the country.

Without exception, all transitional banking systems have experienced challenges and obstacles to their development, which are mostly related to a lack of human capital at the beginning of the transitional process, including a shortage of management capacity. As Fleming has illustrated in the examples of three Baltic states, there were cases of a lack of credit and management skills in the banking sectors of these countries, which consequently gave rise to crises. However, the crises in the Baltic states were compounded by two other factors: the existence of fraud on a massive scale at a number of banks; and the policy followed by the authorities in the early phases of transition of permitting almost free entry into the banking industry.

It had been anticipated that a policy of free entry would rapidly drive down lending rates, and would provide the basis for a banking system founded on competitive principles to exist in parallel with the remnants of the old monobank systems. However, without adequate prudential regulation the result of free entry was to encourage 'wildcat' banking by owners and managers who lacked the skills and incentives to develop soundly run banks, and who often also engaged in large-scale fraud.

The resulting banking crises were sufficiently severe that they threatened to derail the transition process itself, although as Fleming notes they have all now largely been resolved. The degree of success in resolving them, he observes, was a function of the firmness and promptness of the authorities' response once the crisis began to emerge. He argues that banking distress was probably inevitable in the countries of the FSU due to the absence of a previous market-based banking experience.

Non-bank financial sector

The development of a non-bank financial sector is especially relevant in the conditions of transitional countries as a supplement to a weak banking sector. The emergence of a flourishing non-bank sector requires the establishment of entirely new financial markets and institutions, rather than merely the transformation of already existing ones. In their chapter, Norton and Arner emphasized the various obstacles that constrain the development of a non-bank sector in transition economies, with specific reference to the securities markets. Among them are: securities fraud and corruption; bureaucratic insider dominance as well as problems with investment funds (non-profitability of the remaining state-owned enterprises, lack of sufficient information about newly privatized enterprises, the lack of liquidity that characterizes the stock of these enterprises, and so on). Norton and Arner stress the importance of three major conditions for the development of capital markets in the transition economies. These conditions are: the generation of a market economy; the establishment of the rule of law; and the institutionalization of democratic rule.

Practical evidence of such importance is given by Kalyuzhnova in her discussion about the role of pension reform in transitional economies. The shift from the pay-as-you-go (PAYG) pension system, which was the system of the pre-transitional period, to the fully funded (FF) system cannot be effected without the development of additional financial institutions as well as recovery of the real sector of the economy. Kazakhstan has moved further towards establishing a fully funded pension system than practically any other country in the world except Chile. However, in the context of the Kazakhstani experience Kalyuzhnova questions the feasibility of fully funded pension provision in the transition economies given continued problems in the functioning of the real sector of the economy and the absence of minimum preconditions in terms of financial sector development.

Financial system infrastructure

The final, but not last, question addressed in this book concerns the development of an institutional infrastructure which permits the proper functioning of financial markets.

The first such infrastructural issue concerns the development of an appropriate set of accounting standards. Financial markets do not function effectively without accurate and reliable information about major financial indicators of the performance of their potential projects or clients. Roberts bases his analysis on the context of Romanian accounting reform's stated objectives, including the development of the Romanian accounting system in line with the international and the European and International Accounting Standards Committee (IASC) frameworks. Compatibility with the IASC is now widely viewed as being essential if banks and corporations in the transition economies are to have access to the international capital markets. Transitional economies were faced with two possible approaches to accounting reform based on Anglo-Saxon and continental practices respectively. The debate in Romania concerned which of these two approaches should be adopted. In adopting an Anglo-Saxon model of accounting, Roberts argues that the decision was influenced by the government's concern to attract foreign investment to the country. This required making the financial statements of listed companies and new privatized enterprises more comprehensive and transparent to them, and ultimately determined the type of accounting standards adopted.

Another fundamental issue in building market financial infrastructure belongs to effective regulation and supervision. Norton and Arner's chapter reviewed the relevance of the internationally agreed principles for financial regulation, including the Basel Core Principles for Effective Banking Supervision and the IOSCO Objectives and Principles of Securities Regulation. His conclusion was that these various standards and codes are essentially an overlay to other, more fundamental issues, including the existence of a properly functioning legal system. Without these preconditions in place, he argued, the attempt to improve financial regulation through reliance on these codes is unlikely to be successful.

In contrast, Taylor's chapter was less concerned with issues of legal systems and compliance with codes than with what may be termed the political economy of regulation. In particular, it examined the institutional structure necessary to ensure that regulation is effective in the transition economies. Among other matters he considered whether regulation is best placed in the hands of the central bank or assigned to a specialist regulatory agency, and he also considered the design of deposit insurance schemes as well as the appropriateness of prompt corrective action measures. Overarching each of these issues is the fundamental issue of the legitimacy of regulation. Economies that have developed during the last decade in reaction to the excessive role of the state, have frequently neglected the importance of market failure as well as government failure.

Final commentary

The evidence and analysis presented in this book suggest that finance in transition economies is bank-based due to the inheritance of the mono-bank system from the central planning period. Despite the difficulties of developing the securities market under conditions of imperfect information, it is inevitable that Central and Eastern Europe and the CIS require development of both dimensions, namely bank-and securities-based finance.

In order to strengthen economic growth, it is essential to strengthen the banking system and there are two essential elements that underpin this development: a reduction in market power for the remnants of the former monobank system and the increasing role of private participation, especially foreign ownership, in the banking sector. Foreign ownership of leading financial institutions may be politically difficult but in reality provides the most efficient way of bringing about the skills transfer and the development of human capital that banking systems in transition urgently require. The experience of Poland illustrates the importance of permitting foreign entry and competition into banking markets, and the way it can foster the strength of domestic financial systems. Realistically, for the medium term the financial systems of the transitional economies will remain bank-based, therefore improvements in the banking sphere are essential.

Securities markets are undeveloped in practically all transitional economies. Although some progress in enacting legal frameworks for the non-bank financial sector has been achieved, its practical implementation has lagged behind. Effective regulation of these markets would appear to be essential to their successful development. A further issue for investigation is whether the practice in each of the transition economies of setting up its own stock exchange is in the long run the right strategy for economic development. A large number of fragmented securities exchanges, none of which is able to generate sufficient overseas investor interest or to provide the depth and liquidity normally required by portfolio investors, may be inhibiting the ability of the real sector of the economy to attract fresh capital. It is an interesting question whether a smaller number of regionally based exchanges – for example a single securities market for the three Baltic republics – might not in the long run facilitate the ability of firms in these regions to raise capital. But this is a matter that requires further research.

The second decade of transition is likely to be as challenging as the first. It will continue to be influenced by the fact that the whole economic system is organically connected and the illnesses or disease of some of its parts affect the rest. Conversely, improvements in particular sectors can facilitate improvements in other sectors of the economy. Successful transition depends on the ability to create a virtuous circle in which well-planned reforms provide the basis for further reforms; the complementarities of institutions (to use Shrivastava's phrase) need to be fully reflected in the reform process. This volume has attempted to suggest where some of those complementarities have – and have not – been found in the specific case of building effective financial markets and institutions.

Index